CALIFOR

AT COST

CALIFORNIA AT COST

Little Hills Press

©Text - Little Hills Press, 1994
First Published 1991
This edition, **December, 1994**
Editorial Board - Director: Fay Smith.
Assistants: C. Ernest and C. Burfitt.
© Photographs - Fay Smith, C. Burfitt
© Maps - Little Hills Press

Cover by IIC Productions
Printed in Australia
Published by Little Hills Press Pty Ltd,
Regent House, 37 Alexander Street,
Crows Nest NSW 2065 Australia.

ISBN 1 86315 068 4

Published in the UK by:
Moorland Publishing Co Ltd,
Moor Farm Road West,
Ashbourne, Derbyshire,
DE6 1HD. England.

All rights reserved. No part of this publication may be reproduced, stored in a retrieval system, or transmitted in any form or by any means, electronic, mechanical, photocopying, recording or otherwise, without the prior permission in writing of the publisher.

British Library Cataloguing in Publication Data.
A catalogue record for this book is available from the British Library.

DISCLAIMER

Whilst all care has been taken by the publisher and author to ensure that the information is accurate and up to date, the publisher does not take responsibility for the information published herein. The recommendations are those of the author, and as things get better or worse, places close and others open, some elements in the book may be inaccurate when you get there. Please write and tell us about it so we can update in subsequent editions.

CONTENTS

INTRODUCTION
(History, Missions, Climate, Population, Language, Religion, Holidays, Entry Regulations, Embassies, Money, Communications, Miscellaneous) **10**

TRAVEL INFORMATION
(How To Get There, Accommodation, Local Transport, Food, Drink, Shopping, Sport) **33**

LOS ANGELES 45
  Downtown 74
  Hollywood 79
  Westside 90

LOS ANGELES COAST 97
  Malibu 97
  Santa Monica 100
  Venice 100
  Marina del Rey 101
  San Pedro 101
  Long Beach 103
  Catalina Island 104
  The Valleys 106

DISNEYLAND **109**

ORANGE COUNTY 121
Anaheim 121
Buena Park 127
Irvine 133
Newport Beach 133

SAN DIEGO 137
Balboa Park 149
Mission Bay 152
La Jolla 154

THE DESERT 159
Palm Springs 160
Mojave Desert 169

THE CENTRAL COAST 171
Oxnard 171
Santa Barbara 176
Santa Ynez Valley 185
San Luis Obispo 187
San Simeon 193
Big Sur 196

THE MONTEREY PENINSULA 199
Carmel 199
Pacific Grove 205
Monterey 206

SAN FRANCISCO 220

SAN FRANCISCO BAY AREA 263
Oakland 263
Berkeley 265
Marine World Africa USA 266
Muir Woods 268
Tiburon 269

WINE COUNTRY 271
Napa Valley 271
Sonoma Valley 287

SIERRA NEVADA 294
Lake Tahoe 294
Yosemite National Park 302

LIST OF MAPS 309

INDEX 311

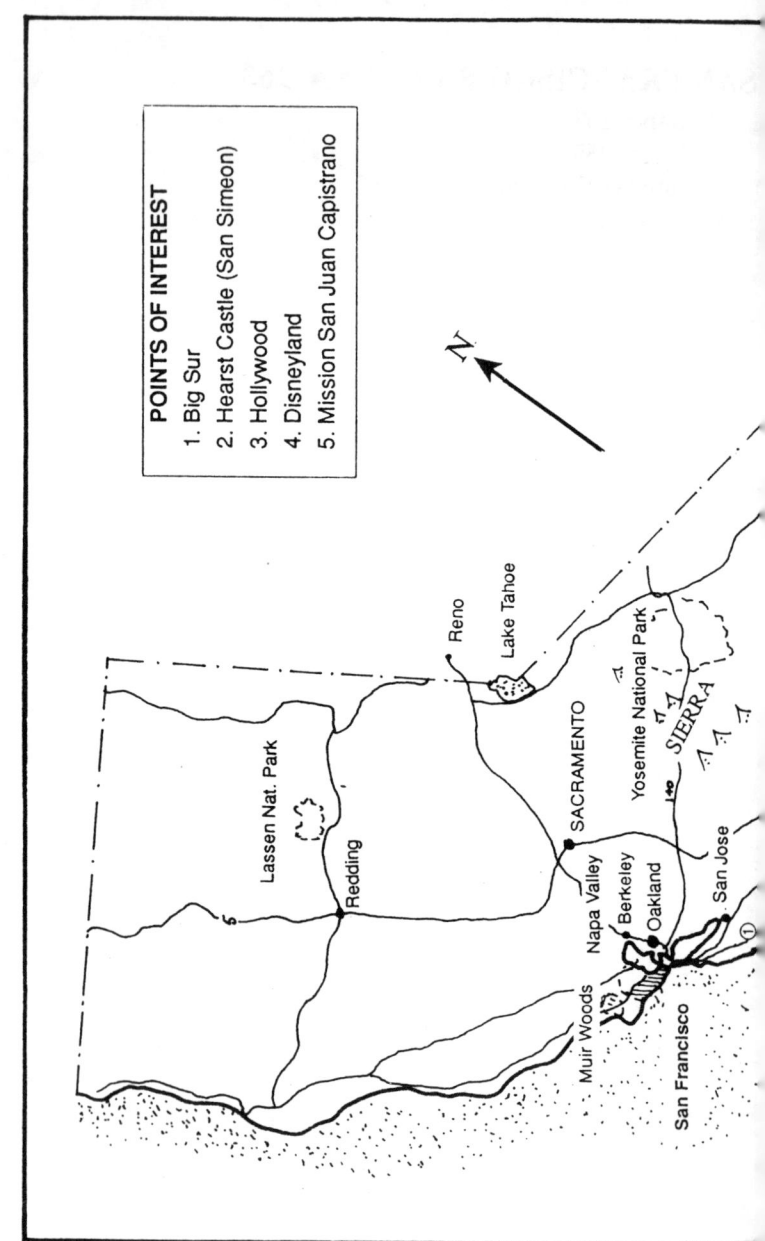

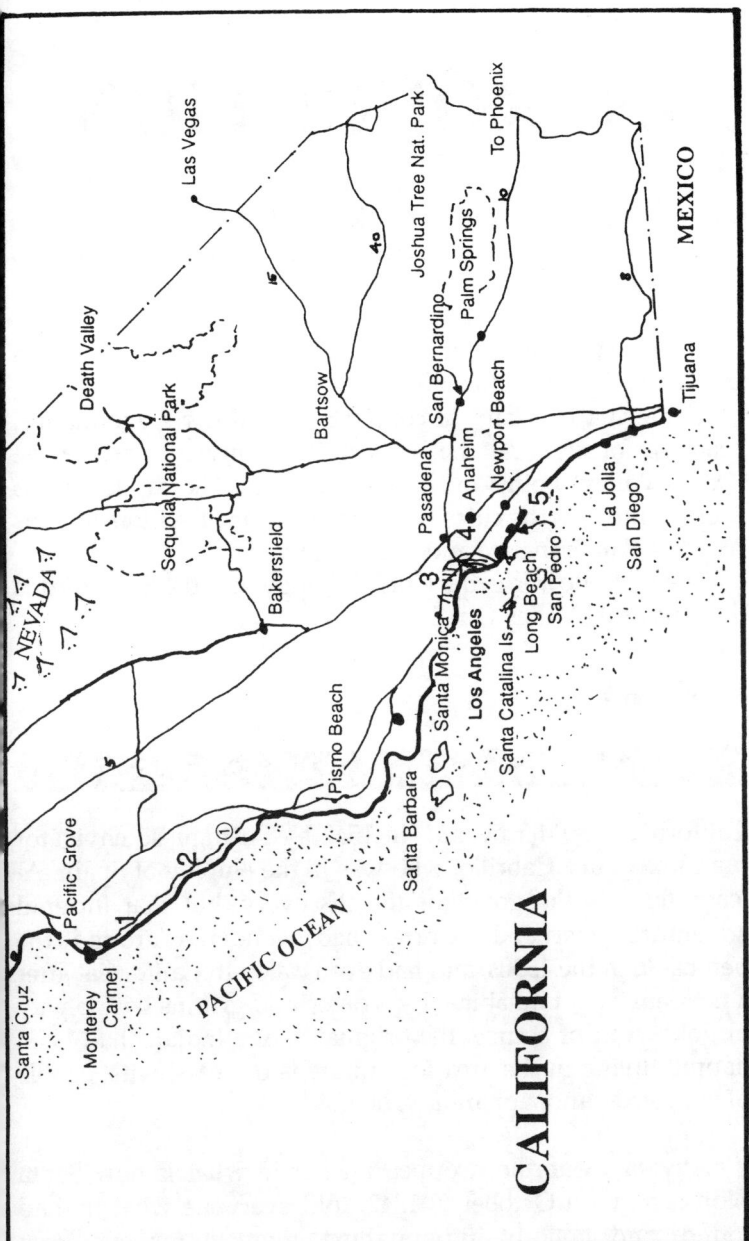

INTRODUCTION

California, the Golden State, lies on the west coast of the United States, and is bordered by Oregon to the north, Mexico to the south, and Nevada and Arizona to the east. It has an area of 411,049 sq km (158,706 sq miles) and a Pacific coastline of 2036km (1265 miles). It is divided into 58 counties, of which San Diego County is the largest.

California is a land of contrasts with deserts, mountains, beaches, forests, and the highest (Mt Whitney) and lowest (Death Valley) points in the United States. The capital city is Sacramento, but the cities that attract the most visitors are Los Angeles, San Francisco and San Diego.

The State flower is the Golden Poppy and the State bird is the California Valley Quail.

HISTORY

Western Discovery

California was 'discovered' in 1542 by Portuguese navigator Juan Rodriguez Cabrillo, who was in the employ of Spain. At least, he gets the gong for the discovery, but that intrepid adventurer Hernando Cortez had wandered around the peninsula in the 1530s, and had even called it 'California' after a fictional island inhabited by women and griffins with plenty of gold. And of course, the original native Indians had been happily living in the area for hundreds of years, with people of both sexes and, apparently, no gold.

Anyway, Cabrillo dropped anchor in what is now Santa Monica Bay on October 9, 1542, told everyone what he had found, and nobody did anything about it for over two hundred years. A few other people subsequently visited, namely Sir Francis Drake, who reached Drake's Bay in Marin County in 1579 and claimed the area for Elizabeth I, who was apparently not interested; and Sebastian Vizcaino, in 1602, who named Santa Catalina, San Diego and San Clemente.

The next people on the scene were the **Franciscan Missionaries**. They arrived in Mexico in 1767, to take over from **the Jesuits** who had been busy with the local Indians since 1697, but were expelled when Spain and Rome had an altercation.

In 1769, Father Junipero Serra decided to go further afield, well north actually, and founded the first Californian mission, San Diego de Alcala, which was originally five miles down the San Diego River from its present location. During the next fifty-four years the Spanish Fathers established a chain of twenty-one missions, stretching for 600 miles from San Diego to Sonoma, north of San Francisco Bay. Each mission, by the way, is alleged to be a day's donkey ride from the previous one. For more information on the missions, see the following section.

Meanwhile, Spain was a bit worried about the Russians who were looking for new territories, so Charles III sent Gaspardi Portola post haste, with a military force, to officially take possession of California for Spain. This was not good news for the Indians, who were already being forced to work harder than they had before in the Missions, and were now introduced to measles, chicken pox, and various venereal diseases. Having no immunity to any of the above, more than half the population perished.

The Town of the **Queen of the Angels (El Pueblo de la Reina de los Angeles)** was established when forty-odd settlers from the provinces of Sonora and Sinaloa, were granted housing lots and growing fields in September, 1781.

Spain's rule came to an end when Mexico declared itself a Republic on September 27, 1821, and took control of California.

Mexico was obviously happy with its acquisition because when the American President, Andrew Jackson, tried to buy it in the 1830s, and offered $500,000, the Mexicans said 'thanks, but no thanks'.

The Californian settlers were obviously not thrilled with being part of Mexico, and a group of them, led by the explorer and army officer, John Fremont, tried to establish a Republic of California in 1846.

Coincidentally, the war between the United States and Mexico broke out the same year, over the Rio Grande and the establishment of Texas. This war was settled on July 4, 1848, with the Treaty of Guadalupe Hidalgo, and in 1850 California became the 31st State in the Union.

The Golden State

Gold had been found in 1842, when the territory was still part of Mexico, at Placeritas Canyon in the San Fernando Valley. But the boom period came several years later with the arrival of half a million Forty-Niners from all around the world. Not many made their fortune from gold, but a lot stayed to reap the rewards offered by the rich soil.

The first orange trees were shipped from Washington in 1873, and along with grapes, formed the basis of a new influx of immigrants. The population swelled again with the discovery of oil in 1892, and in the 1930s thousands of 'Okies' arrived, searching for good farming land to replace their drought-ravaged Mid-West holdings.

The **motion film industry** was by this time well established in California. Originally a New York undertaking, the movie makers decided to move to California for the long hours of sunshine needed for the early pictures, which were mainly filmed outdoors. Hollywood was established, and the rest is well-documented, especially by the film-makers themselves.

Of course, not all California's history has been sunny. At 5.12am on April 18, 1906, an **earthquake** that measured 8.3 on the Richter scale rocked the city of San Francisco and, together with the fifty separate fires that broke out, destroyed three-quarters of the city's houses, and left 452 people dead and 250,000 homeless. The city was quickly rebuilt though, and adopted as its symbol a phoenix rising from the ashes.

During **World War II**, the California coastline became strategically important. The navy established port facilities in San Diego, and defence bases were constructed in Marin County and at Camp Pendleton, Point Mugu, Vandenberg and Fort Ord. In 1942, the US government committed one of the most reprehensible acts in history when it decided to 'relocate' 93,000 Japanese-Americans from the coastal regions to prevent them from aiding the Japanese empire. In fact only one submarine ventured anywhere near California, and the only damage it did was to a wooden pier near Santa Barbara.

After the war the **property developers** moved in and California became the most populous state of the union, and Los Angeles the second largest city.
　　The 1960s brought notoriety to San Francisco's Haight-Ashbury district with its population of drug-taking flower children and hippies, and later in the decade with conservative governor Ronald Reagan at the helm, California was heavily involved in the anti-Vietnam War movement.

During the 70s and 80s, many Asians and Hispanics settled in the state, adding to its multiculturalism and threatening to make it a pluralistic society in the not too distant future.
　　In 1972, the California Coastal Commission was established to slow down development and to preserve the natural beauty of the coastline. Let us hope that it continues to succeed.

NOTES

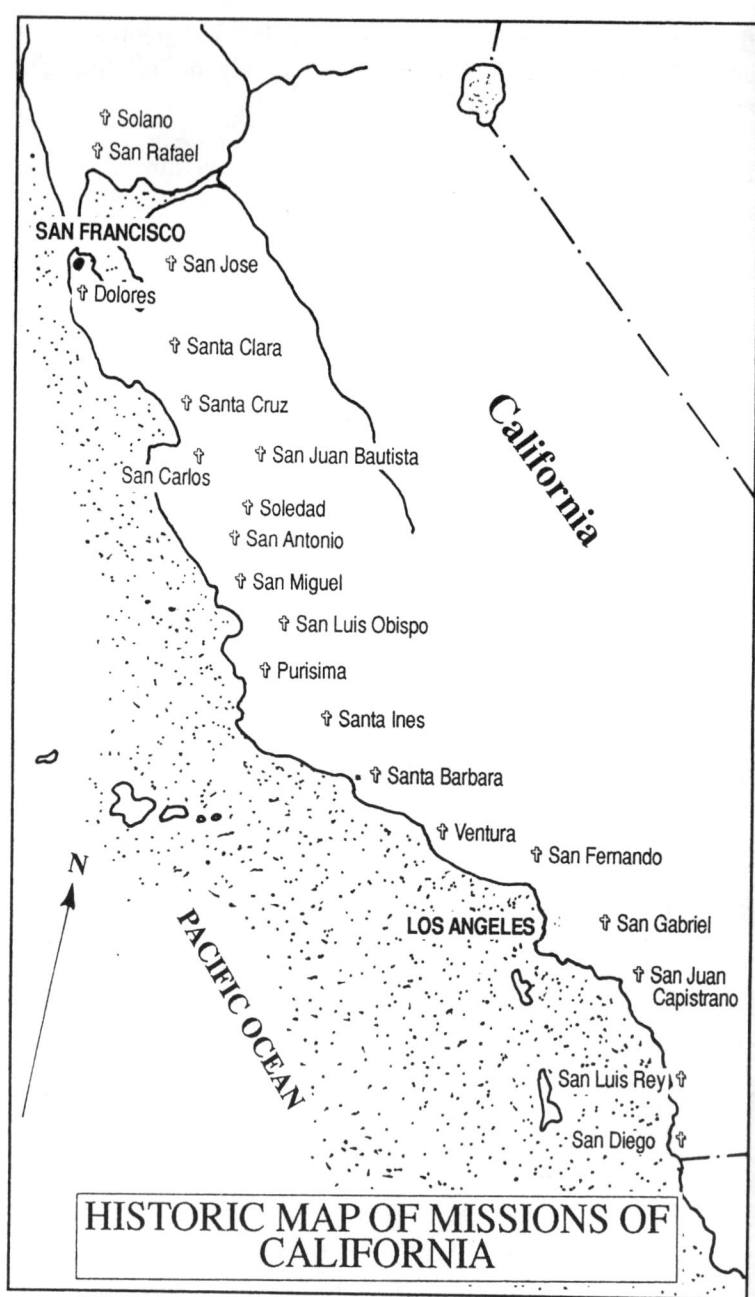

MISSIONS

The Missions were built from San Diego to Sonoma, along the famous Mission Trail, which grew into El Camino Real (The Royal Road), which in turn became Highway 101, and can be followed today. Not all the missions are still standing, and some are being restored, either in part or total.

As mentioned before, the first mission, *San Diego De Alcala*, **was established by Father Junipero Serra** in 1769, on July 16, the last was *San Francisco de Solano* on July 4, 1823. The missions welcome visitors, and a nominal fee is charged. Some have museums and bookshops, and all are photogenic. The following list is in geographical order from south to north.

Mission *San Luis Rey de Francia* was called the 'King of the Missions'. It was founded on June 13, 1798, and by 1830 was the largest and most populous in the mission chain. Situated near the town of San Luis Rey, on a road branching off Interstate Highway 5, it had groves of olive and orange trees, vineyards, 27,000 head of cattle and 26,000 sheep. By 1846, the mission was abandoned because of the action of Mexican politicians, and the property was sold to relatives of the governor. In 1865, President Lincoln returned about 26ha (65 acres) of the mission lands to the church, but it was not until 1892 that restoration work **began.**

The oldest pepper tree in California, planted in 1830, is in the mission grounds. Incidentally, it is only at Mission San Antonio de Pala, former outpost chapel of Mission San Luis Rey, that Mission Indians are still ministered to at an original Spanish site.

Mission *San Juan Capistrano*, probably the best known to people from outside California, was founded on November 1, 1776. Made famous in story and song for its returning swallows, the original church was the most ornate of the mission churches, and took nine years to build. It was only used for six years, however, as it collapsed during an earthquake in 1812. The little chapel that is still standing is called Fr Serra's Church, as it is the only building remaining in the whole mission chain where it is known that Fr Serra actually said Mass.

The buildings and gardens today are truly a picture, and the present church is a favourite place for weddings, to the extent that it is booked out for years in advance. The mission is found on Interstate Highway 5, at the junction of State Highway 74, north of San Clemente.

A word about the swallows - for years they returned each year on or about March 19, St Joseph's Day, to build their mud nests in the ruins of the old mission church. However, in the last few years they have diminished in numbers, and it is thought that pesticides in the area could be the problem. Swallows or not, Mission San Juan Capistrano is definitely worth a visit.

Mission *San Gabriel Arcangel*, September 8, 1771, is in the Los Angeles area in San Marino, on Santa Anita Street, between Valley Boulevard and Mission Road. The old church looks much as it did in the old days, except that after the bell tower fell during an earthquake in 1812, it was replaced with a campanario, or bell well, at the opposite end of the building. This mission has probably the finest collection of mission relics in existence. The hammered copper baptismal font was a gift from King Carlos III of Spain in 1771, and the six altar statues were brought around Cape Horn in 1791.

Mission *San Fernando Rey de España* began on September 8, 1797, and was used as a hospice, or hotel, for travellers between San Gabriel and Ventura. Across the street in Brand Park stands an old mission fountain and a statue of Fr Serra with his arm around an Indian boy. The beautifully restored church and mission gardens belie the fact that at one stage the buildings were used as a warehouse and stable, and the patio as a pig farm. In 1923 church officials returned to begin restoration work, and once the years of neglect were cleaned away, the true majesty of the buildings was revealed. In the 'long building', the huge wine press, smoke room, refectory, and governors' chamber for important guests, are much as in former times.

Mission *San Buenaventura*, founded on March 31, 1782, is located in the main street of the city of Ventura. The mission, now slap bang in the middle of the business district, once was surrounded by orchards, vineyards and fields, and was considered to be the garden spot of all the missions. A reservoir and aqueduct system supplied water to the complex, which extended from the foothills to the edge of the Pacific Ocean. In the garden between the church and the little museum are two huge Norfolk Island pines that are believed to be 100 years old. The museum has two old wooden bells, thought to be unique in California.

Mission Santa Barbara

Mission *Santa Barbara*, the 'Queen of the Missions', was founded on December 4, 1786, and has remained under the control of the Franciscans to the present day. The others were all abandoned one by one after the Mexican decrees robbed the missions of their lands and their control over the Indians.

In the early 1800s the mission had more than 1700 Indian converts living in a village of 250 adobe houses, and due to their efforts the mission was self-supporting. After Mexico took over, the mission became a parish church. The present stone church, which was completed in 1820, is the fourth to stand on the site. The first was a rough, temporary chapel, the second was destroyed by an earthquake in 1812, and no one seems to know what happened to the third.

Another of the missions that is worth a visit, Santa Barbara is in the town of the same name, and just off Highway 101.

Mission *Santa Ines* was founded on September 17, 1804, and is found in the beautiful town of Solvang. It has been called the 'Hidden Gem of the Missions', and the present church, which was completed in 1817, has the original floor tiles and ceiling beams made from sugar pine. The designs on the rear wall of the altar were painted by Indians using native vegetable colours, and have been restored. The statue of Santa Ines (Saint Agnes) over the main altar, is very old, and some of the Latin missals, music books on parchment, and early vestments in the museum, are far older than the mission itself.

Mission *La Purisima Concepcion* began on December 8, 1787, and is now the most completely restored mission in California. Situated near the city of Lompoc, and the Vandenberg Air Force Base, it had been ruined by earthquake and neglect after the end of the mission period, to the extent that when the property was returned to the church, it was sold. Then, in 1935, the restoration work began and now La Purisima Mission State Historic Park boasts 391ha (967 acres) complete with crops and animals of the mission period, and people in period costume plying the old trades, and showing visitors around.

While not as beautiful as some of the others, this is obviously the mission for the history buffs to visit.

Mission *San Luis Obispo de Tolosa,* founded on September 1, 1772, is in the middle of the town of San Luis Obispo on Highway 101, and has survived as a parish church. It was the first mission built with red roof tiles, replacing the thatched roofs which tended to catch fire so easily. Eventually all the missions were endowed with red tiles. The church is beautiful, and with its adjoining buildings occupies a square block, set in modern landscaped gardens.

Mission *San Miguel Arcangel,* July 25, 1797, is on Highway 101, near the little town of San Miguel, about 11km (7 miles) south of Camp Roberts. The old adobe church and long monastery building are remarkably preserved. The ceiling and roof beams, which were brought from mountains 64km (40 miles) away, have protected the church to such an extent that this is the only church where the painted wall and ceiling decorations remain untouched. In 1893 the mission had over a thousand Indian converts, but by 1840, the last of the missionaries had been forced to retire, and by 1846 all of the buildings had been sold. Church authorities regained possession of the main buildings in 1878, and the Franciscans have been in charge since 1928.

Mission *San Antonio de Padua* was established on July 14, 1771, and the old church and entire quadrangle have been restored and rebuilt. It is one of the more remote missions, but can be reached by taking Route G18 off Highway 101 at Bradley.

Mission *Nuestra Senora de la Soledad* was founded on October 9, 1791, and is situated on a road that branches of Highway 101 south of the town of Soledad. Built entirely of adobe, Soledad Mission fell into ruin after its forced abandonment, but the old church, the chapel, and one side of the quadrangle have been restored and rebuilt. Its location, miles from any town, gives a good idea of how remote all the missions would have been in their hey day.

Mission *San Carlos Borromeo* **dates** from June 3, 1770, and was apparently Fr Serra's favourite, as he is buried at his request under the altar in this church. It is situated on State Highway 1, at the mouth of the Carmel Valley, overlooking the sea, and has survived years of neglect. The buildings have now been carefully restored, and the gardens are a delight to behold. Note the Moorish influence in the architecture of the church, unique to the Californian missions.

Mission *San Juan Bautista* was founded on June 24, 1797, has the largest of the old mission churches, and is considered by many to be the most beautiful. Dedicated to St John the Baptist, the church was planned with two side aisles, but between the cornerstone laying in 1803, and completion in 1812, earthquakes caused the original plan to be abandoned. The arches separating nave and aisle were filled with adobe, except for the front two on each side. Subsequent earthquakes damaged the sealed-off aisles severely, which was evident for many years. Restoration work in 1976 opened up the side aisles and completed the church as it was originally planned. The main altar of the church is worth a visit in itself.

The long cloister wing, formerly the padres' quarters, is now a museum. The mission is on Highway 101, about 5km (3 miles) north-west of the town of San Juan Bautista.

Mission *Santa Cruz*, August 28, 1791, prospered for a few years after its founding, then was eclipsed by the town the Spaniards organised for Indians across the river. By 1840 the population of 400 included only about 100 Indians. That year also brought an earthquake and a tidal wave, and the mission was completely demolished. A replica, about half the original size, has been built on the original site, and while quite pretty, it is not high on the list of missions to visit. The church is in the town of the same name, on the coast between San Francisco and Monterey.

Mission *Santa Clara de Asis,* was founded on January 12, 1777, and is situated in the town of Santa Clara south-east of

San Francisco. It was, at one time, the most prosperous mission in the north, although it suffered the same as the other missions when California broke away from Spain. Santa Clara was taken over by the Jesuits in 1851, and has been used as an educational institution ever since. The university chapel standing today was built after the fire of 1926, which followed flood and earthquake, resulting in three former sets of buildings being destroyed.

Mission *Francisco de Asis (Dolores)*, October 9, 1776, is on the corner of 16th Street and Dolores Street in San Francisco's Mission District. The church is the oldest building in San Francisco, having come unscathed through the earthquake and fire of 1906, and the interior is largely unchanged from the original. The old cemetery is the only reminder of earlier times on the outside, as the church is now surrounded by the modern Mission Dolores Basilica and the city.

The original mission was started by one missionary, a Spanish officer and sixteen soldiers, settler families from Mexico, a herd of 200 cattle, plus cowboys, who had followed the overland trail from Monterey to found a fort, a colony and a mission. It was named in honour of St Francis of Assisi, the founder of the Franciscan Order, but the city took that name, and the mission was called after the little lake nearby, Dolores.

Mission *San Jose*, June 11, 1797, is on Highway 101 about 32km (20 miles) north of the city of San Jose and closer to Fremont. It was established as a half-way house between San Jose and San Francisco, across the approach to the San Joaquin Valley, but served more at first as headquarters for Spanish soldiers fighting the Indians. Things changed, though, and in 1831 there were 1877 Indians living and working at the mission. It was never as large as the other missions, but suffered the same hazards of earthquakes and neglect and mostly disappeared. A white New England style church was erected on the site in 1868, and rebuilding of the adobe mission began in 1982. By 1985 the church was finished, and was redecorated in the style of the 1830s.

Mission *San Rafael Arcangel,* December 14, 1817, was the only mission that was founded as a hospital. Situated north of the Golden Gate Bridge, its initial residents were converts from Dolores who had fallen prey to white man's diseases and tended to waste away in the damp and foggy climate of the San Francisco peninsula. Within five years the sanatorium on the sunny north shore had achieved **full** mission status, and had over a thousand healthy converts in its care.

This mission was the first to be secularized, and General Vallejo, the administrator, transferred all mission livestock to his own ranchos. Everything, including the vines and fruit trees, was dug up and taken away, and the mission was forgotten. Recent reconstruction work is being carried out on what experts think is the original site.

Mission *San Francisco de Solano,* the last of the missions, was founded on July 4, 1823. It is ironic that the mission owed its existence to fear of the Russians who were well established along the northern Californian coast, because the Russian traders turned out to be quite friendly, and donated many useful things to the new mission, including the bells. But, nevertheless, the mission was founded to give the governor another military outpost. Several hundred converts followed the Franciscans to Sonoma from Dolores, but the mission prospered only briefly. Its chapel was used as a parish church until 1880, then it was abandoned. In 1910, the remains of the property was purchased as a California Landmark and is now administered as a State Park, on a corner of the restored plaza.

CLIMATE

If you travel in local summer time, you probably won't need an umbrella, and that is the only general statement possible about California weather. In fact, I once arrived at LAX (LA International Airport) on a morning in August when there had been light rain, and it took two and a half hours to get a shuttle to my hotel in Beverly Hills. The only reason given for the long delay was the fact that, as it was raining, many drivers had taken the day off! Given the way the locals drive, and the poor state of the roads, I guess home was the safest place for them.

Los Angeles average temperatures range from 13C (56F) in January to 23C (73F) in July/August, the hottest months. At night, though, it gets pretty chilly year round, so never go out without a jacket of some type.

San Francisco average temperatures range from 11C (51F) in January to 16C (62F) in September, the hottest month, which it has to be agreed is not very hot. On my August visit, it would have been possible to freeze to death on Fisherman's Wharf without a fleecy-lined sweater.

Southern California, from San Luis Obispo to San Diego, doesn't really have a temperature range, although it is slightly warmer in summer.

The further you travel inland, the warmer it becomes, unless you are in the mountains, where it is anyone's guess whether it will be warm or whether it will snow, at any time of the year.

The answer to what kind of clothes to pack is - take some winter and some summer, and be a person for all seasons.

Because of the lack of rain, water shortage is a serious problem. Every hotel in which you stay will have signs begging you not to waste the water, and when you enter a restaurant you will notice that they no longer have those enormous glasses of water on the table that inexperienced travellers feel they must drink before they will be served. It seems unbelievable, but California has no dams or catchment areas, and what water runs off the hills is carefully channelled into the ocean.

POPULATION

The population of the State of California is around 30 million, which means that, roughly, one in every eleven people in the United States lives in California.

The only time the place seems crowded though, is when you are on a freeway in a hurry to get somewhere, and that is probably because there are 17 million registered vehicles in the State. Speaking of freeways, the average person, in the tourist industry at least, seems to be extremely proud of their traffic foul-ups, and tour-bus drivers always take great pains to tell you that you are on freeway number something-or-other because there is a pile up on at least three others.

This seems rather strange to a visitor who has had a hard day at say, Disneyland or Universal Studios, and just wants to get back to a hot shower and a few cold beers, and let someone else worry about the traffic.

LANGUAGE

The laws of the State of California state that the official language is English, but I would imagine that there are numbers of people who wouldn't be able to read the laws to discover that fact. **Basically, the native Californian is easy to understand, and you can work your way around some of the strange pronunciations.**

You also become accustomed to asking for 'regular milk' if you want milk, otherwise you receive some mysterious concoction called 'half-and-half', but half-and-half what, I am not sure.

Asking the man, or woman, on the street for directions can also become confusing. Maybe I'm strange, but I never think to pack a compass when travelling in a large city, and invariably you will be told to walk 'six blocks west' or 'two blocks south', or 'that's on the north side of Sunset, east of UCLA'.

You may well think that you could get your bearings by

looking at the sun, but that is not really a consideration in smoggy Downtown LA.

RELIGION
Freedom of religion is one of the things guaranteed in the Constitution of the United States.

HOLIDAYS
Public Holidays, which are observed throughout the USA are:

January 1 -	New Year's Day
January -	Martin Luther King's Birthday
February -	Washington/Lincoln Day
March/April -	Good Friday
May -	Memorial Day
July 4 -	Independence Day
September -	Labour Day
October -	Columbus Day
November 11 -	Veterans' Day
November (fourth Thursday) -	Thanksgiving
December 25 -	Christmas Day.

ENTRY REGULATIONS
All visitors, except Canadian nationals with an ID card, require a valid passport.

Similarly, all visitors, except Canadian nationals with an ID card, and Mexican nationals with a Mexican passport and a USA Border Crossing Card, require a visa.

Non-immigration visas may be obtained from any US Consulate. They are good for multiple entries for a period of five years, and are free of charge.

No immunizations are necessary when travelling to America.

All import and export currency transactions of over US$10000 must be reported to US Customs, otherwise there are no restrictions on the import and export of either local or foreign currency.

There is a departure tax when leaving the States, but it is built into the airline ticket so it doesn't create any dramas looking for left-over local currency.

> The following may be imported into the USA without incurring duty:
>
> 200 cigarettes or 50 cigars or 2kg of tobacco or proportionate amounts of each
> 1 litre of alcoholic beverage (age 21 or over)
> Gifts or articles up to a value of US$100 if the visit is for more than 72 hours (can be claimed only once every six months).
> Alcoholic beverages are not included in this allowance.

EMBASSIES

Foreign embassies are based in Washington, but there are consular offices in California.

Australia:
Australian Consulate-General, 611 North Larchmont Boulevard, Los Angeles, CA, ph (213) 469 4300.
Australian Consulate-General, One Bush Street, 7th Floor, San Francisco, CA, ph (415) 362 6160.

New Zealand:
NZ Consulate-General, 501 Santa Monica Boulevard, Santa Monica, ph (310) 395 7480
NZ Consulate-General, Alcoa Building, Maritime Plaza, San Francisco, CA, ph (415) 788 7430.

United Kingdom:
British Consulate-General, 11766 Wilshire Boulevard, Los Angeles, CA, ph (310) 477 3322.
British Consulate-General, 1 Sansome Street, San Francisco, CA, ph (415) 981 3030.

Canada:
Canadian Consulate-General, 300 South Grand Avenue, Los

Angeles, CA, ph (213) 687 7432.
Canadian Consulate-General, 50 Fremont, Suite 2100, San Francisco, CA, ph (415) 495 6021.

Singapore:
Contact Singaporean Embassy in Washington or one of the local offices of a Commonwealth country such as Australia for assistance or correct referral.

MONEY

The unit of currency is the US Dollar which is equal to 100 cents. Notes are in denominations of $1, 2, 5, 10, 20, 50 and 100, and coins in 1, 5 (nickel), 10 (dime), 25 (quarter) and 50 cents.

Approximate rates of exchange, which should be used as a guide only, are:

A$1 =	US$0.71
NZ$ =	US$0.50
UK£ =	US$1.80
CAN$ =	US$0.83

COMMUNICATIONS

Full International Direct Dialling facilities are available, and the country code is 1.

Local calls in California are a bit of a mystery.

If you are in, say, Beverly Hills, and wish to telephone someone in Downtown LA, it is not necessarily a local call, even though it is really just down the street. If you are ringing from a phone box, the operator will tell you to deposit more coins to connect the call. If you are ringing from a private phone, or more importantly, your hotel, the charge simply increases without you knowing until you pay the hotel bill.

Strangely, there are not many post offices in the United States, and the ones you find are quite old-fashioned.

You stand in a queue to buy the stamps, then go away and put them on the cards/envelopes, then stand in a queue to give them to the person who sold you the stamps - that's high technology for you.

You can also purchase stamps from machines in hotels and shops, but they are in bulk, and cost 25% more than the face value.

Airmail to Australia, for postcards anyway, takes anything up to four weeks, letters seem to make the trip in just over a week.

The United States publishes more newspapers than any other country in the world.

The most influential 'local' paper in California is the *Los Angeles Times*.

MISCELLANEOUS

Local time is GMT - 8.

Electricity is 110/120 volts AC, 60 cycles.

Electrical appliances not fitted with dual voltage flexibility require an adaptor which is best purchased in your home country.

Credit Cards

Credit cards are widely accepted, and in fact, it is recommended that people travel with at least one major credit card. Even if your accommodation has been pre-paid, some hotels request a credit card number before allotting a room, presumably to cover any miscellaneous extras. The same goes for hiring a car.

Travellers Cheques

It is best to take US Dollar travellers cheques, then you can always cash them at hotels and shops. Strangely though, you can't always cash them at banks. I tried three banks in the Beverly Hills area before I found one that would exchange either an American Express or a Visa travellers cheque, despite the fact that they all advertised that they sold one or the other.

Business Hours

Banks are open Mon-Fri, 9am-3pm.
Offices are open Mon-Fri, 9am-5.30pm.
Shops are usually open Mon-Sat, 9.30am-6pm, except in tourist areas when they are open for much longer hours, and on Sunday as well.
Post Offices are open, depending on their location, daily 9am-5pm.

Health

The water in California, though heavily chlorinated, is safe to drink, the milk is pasteurised, and all dairy products, local meats, poultry, seafood, fruit and vegetables are generally considered safe to eat.

Insurance

It is **absolutely vital that visitors take out some kind of insurance** before leaving home, which covers them for medical emergencies. In fact, sometimes treatment will be declined unless the patient has proof of insurance.

In any case, medical services are so expensive in the States, you could spend the rest of your life paying off the bill. This explains why the premiums are so much higher for a trip to America than to *any other part of the world*.

Also included in your cover should be insurance against theft.

Crime

In the unhappy event that you find yourself a victim of crime, it is essential that you report it to the local police, as soon as possible.

Whether they choose to interview you or not, a crime report will be made and you will be told its number.

You will need a copy of this report for the insurance company when you make a claim, and this copy is best arranged while you are in the States.

How?

Simply telephone the relevant police station and a recorded message will tell you the address to write to, and the amount of money required for the copy.

You can buy a cheque/money order from any post office, and send it to the police, together with a stamped envelope addressed to your home address, and the station will forward a copy of the report to you.

Why?

This saves you having to obtain a US Dollar cheque at home, and also, with a bit of luck, the report will arrive at your home before you do, facilitating your claim.

Tipping

> I'm sure tipping was not invented in America, but they certainly have it down to a fine art.

It doesn't matter if the bell boy scratched your designer luggage, or if the waitress was the surliest person you have ever seen in your life, it is absolutely necessary that you hand over a tip. Most of the time the person giving the 'service' simply holds out his/her hand, takes the money, pockets it and disappears. Occasionally you might get a thank you.

On Tour

When you are on a tour, be it for a full day or only a few hours, part of the spiel will include information on what size tip is expected. In centres like Anaheim, where people are obviously accustomed to Aussies and Kiwis who are not known for their largesse in these circumstances, the tip/gratuity is already included in the bill.

Earthquakes

California has many earthquakes, some that reach the front pages of the newspapers, and some that go unnoticed except by the seismographs. The chances of a visitor experiencing a full-scale earthquake are not great, and in fact the locals in San Francisco will tell you that the quake of 1989 was grossly exaggerated in the press. They say it just caused a bigger than normal traffic jam, which is to be expected when a bridge collapses.

Having said all that, there are a few survival tips to keep in mind in case you are unlucky.

1. If you are in a building, do not run outside, but take cover inside, preferably under a large piece of furniture, away from the windows. If you have to exit the building, use the stairwells, do not enter the elevators.

2. If you are out in the open, stay there, but not near trees, power lines, or the sides of buildings. If you are in amongst a lot of tall buildings, stand in a doorway.

3. If you are in a car, once you are clear of bridges, overpasses, telegraph poles and power lines, pull over to the side and stop, but stay in the car.

Liquor Laws

The legal age for drinking or buying alcohol in California is 21. Proof of age is required. No liquor may be served, purchased or consumed in public establishments between 2am and 6am.

Emergency Telephones

For police, fire, highway patrol, or life-threatening emergencies, dial 911.

Trivia

To people from the rest of the world,
*the light switches in America are all upside down,
*the toilets always seem as if they are going to overflow,
*and there are a million and one ways to turn on a tap. Sometimes, it is easier to have a cold shower than to endeavour to come to grips with the incredible piece of chrome that controls the hot/cold water flow.

NOTES

TRAVEL INFORMATION

HOW TO GET THERE

By Air

For people coming from overseas, this is obviously the best option for travel. Many **'bargain' fares** are available at various times of the year, and usually include very reasonable accommodation.

Some companies offer packages that include return airfares plus six nights in Anaheim, with the opportunity to obtain affordable accommodation at other destinations, such as Los Angeles, San Francisco or Hawaii.

Others can be combined with bus tours to take visitors further afield than California, including such places as Las Vegas, the Grand Canyon, and Denver, or even as far as Florida, New Orleans, New York, or north to Canada.

It is best to contact your travel agent well in advance to find out the availability of these 'specials', and sometimes it is worthwhile changing the dates on which you want to travel to take advantage of them.

California has three international airports - Los Angeles (LAX), San Francisco (SFO) and San Diego (SAN).

British Airways has flights from London

daily to	LAX and SF0,
daily except Tuesday to	SAN.

Air New Zealand has flights to LAX from:

Auckland -	daily.
Christchurch -	daily.
Wellington -	daily.
Brisbane -	Mon, Wed, Thurs, Sun, via Auckland.
Melbourne -	daily, via Auckland.
Sydney -	daily, via Auckland.

Qantas has flights from:

Sydney -	daily to LAX and SFO.
Melbourne -	daily to LAX and SFO.
Adelaide -	daily to LAX and SFO.
Brisbane -	daily to LAX and SFO.
Perth -	daily to LAX and SFO.
Hobart -	daily to LAX and SFO.
Auckland -	daily, except Mon, to LAX.
Honolulu -	Mon, Wed, Sat to LAX and SFO.

Note that all Qantas flights between LAX and SFO are operated by *USAir*.

American Airlines has flights from:

London -	daily to LAX, SFO and SAN.
Montreal -	daily to LAX, SFO and SAN
Vancouver -	daily to LAX and SAN.

United Airlines has flights from:

Auckland -	daily to LAX, SFO and SAN.
Sydney -	daily to LAX, SFO and SAN.
Vancouver -	daily to LAX, SFO and SAN.

Canadian Airlines has flights from:

Vancouver -	daily to LAX, SFO and SAN.
Montreal -	daily to LAX and SFO.
Sydney -	Fri to LAX, Tues, Fri, Sun to SFO.

Air Canada has flights from:

Toronto -	daily to LAX, SFO and SAN.
Montreal -	daily to LAX, SFO and SAN.
Quebec -	daily to LAX and SFO.

Singapore Airlines has flights from:

Singapore -	daily to LAX via Tokyo,
	daily to SFO via Hong Kong.

Cathay Pacific has flights from:

Hong Kong -	daily to LAX non-stop.

Information on transfers from the airports to the various cities is included in the Local Transport section of the particular city.

For those who are already in the United States and wish to visit California, air travel is still probably the best option, given the long distance involved from, say, the East to West Coast. All major domestic carriers service California, and there are domestic airports at Bakersfield, Burbank, Fresno, Imperial, Inyokern/Ridgecrest, Los Angeles, Monterey, Ontario, Santa Ana (John Wayne-Orange County), Palmdale/Lancaster, Palm Springs, Sacramento, San Diego, San Francisco, San Jose, San Luis Obispo, Santa Barbara and Santa Maria.

> For information on schedules and fares, contact any of the following toll free:
>
> | | |
> |---|---|
> | Delta Air Lines, Inc, | ph 800 221 1212 |
> | **Midway Airlines,** | **ph 800 621 5015** |
> | Northwest, | ph 800 328 2216 |
> | **Southwest,** | **ph 800 531 5601.** |

By Rail

Amtrak, the most complete long-distance passenger rail network in America, connects about 500 cities, with over 30 of them in California. They have special deals for round trips between New York and San Francisco, and New York and Los Angeles, as well as excursion fares that allow three stopovers. *They also offer other money-saving special fares,* and for further current information contact them toll free on 800/872 7245.

By Bus

Greyhound connects all the major cities in the United States, and for more information on passes available, see the Local Transport section in this chapter.

ACCOMMODATION

California hosts millions of visitors every year, and has the accommodation facilities to do so, but it is still wise to book in advance. Many organisations hold their conferences in the Golden State, and often book the majority of, if not all, the rooms in a hotel, leaving nothing for the tourist in transit.

Hotel rooms in the US are of a very high standard. A double room usually contains two double beds (sometimes queen size), television, telephone, two comfortable lounge chairs, a table, and plenty of cupboard and drawer space. Sometimes a refrigerator is provided, but only in Anaheim have I ever found tea and coffee making facilities. There is always an ice machine on every floor, and it is best not to have the room near the machine as they are noisy contraptions, especially in the still of the night.

> If you are booking accommodation through a travel agent in your home country, ensure that someone in their office has actually been to the city of your choice, then you can be certain that you are not put in a sleazy neighbourhood.

I met one Aussie couple travelling with young children, who had found themselves booked into a substandard hotel room in the 'red light' district of San Francisco. They were not impressed.

LOCAL TRANSPORT

Air
Refer to the How To Get There section above for details of airports and companies that provide air travel within California.

Rail

Amtrak has a service to Los Angeles and Seattle, Washington, operating out of Oakland, and regular bus services connect from the Transbay Terminal in San Francisco. There is also a service between San Diego and Seattle, with stops between, and one between Los Angeles and Las Vegas.

For Australians:
Amtrak is represented in Australia by Thomas Cook and Walshes World, and they report a big rise in foreign sales.

Southern Pacific has a service from San Francisco to the towns on the Peninsula.

Car

All the major car rental companies are represented in California, and to rent a car you have to be over the age of 16, and have a current driver's licence.

The Automobile Club of Southern California, 2601 South Figueroa Street, Los Angeles, CA 90007, ph (213) 741 3111, has reciprocal arrangements with interstate and overseas Automobile Associations, so take your local membership card with you. In San Francisco contact the California State Automobile Association, 150 Van Ness Avenue, CA 94102, ph 415/565 2012.

> **Traffic drives on the right-hand side of the road, and the wearing of seat-belts is compulsory.**

The speed limit on most streets is 35mph, or as sign-posted. Freeway speed is usually 55mph. You can get a ticket for driving at speeds that are considered to be dangerously slow, as well as for those that seem dangerously fast. It is permissible to turn right at a red light after coming to a complete stop.

Driving in San Francisco is fine if you are into hill starts and dodging cable cars, which, along with pedestrians, have right of way.

Driving in Los Angeles is a challenge, and not to be considered until you have bought a good map and studied the freeway system. Even then it is best to avoid driving in the peak-hour periods.

Hiring a Car

It is advisable to check out what is covered by the insurance policy. Some do not cover collisions, others do not cover burglary. Find out if you can pay waivers to cover these.

Also, make sure that you can drop off the car where you intend to finish your trip.

If you intend to fly out of San Francisco, but picked up your car on arrival at Los Angeles, it is a long drive back if the company you hired from does not have facilities at San Francisco.

Some rental companies offer **24-hour emergency service**, and some who do not have counters at airports have **free transfers** to their offices. If you want to drive yourself, do some research first, ask a lot of questions, and have it all organised before you leave home.

Another consideration is renting a motorhome, and as with cars, find out the facts, and organise it before you leave.

There are many fly/drive holidays on offer from the big package tour companies, which give the opportunity for accommodation vouchers at reasonable rates.

The car rental companies are listed in the sections on the various cities.

Following is a list of approximate driving distances.

From Los Angeles to:

Anaheim -	43km (27 miles)
Lake Tahoe -	**710km (441 miles)**
Oakland -	595 km (370 miles)
San Diego -	**201km (125 miles)**
San Francisco -	628km (390 miles)
San Jose -	**544km (338 miles)**
Santa Barbara -	148km (92 miles)
Yosemite -	**494km (307 miles)**

From San Francisco to:	
Anaheim -	729km (453 miles)
Lake Tahoe -	314km (195 miles)
Los Angeles -	628km (390 miles) inland, 713km (437 miles) coast
Oakland -	16km (10 miles)
San Diego -	818km (508 miles) inland, 893km (555km) coast
San Jose -	82km (51 miles)
Santa Barbara -	507km (315 miles)

Price of Petrol

The price of petrol will vary as you are driving around, and people from "metric" countries will have to remember that the prices advertised are for a gallon, not a litre. It is much cheaper to use a Self Serve outlet, as Full Service can put the price up by over 50c a gallon.

Bus

Greyhound, the name synonymous with bus travel in the US, has many **special deals that can only be purchased outside of North America**, through the local Greyound office, or travel agents. Passes are available for 4 days to 30 days travel.

But, there are a few conditions: no child discounts; mid-week travel only; no daily extensions; additional charges for the round trip journey Flagstaff, Arizona to the Grand Canyon; and additional charges for side trips between Las Vegas, Nevada, and Hoover Dam, Nevada, and between Las Vegas, Nevada and Death Valley, California.

The valid period of the various passes begins on the date of the first trip you make, so if you make your first trip from Los Angeles to, say, San Diego and stay there for three nights, you have blown a 4-day pass. Alternatively, a 4-Day pass from LA to San Francisco is good value for money, and would allow you to stay at three places on the way, eg Ventura, Solvang and Monterey.

The longer 30-Day passes are more suitable for people travelling across the country rather than staying in only California.

Extensions to the passes are available, but they must be purchased at the same time as the original pass.

FOOD

Wherever you travel in California there will be a wide choice of restaurants, coffee shops and fast food outlets, and they will all offer you generous servings.

Generally speaking, the restaurants, both in the hotels and on the streets, are quite expensive, especially when you add on the tip/gratuity.

Names and addresses are given in the sections on the various cities.

In the *Eating Out* sections in some chapters of this guide there is an indication of restaurant prices, rated as follows:

Reasonable = main course under $10

Moderate = main course $10-20

Expensive = main course $20+.

Tip

For breakfast. Small coffee shops and delicatessens abound, and you can get a hearty breakfast for about half the price of that offered in a hotel. And, quite often you get to meet some of the locals and pick up good tips for sightseeing and bus routes, etc.

DRINK

Coca Cola is available, as you would expect, everywhere, and when bought by the glass is about half ice, half Coke. *Be quick to state if you don't want ice, and look at the surprised look on the server.* Often they will refuse to serve you because obviously there is more Coke in a glass without ice than one with it.

The **local beers,** Coors, Millers, Budweiser, are generally quite palatable, but if you are Aussie, British or a Kiwi, and don't want to experiment, **Fosters is quite common.**

Californian wines are very good, particularly *the Chardonnays*.

SHOPPING

The *UK* has its **VAT**,
New Zealand has its **GST**,
Australia tried hard to introduce some form of consumption tax, but has **wholesale tax** instead,
and the *United States* has its **Sales Tax**.

But, in the UK and in New Zealand, it is not treated like some sort of state secret. The price tag either tells you that it has already been added, or that the goods cost so much, and so much tax will be added. In the States, you find something you want to buy and the ticket says, say $25.00, but that is not what you will have to pay.

> *When the sale goes through the cash register, the tax is added. The docket does not say '?% tax = $x', it just says '+ $x'.*

I suppose if you live there and shop there all the time, it all becomes crystal clear, but to the overseas traveller who has already converted the price to their currency to see if the article was worth buying, having to suddenly add on some percentage which is not clear anyway, is extremely frustrating.

> Nevertheless, the **good buys** are **shoes, jeans,** and **cosmetics**. Ladies' and **men's fashion shoes** are much cheaper than elsewhere, including those imported from Italy, and I'm sure that every person leaving California has at least one pair of *Reeboks* in their luggage. **Jeans** are about half the price you'd pay in Australia and the United Kingdom, and there is much more variety in design and styles.

Cosmetics, particularly *Revlon*, are also less expensive, and there are two types. The *department stores* stock one range, and the *pharmacists* (no longer usually called 'drug stores') stock another, and that is where you pick up the good bargains in lipsticks, foundations, eye shadows and mascaras. **Perfumes**, which were once high on everyone's shopping list, are now not much cheaper than anywhere else.

SPORT

The main spectator sports are, of course, Baseball, Football and Basketball, and details of where you can attend games are in the sections on the various cities.

There are many golf courses in the State, and these are also covered in the city sections.

Other sporting facilities available include tennis courts, jogging tracks, horseriding, snow skiing, and then, of course, there are the beaches.

NOTES

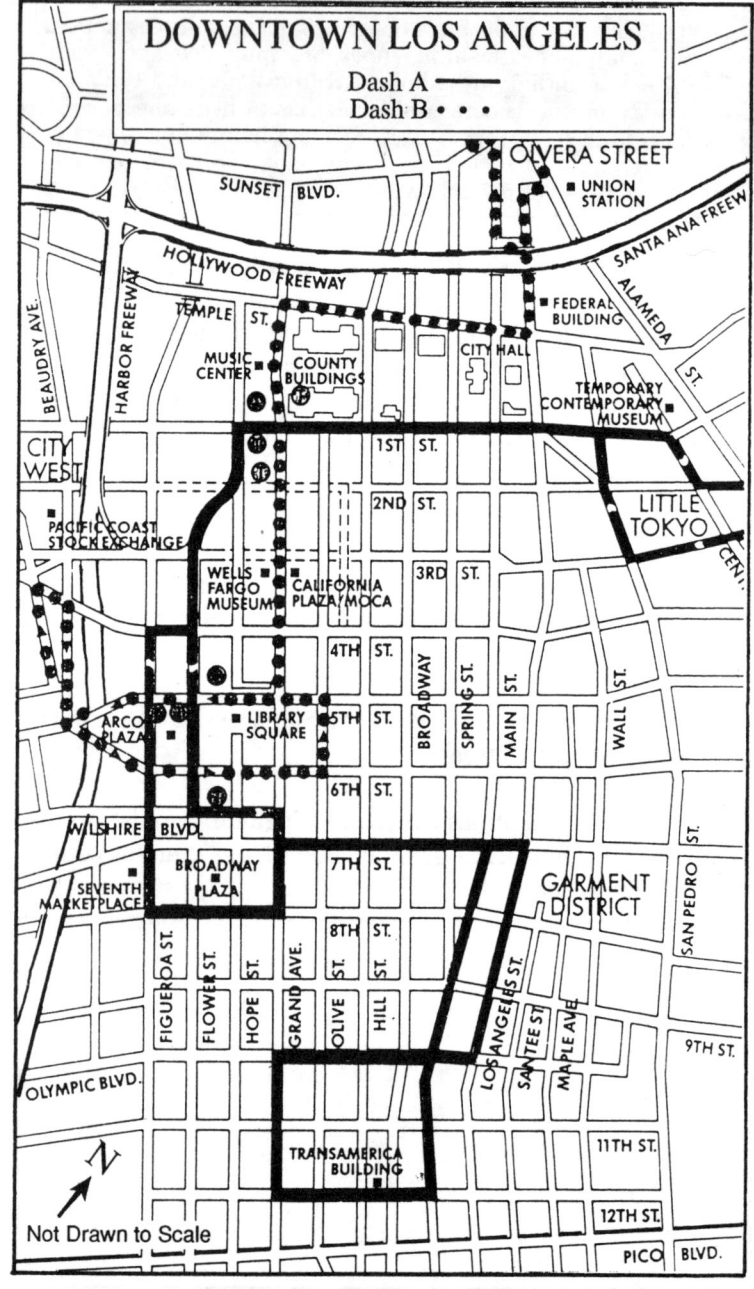

LOS ANGELES

The city of Los Angeles has an area of 1205 sq km (465 sq miles), and a population of 3.4 million. It is roughly divided into eight areas - Downtown, Hollywood, West Hollywood, Beverly Hills, West Los Angeles, Santa Monica and the Coast, The Valley, and Pasadena. The Los Angeles area includes desert regions, mountain ranges and 116km (72 miles) of beaches.

Los Angeles was founded by a group of eleven families, who would not in their wildest dreams have imagined the city as it is today. To most people it evokes an idea of excitement and glamour, probably because of the movie industry, and to some it is simply the home of Disneyland, which is actually 43km (27 miles) out of LA in the town of Anaheim.

For the first-time visitor arriving by plane, the thick pall of smog that you fly through before landing is quite daunting, and when you are travelling around LA you will notice that the tall buildings are invisible only a few kilometres from the city centre. Many reasons are given for the smog - something to do with the wind currents, the proximity of the ocean and the hills, the number of cars on the road, etc - but I have visited many cities in the world with similar topography that do not have the same smog problem. Presumably the local authorities are doing something about it, and the rest of the world will learn from their findings.

HOW TO GET THERE

Getting to Los Angeles is covered in the Travel Information chapter.

TOURIST INFORMATION

The Downtown Los Angeles Visitor Information Center, 685 South Figueroa Street (between Wilshire Boulevard and Seventh Street), Los Angeles, CA 90017, ph (213) 689 8822, is open Mon-Fri 8am-5pm, Sat 8.30am-5pm. The staff here are extremely helpful, going beyond the call of duty to make sure that your stay in LA is all you want.

The Hollywood Visitor Information Center, The Janes House, Janes Square, 6541 Hollywood Boulevard, Hollywood, CA 90028, ph (213) 689 8822, is open Mon-Sat 9am-5pm, and is also worth visiting.

ACCOMMODATION

There are far too many hotels in LA to list them all here, so the following is a selection, with prices for a double room per night, in **US Dollars**, which should be used as a guide only.

DOWNTOWN

Telephone Area Code is 213.

I would not really recommend staying in the Downtown area.

It is close to the shops, marts, museums and theatres, but is not the area where you would go for a walk at night, in fact, you have to be careful even through the day. Nevertheless, **if you desperately want to stay in the centre of the city, here are some locations,** but, please, leave your valuables in the hotel safe when venturing out.

Checkers Hotel Kempinski, 535 South Grand Avenue, ph 624 0000 - very central - 190 rooms, restaurant, cocktail lounge, swimming pool - $200-285.

The Biltmore Hotel, 506 South Grand Avenue (at Sixth Street), ph 624 1011 - very central - 700 rooms, restaurants, cocktail lounges, swimming pool, courtesy airport bus - $185-250.

Radisson Wilshire Plaza, 3515 Wilshire Boulevard, ph 381 7411 - in the Wilshire business corridor - 364 rooms, restaurants, cocktail lounge, swimming pool - $130-170.

Los Angeles Athletic Club, 431 West Seventh Street, ph 625 2211 - deluxe city club, built in 1904, with extensive fitness facilities - 60 rooms, restaurant, cocktail lounge, swimming pool - $120-150.

Holiday Inn City Center, 1020 South Figueroa Street, ph 748 1291 - close to downtown shopping and the California Mart - 195 rooms, restaurant, cocktail lounge, pool, airport bus service - $95-135.

Holiday Inn Downtown, 750 South Garland Avenue, ph 628 5242 - near shopping, California Mart, USC, LA Coliseum and Sports Arena - 202 rooms, restaurant, cocktail lounge, pool, airport bus service - $90-110.

Figueroa Hotel, 939 South Figueroa Street, ph 627 8971 - one block from Convention Center - 280 rooms, restaurants, cocktail lounges, swimming pool, airport bus service - $72-120.

Kawada Hotel, 200 South Hill Street, ph 621 4455 - European-type hotel - 115 rooms, restaurant, cocktail lounge, - $62-95.

Inntowne Hotel Los Angeles, 925 South Figueroa Street, ph 628 2222 - near Convention Center - 170 rooms, restaurants, cocktail lounge, swimming pool, airport bus service - $69-86.

Howard Johnson Downtown, 1640 Marengo Street, ph 223 3841 - 2 miles from Downtown - 122 rooms, restaurant, cocktail lounge, swimming pool - $56-64.

Royal Host Motel, 901 West Olympic Boulevard, ph 626 6255 - one block from Convention Center - 54 rooms, meal coupon for restaurant next door - $36-50.

Motel de Ville, 1123 West Seventh Street, ph 624 8474 - three blocks from Convention Center - 60 rooms, restaurant, swimming pool - $35-45.

HOLLYWOOD

Telephone Area code is 213.
North Hollywood and Universal City Area Code is 818.

Sheraton Universal Hotel, 333 Universal Terrace Parkway, Universal City, ph 908 1212 - in the heart of the entertainment industry - 444 rooms, restaurants, cocktail lounges, swimming pool - $165-225.

Hollywood Roosevelt Hotel, 7000 Hollywood Boulevard, Hollywood, ph 466 7000 - on Walk of Fame, opposite Chinese Theatre -322 rooms, restaurants, cocktail lounges, swimming pool, airport bus service - $100-110.

Holiday Inn Hollywood, 1755 North Highland Avenue (at Hollywood Boulevard), Hollywood, ph 462 7181 - minutes from Downtown LA, Beverly Hills and University City - 470 rooms, restaurants, cocktail lounges, swimming pool, airport bus service - $89-132.

The Beverly Garland's Holiday Inn, 4222 Vineland Avenue, North Hollywood, ph 980 8000 - near Universal Studios - 258 rooms, restaurant, cocktail lounge, swimming pool, tennis, airport bus service - $70-105.

Best Western Hollywood Plaza, 2011 North Highland Avenue, ph 851 1800 - near Mann's Chinese Theatre - 82 rooms, swimming pool - $62-85.

Dunes Wilshire Motor Hotel, 4300 Wilshire Boulevard, LA, ph 938 3616 - minutes from Miracle Mile, Beverly Hills, LA Convention Center - 58 rooms, coffee shop, swimming pool - $54-65.

Dunes Sunset Motel and Restaurant, 5625 Sunset Boulevard, LA, ph 467 5171 - near Mann's Chinese Theatre - 57 rooms, restaurant, cocktail lounge - $54-65.

Saharan Motor Hotel, 7212 Sunset Boulevard, Hollywood, ph 874 6700 - surrounded by restaurants, nightclubs, theatres and shopping - 63 rooms, swimming pool - $35-55.

Hollywood Downtowner Motel, 5601 Hollywood Boulevard, Hollywood, ph 464 7191 - close to Hollywood Freeway and major attractions - 30 rooms, swimming pool - $38-48.

WESTSIDE

(Beverly Hills, Century City, Westwood)
Telephone Area Code is 310.

Four Seasons Hotel at Beverly Hills, 300 South Doheny Drive, at Burton Way, ph 273 2222 - in quiet neighbourhood close to Rodeo Drive, Beverly Center and Melrose Avenue - 180 rooms, restaurants, cocktail lounge, swimming pool - $280-325.

Beverly Hills Ritz Hotel, 10300 Wilshire Boulevard, ph 275 5575 - modern European decor in central position - 100 suites, restaurant, cocktail lounge - $115-290.

J.W. Marriott Hotel at Century City, 2151 Avenue of the Stars, ph 277 2777 - luxury, in Century City, adjacent to Beverly Hills - 367 rooms, restaurant, cocktail lounge, swimming pools - $195-250.

The Beverly Hilton, 9876 Wilshire Boulevard, Beverly Hills, ph 274 7777 - near Rodeo Drive shops and Century City - 578 rooms, restaurants, cocktail lounges, swimming pool - $155-255.

Holiday Inn Brentwood/Bel Air, 170 North Church Lane, ph 476 6411 - near UCLA - 207 rooms, restaurant, cocktail lounge, swimming pool - $98-150.

Hotel Del Capri, 10587 Wilshire Boulevard, LA, ph 474 3511 - minutes from Beverly Hills, Century City and Santa Monica beaches - 35 rooms, swimming pool - $85-105.

Howard Johnson Plaza-Culver City, 5990 Gren Valley Circle, Cluver City, ph 641 7740 - 200 rooms, restaurant, cocktail lounge, swimming pool - $65-89.

Best Western Royal Palace, 2528 South Sepulveda Boulevard, LA, ph 477 9066 - 6km from beach, 3km from Century City - 55 rooms, swimming pool - $55-75.

SANTA MONICA

Telephone Area Code is 310.

Shutters on the Beach, 1 Pico Boulevard, ph 458 0030 - panoramic views of the coast - 186 rooms, restaurant, cocktail lounge, swimming pool - $225-375.

Loews Santa Monica Beach Hotel, 1700 Ocean Avenue, ph 458 6700 - in walking distance of Santa Monica Pier - 349 rooms, restaurants, cocktail lounge, swimming pool - $195-300.

Malibu Beach Inn, 22878 Pacific Coast Highway, Malibu, ph 456 6444 - 44 rooms, continental breakfast - $125-200.

The Georgian - A Grand Heritage Hotel, 1415 Ocean Avenue, ph 395 9945 - in downtown Santa Monica - 56 rooms, continental breakfast included - $125-175.

Channel Road Inn, West Channel Road, Santa Monica, ph 459 1920 - one of the most romantic inns in the country - 14 rooms, full breakfast included - $95-180.

The Sovereign Hotel at Santa Monica Bay, 205 Washington Avenue, ph 395 9921 - 2 blocks north of Wilshire Boulevard - 22 rooms, continental breakfast included - $49-99.

MARINA DEL REY

Telephone Area Code is 310.

Doubletree Hotel Marina del Rey, 4100 Admiralty Way, ph 301 3000 - panoramic views, 8km north of LAX - 300 rooms, restaurants, cocktail lounges, swimming pool - $170-210.

Marina del Rey Hotel, 13534 Bali Way, ph 301 1000 - water on three sides of hotel, 8km north of LAX - 154 rooms, restaurants, cocktail lounge, swimming pool - $140-210.

Marina Del Rey Marriott, 13480 Maxella Avenue, ph 822 8555 - ten minutes from LAX, close to Villa Marina and Fisherman's Village - 283 rooms, restaurant, cocktail lounge, swimming pool - $100-159.

Marina International Hotel & Bungalows, 4200 Admiralty Way, ph 301 2000 - near Venice Beach, 8km from LAX - 94 rooms, restaurant, cocktail lounge, pool, courtesy airport bus -

$125-145, bungalows $185-250.
Jolly Roger, 2904 Washington Boulevard, ph 822 2904 - in walking distance of Marina del Rey, less than 2km to ocean beaches - 82 rooms, swimming pool, continental breakfast included - $50-75.

VENICE

Telephone Area Code is 310.
Marina Pacific Hotel and Suites, 1697 Pacific Avenue, ph 452 1111 - near beach community - 92 rooms, restaurant - $80-120.
Cadillac Hotel, 401 Ocean Front Walk, ph 399 8876 - on the beachfront, tours to Disneyland, Hollywood and studios - 40 rooms - $54-64.

AIRPORT AREA

Telephone Area Code is 310.
Sheraton LAX, 6101 West Century Boulevard, ph 642 1111 - modern hotel near beaches and freeways - 716 rooms, restaurants, sushi bar, cocktail lounge, swimming pool - $130-150.
Holiday Inn-LAX, 9901 South La Cienega Boulevard, ph 649 5151 - off 405 Fwy - 402 rooms, restaurant, cocktail lounge, swimming pool - $79-102.
Howard Johnson LAX, 8620 Airport Boulevard, ph 645 7700 - one mile from LAX - 150 rooms, restaurant, cocktail lounge, swimming pool - $75-85.
Hampton Inn, 10300 La Cienega Boulevard, Inglewood, ph 337 1000 - 150 rooms, continental breakfast included - $65-85.
Best Western Airpark Hotel, 640 West Manchester Boulevard, Inglewood, ph 677 7378 - near LAX, shopping, restaurants and Hollywood Park Racetrack - 64 rooms, swimming pool, courtesy airport bus - $58-82.
Quality Hotel LAX, 5249 West Century Boulevard, LA, ph 645 2200 - 1 mile from LAX - 270 rooms, restaurant, cocktail lounge, swimming pool - $49-89.
Days Inn Airport Center, 901 West Manchester Boulevard,

Inglewood, ph 649 0800 - near beaches, shopping and Hollywood Park Racetrack - 36 rooms, restaurant, swimming pool - $47-59.

SOUTH BAY AND BEACH CITIES

Telephone Area Code is 310.

Holiday Inn Crowne Plaza, 300 North Harbor Drive, ph 318 8888 - 11km south of LAX, ocean view resort - 339 rooms, restaurant, cocktail lounges, swimming pool, airport bus service - $135-180.

Portofino Inn, 260 Portofino Way, Redondo Beach, ph 379 8481 - only oceanfront hotel in King Harbor - restaurants, cocktail lounges, swimming pool - $129-149.

Barnabey's Hotel & Restaurant, 3501 Sepulveda Boulevard, Manhattan Beach, ph 545 8466 - 2km from beach and 3km south of LAX - 120 rooms, restaurant, cocktail lounge, swimming pool, courtesy airport bus - $119-159.

Holiday Inn Torrance Gateway, 19800 South Vermont Avenue, Torrance, ph 781 9100 - located on travel routes that connect the area's most popular destinations - 301 rooms, restaurant, cocktail lounge, swimming pool - $95-115.

Western Sunrise, 400 North Harbour Drive, Redondo Beach, ph 376 0746 - across from King Harbor Marina and beaches - 109 rooms, restaurant, swimming pool - $95.

Redondo Beach Pier Travelodge, 206 South Pacific, Redondo Beach, ph 318 1811 - near the pier, King Harbor and shopping - 35 rooms, swimming pool - $58-70.

Best Western Galleria Inn, 2740 Artesia Boulevard, Redondo Beach, ph 370 4353 - near shopping, restaurants and South Bay beaches - 27 rooms, continental breakfast included - $52-68.

Sea Horse Motel, 233 North Sepulveda Boulevard, Manhattan Beach, ph 376 7951 - in walking distance of beaches and shops - 33 rooms, restaurant, swimming pool - $40-58.

SAN FERNANDO VALLEY

Telephone Area Code is 818.

Airtel Plaza Hotel, 7277 Valjean Avenue, Van Nuys, ph 997 7676 - at Van Nuys airport - 249 rooms, restaurant, cocktail lounge, swimming pool - $99-160.

Sportsmen's Lodge, 1285 Ventura Boulevard, Studio City, ph 769 4700 - near Universal Studios and Hollywood - 180 rooms, restaurant, cocktail lounge, swimming pool - $94-114.

Holiday Inn Mid-San Fernando Valley, 8244 Orion Avenue, Van Nuys, ph 989 5010 - freeway access to entire LA area - 126 rooms, restaurant, cocktail lounge, swimming pool - $64-125.

Warner Gardens Motel, 21706 Ventura Boulevard, Woodland Hills, ph 992 4426 - in Warner Center business comples with easy access to Hollywood, Beverly Hills and Malibu - 40 rooms, coffee shop, swimming pool - $46-54.

St George Motor Inn, 19454 Ventura Boulevard, Tarzana, ph 345 6911 - in the heart of the valley - 51 rooms, swimming pool, continental breakfast included - $44-55.

SAN GABRIEL VALLEY

The Ritz-Carlton, Huntington Hotel, 1401 South Oak Knoll Avenue, Pasadena, ph (818) 568 3900 - luxury landmark - 358 rooms, restaurants, cocktail lounge, swimming pool, tennis courts - $135-210.

Red Lion Glendale, 100 West Glenoaks Boulevard, Glendale, ph (818) 956 5466 - near Gene Autry Museum - 338 rooms, restaurants, cocktail lounges, swimming pool - $125-155.

Holiday Inn Express, 705 North San Gabriel Boulevard, Rosemead, ph (213) 726 2227 - near shopping, cinema complex, park and golf - 70 rooms, swimming pool, breakfast inlcuded - $59-69.

Comfort Inn-Eagle Rock, 2300 West Colorado Boulevard, LA, ph (213) 256 1199 - near Pasadena's Rose Bowl and Dodger Stadium - 58 rooms, continental breakfast included - $48-100.

SANTA CLARITA VALLEY

Valencia Hilton Garden Inn, 27710 The Old Road, Valencia, ph (805) 254 8800 - closest hotel to Six Flags Magic Mountain - 148 rooms, restaurant, cocktail lounge, swimming pool - $79-125.

LOCAL TRANSPORT

From the Airport

Los Angeles International Airport (LAX) is located near the coast, 27km (17 miles) from Downtown LA, and there are several companies that operate shuttle services to various areas and hotels. After you exit the terminal, you will notice an **information kiosk** on your right, and the person locked in there will direct you to a shuttle stop across a lane of traffic.

> If you have had a long flight, be particularly careful when crossing the traffic lane, especially if this is your first brush with traffic driving on the right, because they are coming at you from the wrong way.

At **the shuttle stop** there is a person, with a hand-held gizmo who can apparently contact the various mini-buses, and tell you how long you will have to wait.

If you already have a *pre-paid shuttle transfer* to your hotel, you will have to wait until an empty mini-bus from that company stops in front of you.

If you have *no such arrangement,* the person in charge of the shuttle stop will flag down an empty bus that has your destination area on a sign.

Check the price before you get in the bus, but be assured that it is going to be much less expensive than a taxi, especially if you are staying in, say, Anaheim. If you are staying in a private home, the shuttle will still drop you at the door.

If you are going to fly out of LAX on your return trip, book your shuttle to the airport at least 24 hours in advance.

The following companies have shuttle services to/from LAX:
Diva, 400 South Beverly Drive, Beverly Hills, ph (310) 278 3482.
LA Deer Services, 250 East First Street, ph (213) 617 8645.
Prime Time Shuttle, 7955 San Fernando Road, Sun Valley, ph (818) 504 3600.
S&L Transportation & Hospitality Services, PO Box 2088, Canoga Park, ph (310) 556 1853.
Shuttle Trak, 9100 Sepulveda Boulevard, Westchester, ph (310) 216 9186.
Super Shuttle Inc, 531 South Van Ness Avenue, Torrance, ph (310) 782 6600, (213) 775 6600.

Bus

Bus transportation is provided by the Southern California Rapid Transit District (RTD) and several smaller municipal organisations. For information on all RTD services and routes, ph (213) 626 4455, or call into their ticket office at 419 South Main Street, LA, where they have maps and schedules. They also have another office in ARCO Towers, 515 South Flower Street, LA.

The basic fare is $1.10 (55c for over 65s with proof of age), and you have to **have the exact fare as no change is given.** Transfers are 25c each.

> *Boarding a public bus for the first time in the States is a bit of a culture shock. I guess we always expect America to have the latest and the best, but this certainly does not apply to their buses. The vehicles are old and dirty, the insides covered with graffiti, and the bus drivers can be rather less than charming.*

The Downtown Area Short Hop (DASH) shuttle system operates in the central city area, and links major business, government, retail and entertainment centres. Five routes are in operation, and the buses run at five to twenty minute intervals Mon-Fri 6.30am-6.30pm, Sat 10am-5pm. Again the exact fare is required, this time 25c with transfers free.

Rail

Los Angeles is in the process of constructing a light rail transportation system that will connect Downtown LA with outlying districts, and the Metro Blue Line rail service between Downtown and Long Beach is already in operation, 6am-9pm daily.

The city's first subway, the Metro Red Line, runs between historic Union Station and Westlake/MacArthur Park at Wilshire and Alvarado boulevards. The Red Line also connects with the Blue Line at Downtown's Seventh Street Station.

The entire Metro Rail System is expected to be completed in the next years and will cover 300 miles of track, including light rail, subway and commuter rail.

Taxi

Taxi stands are found at airports, train and bus terminals, and at major hotels. Otherwise, you have to book them by phone, as they will rarely pull over when hailed. Fares are $1.90 flagfall, plus $1.60 per mile, plus 15% tip. The average fare from LAX to Downtown LA is between $24-$28 plus $3.60-4.20.

In the Downtown area there is a "One-Fare Zone", bounded by the Harbor Freeway to the west, Main Street to the east, Pico Boulevard to the south and the Hollywood Freeway to the north. Taxi travel in this zone costs a flat $3.50. For more information contact Checker Cab, ph (213) 221 2455, or LA Taxi, ph (213) 627 7000.

Car

Before you head off for the rental agency, read the section on driving in the Travel Information chapter.

Peak hour driving times in LA are 7.30-10.30am and

3.00-6.30pm, and it is advisable to stay off the freeways during these periods. Traffic conditions are reported on many radio stations, but the most frequent coverage is supplied by KNX/1070-AM and KFWB/980-AM.

Fortunately, the directional signs on the freeways state the names of the destinations, rather than the directions, which makes it easier for overseas travellers. The numbers and names of the freeways are as follows:

1	Pacific Coast Highway (coastal route)
5	Golden State/Santa Ana Freeway (north/south)
10	Santa Monica/San Bernardino Freeway (east/west)
60	Pomona Freeway (runs east/west)
91	Artesia/Redondo Freeway (runs east/west)
101	HollywooFreeway(runs north/south)
101	Ventura Freeway (runs east/west)
110	Harbor/Pasaden Freeway (runs north/south)
134	VenturaFreeway(runs east/west
170	Hollywood Freeway(runs north/south)
210	Foothill Freeway (runs east/west)
405	San Diego Freeway (runs north/south)
605	San Gabriel River Freeway (runs north/south)
710	Long Beach Freeway (runs north/south)

Street parking is prohibited in Downtown LA during the day, so it is wise to find out if your hotel has a parking area.

Alamo Rent A Car, 9020 Aviation Boulevard, Inglewood, CA 90301, ph (213) 649 2245. Agents in Australia are General Travel Marketing, ph (02) 436 0566. Excellent rates if booked and paid for outside the USA.

Avis LAX Rent-A-Car, 9217 Airport Boulevard, LA, 90045, ph (310) 646 5600.

Budget Rent A Car-LAX, 9775 Airport Boulevard, Los Angeles, CA 90043, ph (310) 649 7500.

Dollar Rent-A-Car, 100 North Sepulveda Boulevard, El Segundo, CA 90245, ph (310) 535 7500.

Enterprise Rent-A-Car, 17210 South Main Street, Carson, CA 90749-5015, ph (310) 329 3030.
The Hertz Corp, 9029 Airport Boulevard, Los Angeles, CA 90045, ph (310) 646 4861.
Midway Rent-A-Car, 2926 Wilshire Boulevard, Los Angeles, CA 90010, Ph (213) 487 470; 4900 Century Boulevard, Inglewood, CA 90301, ph (310) 673 0700; 8420 Sunset Boulevard, Los Angeles, CA 90069, ph (213) 650 5823; 4201 Lankershim Boulevard, North Hollywood, CA 91602, ph (818) 985 9770.

EATING OUT

Los Angeles has the reputation of being one of the world's leading restaurant cities, and if this means that there are a lot of restaurants, it is well deserved. Whether the quality of the food lives up to the reputation is for each individual to decide. Nevertheless, one plus for dining in the 'in' restaurants is that you may find yourself in the same room as your favourite 'star'. I hasten to stress 'in the same room', not 'at a nearby table', as where you will be seated depends on who you are and how many people would recognise you. After all, the movie stars are the closest thing the United States has to royalty.

Many restaurants in LA take advantage of the weather and have outdoor seating with the regulation greenery, others rely more on ostentatious, dare I say gaudy, decor. *Whatever type of eatery you choose, remember to take your credit card, or a well-stacked wallet.*

More and more restaurants, even small, almost coffee shop types, offer valet parking. If you are driving yourself around, enquire about this option when you phone to make a reservation, which incidentally is always a good idea.

Following is a selection of restaurants in the various areas, rated

Reasonable (under $10 evening main course),
Moderate ($10-20) and
Expensive ($20+), and

including credit cards accepted (Amex = American Express; DC = Diners Club; MC = Mastercard; V = Visa).

The *ratings* should be used as a guide only because it is impossible to gauge if a restaurant will suddenly decide to go upmarket, or to down-grade.

DOWNTOWN

Continental

Little Joe's Restaurant, 900 North Broadway, ph (213) 489 4900 - open Mon-Sat 11am-9pm - LA's oldest Italian eatery - **Reasonable** - Amex, DC, MC, V.
Velvet Turtle, 708 North Hill Street, ph (213) 489 2555 - open Mon-Fri 11am-3pm, Mon-Thurs 5-10pm, Fri-Sat 5-10.30pm, Sun 4-9pm - Seafood and prime rib specialties - **Moderate** - Amex, DC, MC, V.
The Tower Restaurant, 1150 South Olive Street, ph (213) 746 1554 - lunch Mon-Fri 11.30am-2pm, dinner Mon-Sat 5.30-10pm - Seafood specialty - **Expensive** - Amex, DC, MC, V.
Tam O'Shanter Inn, 2980 Los Feliz Boulevard, ph (213) 664 0228 - lunch Mon-Fri 11am-3pm, dinner Mon-Thurs 5-10pm, Fri-Sat 5-11pm, Sun 4-10pm, Sun brunch 10.30am-2.30pm - Scottish pub atmosphere, prime rib & roast duckling specialties - **Moderate** - Amex, DC, MC, V.

American

Checkers Restaurant, Checkers Hotel, 535 South Grand Avenue, ph (213) 624 0000 - open Mon-Thurs 6.30am-10pm, Sat 8am-10pm, Sun 8am-9pm - contemporary American cuisine, seasonal specialties - **Moderate** - Amex, DC, MC, V.

Epicentre Restaurant & Lounge, Kawada Hotel, 200 South Hill Street, ph (213) 625 0000 - open Mon-Sat 6am-midnight, Sun 7am-2.30pm - earthquake decor, free-range chicken, homemade pasta, seafood - **Moderate** - Amex, MC, V.

Garden Restaurant at Lawry's California Center, 570 West Avenue 26, ph (213) 225 2491 - open daily 11am-3pm, 4.30-9pm - specialties Mexican and California barbecue - **Reasonable** - Amex, MC, V.

Engine Co. No. 28, 644 South Figueroa Street, ph (213) 624 6996 - open for lunch Mon-Fri, Dinner Mon-Sat - a 1912 firehouse is a popular night spot - **Moderate** - Amex, DC, MC, V.

Homers Bar & Grill, 444 South Flower Street, Concourse Level, ph (213) 624 6880 - open Mon-Fri 7am-10pm, Happy Hour 4-7pm - pizza, pasta, salads - **Moderate** - Amex, MC, V.

Pacific Dining Car, 1310 West Sixth Street, ph (213) 483 6000 - open daily, 24 hours - steak, Maine lobster and seafood - **Expensive** - Amex, MC, V.

HOLLYWOOD

Continental

Musso & Frank Grill, 6667 Hollywood Boulevard, ph (213) 467 7788 - open Tues-Sat 11am-11pm - oldest restaurant in Hollywood - **Reasonable** - Amex, DC, MC, V.

Chianti Cucina e Ristorante, 7383 Melrose Avenue, ph (213) 653 8333 - open for dinner nightly - good atmosphere and fine Italian cuisine - **Expensive** - Amex, MC, V.

Al Amir, 5750 Wilshire Boulevard, ph (213) 931 8740 - open for lunch Mon-Fri, dinner Mon-Sat - Middle Eastern cuisine - **Moderate** - Amex, DC, MC, V.

American

Morton's, 8800 Melrose Avenue, West Hollywood, ph (310) 276 5205 - open for dinner Mon-Sat - owned by the creator of the Hard Rock Cafe, and visited by many movie people - changing menu - **Moderate** - Amex, DC, MC, V.

Pink's Hot Dogs, 709 North La Brea Avenue, ph (213) 931 4223 - open daily 7am-2.30am - over 20 varieties of hamburgers and hot dogs, movie star clientele (not guaranteed every day) - **Reasonable** - no credit cards.

Kings Road Cafe, 8361 Beverly Boulevard, West Hollywood, ph (213) 655 9044 - open for breakfast, lunch and dinner daily, late summer Wed-Sat - **Reasonable** - no credit cards.

WESTSIDE

Continental

The Bistro Garden, 176 North Canon Drive, Beverly Hills, ph (213) 550 3900 - open Mon-Sat 11am-3pm, 6-11pm - very popular - **Expensive** - Amex, DC.

The Bistro, 246 North Canon Drive, Beverly Hills, ph (213) 273 5633 - open Mon-Sat 6-11pm - known world-wide for good food and service - **Expensive** - Amex, DC, MC, V.

Celestino's, 236 South Beverly Drive, Beverly Hills, ph (213) 859 8601 - open Mon-Fri 11.30am-3pm, Mon-Sat 5.30-11pm, Sun 5.30-10pm - Italian with excellent wine list - **Moderate** - Amex, DC, MC, V.

Champagne Bis, 10506 Little Santa Monica Boulevard, Century City, ph (310) 474 6619 - open Tues-Fri 11.30am-2.30pm, Tues-Sun 6-10.30pm - French and Californian cuisine, nationally acclaimed - **Expensive** - Amex, DC, MC, V.

Jimmy's Restaurant, 201 Moreno Drive, Beverly Hills, ph (310) 552 2394 - open Mon-Fri 11am-3pm, Mon-Sat 6pm-midnight - specialties fresh seafood and rack of veal - **Expensive** - Amex, DC, MC, V.

Larry Parker's 24 Hour Diner, 206 South Beverly Drive, Beverly Hills, ph (310) 274 5655 - open daily, 24 hours - enormous menu choice, 50s music, colourful staff - **Reasonable** - Amex, DC, MC, V.

American

Carroll O'Connor's Place, 369 North Bedford Drive, Beverly Hills, ph (310) 273 7585 - open for lunch and dinner Mon-Sat, supper Fri-Sat, brunch Sun - a Beverly Hills landmark - **Moderate** - Amex, MC, V.

J.W.'s Restaurant, J.W. Marriott Hotel at, 2151 Avenue of the Stars, Century City, ph (310) 277 2777 - open daily, Mon-Fri 6.30am-10/30pm, Sat-Sun 7am-10.30pm - daily specials - **Moderate** - Amex, DC, MC, V.

COASTAL

Continental

Knoll's Black Forest Inn, 2454 Wilshire Boulevard, Santa Monica, ph (310) 395 2212 - open Tues-Fri 11.30am-3pm, Tues-Sun 11.30am-10.30pm - **Moderate** - Amex, DC, MC, V.

Papadakis Taverna Inc, 301 West Sixth Street, San Pedro, ph (310) 548 1186 - open nightly 5-10pm - Greek, well-known across the country - **Moderate** - DC, MC, V.

Riva Restaurant, Loews Santa Monica Beach Hotel, 1700 Ocean Avenue, Santa Monica, ph (310) 458 6700 - open Mon-Sat 6-10.45pm, Sun brunch - Italian, good views, great wine list - **Expensive** - Amex, DC, MC, V.

Wallaby Darned, 617 South Centre Street, San Pedro, ph (310) 833 3629 - open for lunch and dinner daily, breakfast Sat-Sun - features Aussie tucker, and more importantly, Aussie wines - **Reasonable** - MC, V.

American

Michael's Restaurant, 1147 Third Street, Santa Monica, ph (310) 451 0843 - open Tues-Fri noon-2pm, 6.30-9.45pm, Sat-Sun 10.30am-2pm, 6.30-9.45pm - French and American cuisine - **Expensive** - Amex, DC, MC, V.

Bob Burns Restaurant, 202 Wilshire Boulevard, Santa Monica, ph (213) 829 0093 - open Mon-Thurs 11am-11pm, Fri-Sat

5-midnight, Sun 11am-3pm - California cuisine, extensive wine list, music - **Moderate** - Amex, DC, MC, V.

Chart House Malibu, 18412 Pacific Coast Highway, Malibu, ph (310) 454 9321 - impressive views, seafood, rack of lamb - **Moderate** - Amex, DC, MC, V.

Chez Melange, Palos Verdes Inn, 1716 South Pacific Coast Highway, Redondo Beach, ph (310) 540 1222 - open Mon-Thurs 7am-11pm, Fri 7am-11.30pm, Sat 7.30am-11.30pm, Sun 8am-2.30pm, 5-10.30pm - nouvelle cuisine, fine wine and champagne bar - **Moderate** - Amex, MC, V.

DC3 Restaurant, 2800 Donald Douglas Loop North, Santa Monica, ph (310) 399 2323 - open Mon-Fri 11.30am-2.30pm, nightly 6-10.30pm, Sunday 11am-2.30pm - at Santa Monica airport, great meat dishes - **Expensive** - Amex, DC, MC, V.

THE VALLEYS

Continental

The Bistro Garden at Coldwater, 12950 Ventura Boulevard, Studio City, ph (818) 501 0202 - open for lunch Mon-Fri, dinner nightly - French brasserie-style - **Moderate** - Amex, DC, MC, V.

Pappagallo, 42 South Pasadena Avenue, LA, ph (818) 578 0224 - open Tues-Sat 11.30am-2.30pm, Sun, Tues-Thurs 5-10.30pm, Fri-Sat 5-11.30pm - Northern Italian and California cuisine - **Moderate** - Amex, DC, MC, V.

Val's Restaurant, 10130 Riverside Drive, Toluca Lake, ph (818) 508 6644 - open Mon-Fri 11.30am-10pm, Sat 5.30-10pm - Continental/French cuisine, renowned chef - **Moderate** - Amex, DC, MC, V.

American

Sportmen's Lodge Restaurant, 12833 Ventura Boulevard, Studio City, ph (818) 984 0202 - open Tues-Sun 5.30-10.30pm - prime rib, steaks, fresh fish - **Reasonable** - Amex, MC, V.

ENTERTAINMENT

As mentioned in the Accommodation section, most hotels have one or more cocktail lounges. Usually these are equipped with several television sets, strategically placed so that it is impossible to sit anywhere where you are not confronted with one. Some sets are tuned into the sport of the moment (baseball in summer, football in winter), the rest are occupied with MTV, a never-ending range of music video clips. The time for **the Happy Hour varies from hotel to hotel**, and may or may not offer drinks at reduced prices, but does offer extremely tasty snacks, both hot and cold, which allow guests to forestall dinner for a few hours, or completely.

Dinner Theatres

For a city of its size, Los Angeles does not have many venues of this type, so naturally it is necessary to book well in advance. Here are some names and addresses.

El Cid Show Restaurant, 4212 West Sunset Boulevard, Hollywood, ph (213) 668 0318. This authentic replica of a 16th century Spanish tavern was built in 1900, and is open Wed-Sun 6.30pm-1.30am. The dinner prices are Moderate, and the entertainment includes dancers, singers and guitarists in true Spanish style. Amex, MC, V.

La Cage LA, 643 North La Cienega Boulevard, West Hollywood, ph (310) 657 1091. An elegant supper club featuring celebrity female impersonators and great French cuisine. Open Sun-Thurs 7pm for dinner (show begins at 9.15pm), Fri-Sat 6pm for dinner (two shows nightly). Amex, DC, MC, V.

Il Vittoriale, 2035 North Highland Avenue, Hollywood, ph (213) 480 3232 - participatory theatre. The audience follows characters from room to room, so wear comfortable shoes. Open Tues-Fri 7.30-10.30pm, two shows on Sat-Sun 2-5pm and 7.30-10.30pm. Entry, which includes wine, champagne, dinner buffet, coffee and dessert is Tues-Thurs $65, Fri $75, Sat-Sun $85, Amex, MC, V.

Comedy Venues

Since you are in the entertainment capital of the world, why not take some time out for a good laugh. Here are a few ideas.

The Comedy Store, 8433 Sunset Boulevard, Hollywood, ph (213) 656 6225 - open nightly 7.30pm-2am. This establishment has three rooms to choose from - the Mainroom, Original Room, or Bellyroom-Headliner. For advance ticket purchase, ph (213) 480 3232. Cover charge is $6-14, Amex, MC, V.

The Comedy & Magic Club, 1018 Hermosa Avenue, Hermosa Beach, ph (310) 372 1193, open Sun-Fri 6pm, Sat 5pm. Topline performers and Continetal menus for both cafe and showroom dining. Cover charge $8-15, Amex, MC, V.

Igby's, 11637 West Pico Boulevard, LA, ph (310) 477 3553. Stand-up comics perform nightly, and often surprise guest artists drop by. Shows are at 8pm nightly, with an extra at 10.30pm on Fri-Sat. Cover charge $7-10, Amex, DC, MC, V.

Improvisation, 8162 Melrose Avenue, West Hollywood, ph (213) 651 2583. This is where people like Bette Midler and Robin Williams honed their skills for the big time. Open nightly 6pm-2am. Cover charge $8-11, MC, V.

Casinos and Card Clubs

If the word 'casino' makes you think of roulette wheels and slot machines, think again. These clubs are devoted to card games, and they play for big money. You can pick up a booklet at each venue that outlines the rules of the various forms of poker, or whatever, and if you can understand them, maybe you should try your luck. Even if you don't want to participate in the games, it is fascinating to watch others lose their money.

The Bicycle Club, 7301 Eastern Avenue, Bell Gardens, ph (818) 806 4646. Situated out of LA, this is one of the largest card casinos in Southern California, with 170 tables offering American and Asian card games. Poker instruction is available, and the complex includes a beauty salon, gift shop

HOLLYWOOD

and Asian restaurant. Open daily, 24 hours.
Commerce Casino, 6131 Telegraph Road, Commerce, ph (213) 721 2100 (Downtown). Also open 24 hours a day, and features poker and a variety of Asian card games. This complex includes a gourmet restaurant, a New York style deli, beauty salon, gift shop and lounge. DC, MC, V.
Normandie Gambling Casino & Dinner Theatre, 1045 West Rosecrans Avenue, Gardena, ph (310) 715 7400 (Coastal). Featured as 'Vegas in LA', this casino offers 60 gambling tables and spectacular musical shows. The dinner specialties are steaks and seafood, and everything is open 24 hours a day. Amex, MC, V.
The Regency Card Club and Casino, 4901 Eastern Avenue, Bell, ph (818) 265 1500 (out of LA), features Asian games, including Pang, Pai Gow and Asian Poker, and Asian food in elegant surroundings. Also open 24 hours a day, but take your money with you.

Theatres

Los Angeles is home to many theatres and concert venues. For up-to-date information on performances, check the "Calendar" section of the *Los Angeles Times*, or the free *L.A. Weekly*, which is out each Thursday and available at convenience and liquor stores. The following list will whet your cultural appetite.

Beverly Hills Playhouse, 254 South Robertson Boulevard, Beverly Hills, (310) 855 1556 - classic dramas and new works.
Globe Playhouse, 1107 North Kings Road, West Hollywood, ph (213) 654 5623 - half-scale replica of the original Globe has the classics.
Henry Fonda Theatre, 6126 Hollywood Boulevard, Hollywood, ph (213) 410 1062 - established dramatic and musical works.
James A. Doolittle Theatre, 1615 North Vine Street, Hollywood, ph (213) 972 0700 - top name artists in dramas from Broadway and Hollywood.
Los Angeles Theatre Center, 514 South Spring Street, LA, ph

(213) 627 5599 - this restored 1916 bank building has four threatres and presents some of the nation's most innovative live theatre.

Pantages Theatre, 6233 Hollywood Boulevard, Hollywood, ph (213) 460 1700 - a one-time movie house, this theatre now has major productions, including Broadway imports.

Pasadena Playhouse, 39 South El Molino Avenue, Pasadena, ph (818) 792 8672 - situated about 16km (10 miles) from Downtown LA, this theatre presents a variety of plays.

Second City, 214 Santa Monica Boulevard, Santa Monica, ph (310) 451 0621 - the resident troupe presents sketches and improvisational comedy.

Shubert Theatre, ABC Entertainment Center, 2020 Avenue of the Stars, Century City, ph (310) 201 1500 - has Broadway and London imports, many with original casts.

Westwood Playhouse, 10886 Le Conte Avenue, Westwood, ph (310) 208 5454 - new plays and Broadway productions.

Wilshire Theatre, 8440 Wilshire Boulevard, Beverly Hills, ph (213) 410 1062 - Broadway imports, plays and musicals.

The Music Center, 135 North Grand Avenue, LA, ph (213) 972 7211 - has three theatres: Ahmanson Theatre, which presents the big shows, e.g. *The Phantom of the Opera*; Dorothy Chandler Pavilion, home of the Oscars, features plays, dance and music; Mark Taper Forum, presents original productions and contemporary dramas.

Music and Dance

Greek Theatre, 2700 North Vermont Avenue, Griffith Park, ph (213) 665 5857, tickets ph (213) 410 1062 - an outdoor amphitheatre which hosts a variety of pop and classical groups during the season (May through September).

Hollywood Bowl, 2301 North Highland Avenue, Hollywood, ph Information Hotline (213) 850 2000, tickets ph (213) 480 3232 - summer home of the Los Angeles Philharmonic. A new addition is the Hollywood Bowl Orchestra, which was created to preserve America's musical heritage from Hollywood, Broadway, and the concert hall.

The Bowl has thirteen picnic areas, and three food outlets - the elegant Patio Restaurant ($10 to $25 per person, MC, V); the takeaway Hacienda for Mexican-style snacks; and the Deli for sandwiches. The most popular eating experience, though, is picnicking under the stars. You can take your own munchies, or you can order a picnic basket from the Bowl (by 4pm the day before you are attending).

If your concert tickets are for Box Seats, the baskets will be delivered to the box; if you have Bench Seats, you can pick up the baskets at the Picnic Basket Pick-Up Building, and eat at your seats or at any of the picnic areas. Dining as the sun goes down in the pre-concert atmosphere is truly a great experience. The baskets cost between $15 and $25 per person, and you can pay with cash, MC or V. For information and orders, ph (213) 851 3588.

Getting to the Bowl is easy as there are many BowlBus Shuttle Services and BowlBus Park & Ride routes. The Information Hotline above (850 2000) will give you all the details of services and pick-up points. If you arrive early, you may have time to visit the Hollywood Bowl Museum, open Tues-Sat 9.30am-4.30pm, to 8.30pm on concert nights. The Museum is next to the Patio Restaurant, and has displays from the permanent collection and special exhibitions. Admission is free, and for more information ph (213) 850 2058.

Hollywood Palladium, 6215 Sunset Boulevard, Hollywood, ph (213) 962 7600 - features music groups from rock to Latin.
Pasadena Civic Auditorium, 300 East Green Street, Pasadena, ph (818) 449 7360 - has a varied schedule of dance, music, opera, ballet and theatrical productions.
Shrine Auditorium, 665 West Jefferson Boulevard, Los Angeles, ph (213) 749 5123 - hosts touring companies, ballet, opera and folk groups.
Wilshire Ebell Theater, 4401 West 8th Street, LA, ph (213) 939 1128 - classical music concerts, plays and musicals.

Wiltern Theater, 3790 Wilshire Boulevard, LA, ph (213) 380 5031 - a restored art deco movie house has pop, jazz and classical concerts.

Movies

As you would expect, there are cinemas all over the city (for example there are thirteen movie theatres in the Beverly Center shopping centre), and currently there is a lot of restoration work being done on the 'movie palaces' of an earlier era.

The *Los Angeles Times* "Calendar" section has a list of all movies currently playing, with a parental guide, and times and locations, plus information on movies in production and new faces in the industry. One theatre that you will be visiting anyway is Mann's Chinese Theatre, 6925 Hollywood Boulevard, Hollywood, ph (213) 461 3331, so why not see a first-run movie while you are there. It is open daily noon-midnight.

TV Shows

Depending on the time of the year you visit LA, you might be able to attend the taping of a TV show. Most sitcoms break for the summer, but talk and game shows are taped all year. Often reservations must be made well in advance, and tickets for many shows can only be obtained through Audiences Unlimited, which has a ticket booth at Fox Television, 5746 Sunset Boulevard. The ticket window is actually on Van Ness Avenue, just south of Sunset. For up-to-date ticket information, ph (818) 506 0043.

For additional taping and tour details, contact:
  ABC Television - (213) 520 1ABC
  CBS Television City - (213) 852 2458
  NBC Television - (818) 840 3537
  Paramount Television - (213) 956 5575
  Warner Bros Studios - (818) 954 1744.

SHOPPING

Shopping venues in Los Angeles range from the up-market designer label boutiques and salons on **Rodeo Drive,** to the cut-price garment and jewellery districts in the Downtown area, with all manner of shops and shopping centres in between.

Even if you can't afford to shop on Rodeo Drive, Beverly Hills, it costs nothing to look, and the shops and the goods they offer represent the ultimate in luxury and wealth, as do the customers. Incidentally, the drive is pronounced 'rodayo', not the same way as the cattle round-up.

Department Stores

The Broadway has forty-three stores from Santa Barbara to San Diego, which are open Mon-Fri 10am-9pm, Sat 10am-7pm, Sun 11am-7pm, and accept Amex, MC and V.

Bullock's has eleven locations throughout the Los Angeles area, and the times vary with the different centre open hours.

I. Magnin has two outlets in LA - 3050 Wilshire Boulevard, LA (Downtown); and 9634 Wilshire Boulevard, Beverly Hills. They are open Mon-Sat 10am-6pm (Thurs to 8pm), Sun noon-5pm, and accept Amex, MC and V.

Saks Fifth Avenue, 9600 Wilshire Boulevard, Beverly Hills, has six floors of luxury goods and is open Mon-Sat 10am-6pm, Sun noon-5pm. Amex, DC, MC, V.

Nordstrom is a Seattle-based company that has only opened stores in California in the last ten years or so. They are very good for fashion for both sexes, and have a good reputation for service. Check out their store at Westside Pavilion.

Shopping Centres

Beverly Center, 8500 Beverly Boulevard (at La Cienega Boulevard), LA, ph (213) 854 0070, has 200 international shops, Bullock's and The Broadway department stores, 14 movie theatres and ten restaurants, including the Hard Rock Cafe (ph 276 7605). It is open Mon-Fri 10am-9pm, Sat 10am-8pm, Sun 11am-6pm.

Century City Shopping Center & Marketplace, 10250 Santa Monica Boulevard, Century City, ph (213) 277 3898, is an open-air mall with sidewalk cafes, over 80 shops, The Broadway and Bullock's department stores, several cinemas, and the Festival Marketplace. It is open Mon-Fri 10am-9pm, Sat 10am-6pm, Sun 11am-6pm.

Seventh Market Place, Figueroa Street (between Seventh and Eighth Streets), Downtown LA, ph (213) 955 7150, has Bullock's department store, May Company, and 50 specialty shops and restaurants. It is open Mon-Fri 10am-7pm, Sat 10am-6pm, Sun (department stores and selected stores) noon-5pm.

10800 West Pico Boulevard, Westside, ph (310) 474 6255, has 180 shops, branches of Nordstrom, Robinsons-May, and a four-screen cinema.

Farmers Market, 6333 West Third Street, Los Angeles, ph (213) 933 9211, open in summer Mon-Sat 9am-7pm, Sun 10am-6pm; in winter Mon-Sat 9am-6.30pm, Sun 10am-5pm.

A lot of tours of Los Angeles call into Farmers Market, usually for lunch, and you have to wonder, 'Why?', although I must admit I had probably the best corned beef sandwich I have ever tasted.

The main emphasis of the market is, naturally enough, on food - the type you take home and serve up in some form to the family. Hardly the shopping mecca for people staying in hotels with no cooking facilities. There are twenty-one kitchens from which you can choose something to eat, then you can fight for a table, which, because of the 'bus your own table' system, will probably be next to the rubbish bin.

There are quite a few clothing, jewellery and specialty shops and art galleries, but it all looks a bit 'touristy', even downright 'yuk'. Still, many people walk away with bulging bags so maybe I am just not a dedicated shopper.

Shopping Districts

The Garment District is roughly bounded by Olympic Boulevard, Main Street, 7th Street and Maple Avenue in Downtown Los Angeles. Here there are many outlets offering discounts from 25% to 75% on department and specialty store prices.
For example, the California Apparel Mart is on South Los Angeles Street, between Olympic and 9th, but this is for trade buyers only.

The Cooper Building is at 860 South Los Angeles Street, Downtown, and is open to everyone. The latter has thirty-five shops offering ladies' fashions, fifteen with men's wear, nine with teenagers', five with children's, two lingerie shops, eleven accessory shops, three offering cosmetics, two hosiery, two gifts and one home furnishings.

There are also five restaurants in case shopping makes you hungry.

The Cooper Building itself is partly taken up with offices, and the shops are on the ground, mezzanine, second, third, fourth, fifth, sixth and eleventh floors. There's a receptionist in the lobby who will help you become orientated.

The Jewellery District is roughly along Olive and 6th Streets, and you'll find shop after shop filled with beautiful pieces of jewellery, mostly gold, set with every kind of stone imaginable, at very reasonable prices. It is a veritable treasure trove, but I must give a word of warning here. The shops themselves have armed guards keeping an eye on the goods, but in the streets it is a jungle.

Tip

Do not wear any good jewellery when you visit this area, and keep a tight grip on your handbag. While I was there on one trip, a lady had two gold chains stolen. She was walking north along Olive Street and a young hooligan, running the other way, literally ripped them from her neck. The police were called, but, with so many people around, there was not much they could do. OK, that sort of thing can happen anywhere, but it still leaves a nasty taste in your mouth, so be warned!

Melrose Avenue, West Hollywood, has about 2km of boutiques and bistros beginning around La Brea Avenue and reaching to around La Jolla Avenue. It is worth a visit for the trendy gals and guys.

The above is really only the tip of the iceberg as far as shopping opportunities go, but it will give you a starting point. Keep in mind, though, the tax that will be added to the ticketed price.

SIGHTSEEING
The best place to begin sightseeing is where it all began, so the first district to visit is Downtown.

DOWNTOWN LOS ANGELES

El Pueblo de Los Angeles Historic Park
The park covers four blocks and is bordered by Sunset Boulevard, Macy Street, Hill Street, Arcadia Street, and Alameda Street. Alameda Street also has the entrance to Union Station, just opposite the park. 'Pueblo', by the way, is Spanish for 'village'.

Nothing remains of the huts built by the original eleven families, but the buildings now in the park are all interwoven with the early history of the city. There is a Visitors Centre in Sepulveda House in Olvera Street, ph (213) 628 0605, and they have brochures, and screen a movie entitled *Pueblo of Promise* Mon-Sat at 11am and 2pm.

You can also join **free guided walking tours** of the park, which start at the Park's Docent Center, 130 Paseo de la Plaza, next to the Fire Station on the south side of the Plaza. They are conducted Tues-Sat, on the hour, between 10am and 1pm.

The *Avila Adobe* (1818) and the old Plaza Catholic Church, *Nuestra Senora La Reina de Los Angeles*, (1818-22) are two of the oldest buildings. The Adobe, on Olvera Street was a residence for more than forty years, then it was used as a boarding house, then a restaurant. The first brick homes were constructed in the 1850s, and the *Pelanconi House* (1855-57) on Olvera Street is a fine example of that period.

Floods and a severe drought during the 1860s caused many ranchers to lose their lands, and the Plaza area to lose most of its California residents. Pio Pico, the last Mexican governor of California built the *Pico House*, a grand hotel, in 1869-70 in an effort to revamp the Plaza, and soon after the *Merced Theatre* was built next door. Both these establishments were popular for a while, then declined along with the rest of the area.

The real estate boom of the 1880s saw a revival of the area with the building of the city's first official fire station, *Firehouse No 1*, and *Sepulveda House*, a two-storey Victorian structure that was built on Main Street with a rear entrance on Olvera Street. In 1890, the *Garnier Block* was built, then in 1904 the Los Angeles Railway Company built the *Plaza Substation* on a lot between Olvera and Los Angeles Streets.

Despite these efforts, when Mrs Christine Sterling visited the Plaza in 1926, she found the area to be a slum, and began camp aigning to preserve Los Angeles' heri-tage. With the help of influential citi-zens, including Harry Chandler, she saved the Avila

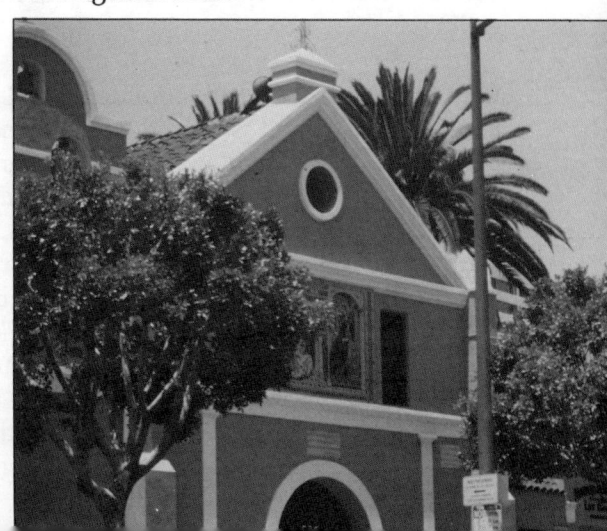

Adobe from demolition, and, in 1930, began a Mexican marketplace in Olvera Street. She then caused the Adobe to be renovated, and brought fiestas and life back to the Plaza. Over twenty years later she was able to persuade the State, County and City governments to dedicate the area as an historic park.

> *Olvera Street* is now a pedestrian mall, and the little shops and cafes, naturally enough, offer Mexican treats. It's a good place to pick up a leather bargain, or sample some authentic Mexican food if you are not going to be heading 'south of the border'.

The Park has two car parks, but they are usually full early in the morning, so public transport is probably your best bet.

Union Station is also on Alameda Street, across from El Pueblo, and was built in 1939, the last of the grand old railroad stations to be built in the United States. Railway stations are not usually on sightseeing itineraries, but it is worth crossing the street to visit this scene of many movies, including the one in which it virtually starred with William Holden and Nancy Olsen. Movie fans will recall many tearful goodbyes and happy reunions the minute they walk through the doors.

The interior is enormous, with marble floors and high, high ceilings.

City Hall is in the block bounded by Main, Temple, Spring and 1st Streets, and is over the Santa Ana Freeway and one block south of El Pueblo. Does it look familiar? If so, you are showing your age. It was used as the *Daily Planet* building in the old TV *Superman* with George Reeves, and in the opening shots of that other old favourite *Dragnet*.

Also in the area are **Times Mirror Square**, on Spring and 1st Streets, the home of the *Los Angeles Times*, and the **Music Center**, 135 North Grand Avenue. The Music Center complex is made up of the Ahmanson Theatre, the Mark Taper Forum, and the Dorothy Chandler Pavilion, which is the focus of the world's attention on Academy Awards night.

Little Tokyo is bounded by Los Angeles, Temple, 3rd and Alameda Streets, and dominated by the Japanese American Cultural and Community Center, home to the Japan American Theatre which stages musical, dance and dramatic performances. The Center also has a gallery, a library, and the Garden of the Clear Stream, a typical Japanese garden. The area also has the Nishi Hongwangi Buddhist Temple, off Central Street, the Little Tokyo Tower, the Union Church, and shopping plazas and restaurants.

The Biltmore Hotel, 515 South Olive Street, ph (213) 624 1011, is opposite Pershing Square, an inner-city park that has had much restoration work done. The Biltmore was designed by the same architects that worked on the Waldorf Astoria in New York, and opened in 1923. Although it is in the vicinity of the Jewellery District, an area where it is wise to keep an eye out for muggers, The Biltmore is an elegant hotel in the grand old tradition. In 1927, its Crystal Ballroom was the birthplace of the Academy of Motion Picture Arts and Sciences, and it was there that the design of the Oscar statuette was devised by MGM art director Cedric Gibbons.

The Financial District is bounded by 3rd and Olive Streets, Wilshire Boulevard and Figueroa Street. The *Central Library*, 5th Street and Grand Avenue, was built in 1925, and its art deco structure stands out among the surrounding glass and steel of more modern edifices.

Nearby is the recently completed *First Interstate World Center*, on 5th and Hope Streets, the tallest building on the West Coast; the *ARCO/Bank of America* twin towers complex, 515 South Flower Street, with its underground shopping plaza; and the ultra-modern *Bonaventure Hotel*, 404 South Figueroa Street, that is used in many TV shows and movies.

You can get a good view of the Financial District from the *Security Pacific Plaza*, 333 South Hope Street, where a 1.5ha (3.5 acres) park surrounds the 55-storey building. Adjacent to the Plaza is the *Wells Fargo Center*, 333 South Grand Avenue, which has the *Wells Fargo History Museum* on the atrium level (open Mon-Fri 9am-5pm); and nearby, at 250 South Grand Avenue, is the $1.2 billion *California Plaza* complex, which houses the *Museum of Contemporary Art*.

Exposition Park is between Exposition Boulevard and Figueroa Street, south of the University of Southern California, and a fair step from the Financial District. The park has quite an outstanding collection of cultural attractions: the *Los Angeles Memorial Coliseum*, 3911 South Figueroa Street, ph (213) 747 7111; the *Los Angeles Sports Arena*, 3939 South Figueroa Street, ph (213) 748 6131; the *California Museum of Science and Industry*, 700 State Drive, ph (213) 744 7400, which has permanent and changing exhibits, including a simulated earthquake, and screens science-related films in the five-storey Mitsubishi IMAX Theater; the *Natural History Museum of Los Angeles County*, 900 Exposition Boulevard, ph (213) 744 3466, has permanent exhibits that include the skeletons of two dinosaurs, fossils, and many items devoted to early American and Californian history.

While you are still in the Downtown area, there are a couple of places worth visiting, but I have left them to last because they are on the way to Hollywood.

Chinatown is within walking distance of Union Station and Olvera Street, to the north-east. Situated between Hill Street and North Broadway (north of Sunset Boulevard), Chinatown is pretty much like any other Chinese district in any other city - hundreds of shops featuring Asian products, and dozens of restaurants offering *dim sum* and other Chinese delicacies.

Dodger Stadium is on Elysian Park Avenue, to the west of Chinatown, and is the home of the Los Angeles Dodgers, who were originally the Brooklyn Dodgers. If you are in LA between April and September, and a visit to a baseball game is on your agenda, phone (213) 224 1400 for tickets. The stadium is enormous and overlooks the skyline of Downtown from Chavez Ravine, in *Elysian Park*. The park is the second largest in LA, with an area of 243ha (600 acres). Nearby is the small *Echo Park*, with an area of 11ha (26 acres), in which is the Angelus Temple that is styled after the Mormon Tabernacle in Salt Lake City.

HOLLYWOOD

To most people, the name 'Hollywood' conjures up visions of glamour and beautiful people doing outrageous things. This may have been the case in the past, but now Hollywood is a bit of a disappointment.

The first sight of the famous **Walk of Fame** along Hollywood Boulevard, between Gower and Sycamore Streets, is exciting, and everyone looks for their favourites among the nearly 1900 greats of film, TV, radio, theatre and popular music that are represented. But when you discover that the stars nominate themselves to a selection committee of the Hollywood Chamber of Commerce, and even pay around $4000 for the privilege of having their name engraved on the footpath, it takes a lot of the shine off it.

Incidentally, when you do visit the Walk of Fame, take note of the symbol underneath the name of the star. It signifies the area of entertainment in which the person has been honoured. For example, Harrison Ford has the projector, for a star of films, while Bette Midler has a record, the sign for a recording star. Some plaques have a combination of symbols. Along the Walk of Fame there are a couple of murals, but I don't think that they add to the area in any shape or form. One is at the corner of Hudson Avenue, the other at Wilcox Avenue.

80 CALIFORNIA AT COST

Mann's Chinese Theatre, (formerly Grauman's Chinese Theatre), 6925 Hollywood Boulevard, is always high on everyone's agenda too, but the forecourt, where the stars' foot and hand prints, and in some cases, hoof and other parts of the anatomy prints, are preserved for posterity, is always so crowded with tourists that it is impossible to take the photo you want, so you invariably have to settle for one of the not-so-popular stars. And, either the concrete has shrunk, or most of those tall cowboys had very small feet.

Then there's the famous **Hollywood sign** on Mount Lee, at the north end of Beachwood Drive. Was it erected on the hilltop to signal that this was the entertainment capital of the world? No! It was erected as an advertising sign for a real estate property development and the original sign said 'Hollywoodland'. The 'land' was removed early in the piece (in the 1940s). When the sign fell into total disrepair a few years ago, a bunch of movie stars got together and financed the erection of a new sign. So, I guess, you could now say it is authentic.

Other 'famous' landmarks are 'Hollywood and Vine' and 'Sunset Strip'. **Hollywood and Vine** is an unremarkable intersection where the old dilapidated Hollywood Palace Theater stands; and **Sunset Strip** is the section of Sunset Boulevard between Crescent Heights Boulevard and Doheny Drive, and all those fans of the old *Seventy Seven Sunset Strip* will look in vain for Dino's - it has been demolished.
In fact, horror of horrors, the area is now known more for its gay bars and nightclubs.
And don't walk or drive around looking for Schwab's Drugstore. It used to be at 8024 Sunset, but has also been completely demolished. Even if Lana Turner wasn't discovered there, and it was just a story put out by the studio publicity people, the Drugstore certainly became a household name, and it is pity that someone didn't step in and save it.

Hollywood flows into **West Hollywood**, which in turn flows into **Beverly Hills**. In fact, there is one street where the houses on one side (in Beverly Hills) are worth almost twice as much as the houses on the other side (in West Hollywood). Beverly Hills is 'famous' as the district where the movie stars live, but if you take a tour of the stars' homes, you will find that the commentary tells you who once lived in the homes, rather than who lives there now. In fact, the area is now populated by lawyers, bankers, and other wealthy people, but the homes are still worth oohing and aahing over.

Having said all that, Hollywood has some amazing attractions, unlike those anywhere else in the world, and, as with Downtown, there are so many buildings and streets that look familiar because you have seen them in films.

MOVIE AND TELEVISION STUDIOS

> Universal Studios is, in my opinion, *the numero uno place to visit*, and I have never heard of anyone coming away disappointed.

Allow as much time there as possible, and you still will have to miss out on something. Situated on Lankershim Boulevard at the Hollywood Freeway, Universal City, ph (818) 508 9600, Universal Studios are open daily, but the hours change, so it is best to phone and check the day before if you want to make an early start. **Admission is $29.00 adults, $23 children 3-11. Two-day passes are also available, and if you want to see and experience everything, these are worth considering.**

It should be mentioned that most of the local tourist guides list Universal Studios as an amusement park, in the same category as Disneyland, not under the Television & Motion Picture Studios section.

Universal is the largest working movie studio in the country (170ha - 420 acres) and is on two levels, the Entertainment Center on top of the 'hill', and the Studio

Center in the valley below. The two are joined by the longest escalator in the world, which, I hasten to add, is in sections and not the least bit daunting for those, such as I, who have a fear of heights. While I use the term 'working studio', do not expect to actually see a movie being shot while you are there.

Over 3 million people per year visit the studios, and it would not do much for a movie to have several thousand people standing around watching (unless they wanted a mob scene). If you visit during production time, however, you may be iucky enough to see the taping of a television show, and information will be in the Entertainment Schedule in the Studio Guide you receive on entry.

In any case, you will get to see actual locations for shows, for example, the house where Jessica Fletcher (Angela Lansbury) lives at Cabot Cove in *Murder She Wrote* is actually on a back lot. And the town hall and square used in all the *Back To The Future* movies is there in all its glory. (It is not until the guide tells you that you realise that this town square has been used in many movies, with little change, eg *The Music Man*, with Robert Preston.)

The exhibits are constantly being altered and added to, and some parts of the tram ride may be excluded if a lot is being used for taping, but in any case, a great time will be had by all, young and old.

What to do

After going through the turnstiles and collecting your Studio Guide booklet, walk basically straight ahead to the Stairway Escalator which will take you down to the lower level and the Studio Tram Ride Entrance.

The tram ride is a must. Do not be put off if there are hundreds of people ahead of you waiting to board the trams, they leave every couple of minutes. Actually, they are not trams in the accepted sense, but rather motorised people-movers.

The ride takes you through the back lot and lets you into many movie secrets. You will visit many countries, experience a flash flood, a spectacular earthquake, and an avalanche, and meet King Kong, Jaws, and other "characters". The last tram departs at 6.15pm.

Also in the lower Studio Center is a *Special Effects Show* featuring the latest state-of-the-art special effects (open 8am-7.30pm); a chance to board a starbound bike and fly with *ET*; or experience "Back to the Future - The Ride".

The upper Entertainment Center level has six venues offering such shows as *The Riot Act*, a stuntmen show; *Adventures of Conan*, complete with dungeons and dragons; *Miami Vice Action Spectacular*, a live show with all the elements of the TV series;
Animal Actors' Stage; Star Trek Adventure, with audience participation; *An American Tail*, featuring Fievel and all his friends (first show starts at 10am, last at 9.30pm).

These times are for the summer season - in winter the studios are open for much shorter hours.

New attractions are being added to the list every year and the new one now is the *Flintstones' Show*, a very extensive live stage show, featuring the characters from the television show and the movie.
Add to all that a total of -
*eighteen refreshment and food outlets (from glamorous restaurants to snack bars);
*twenty-five shopping opportunities;
*and the chance to have your photo taken with Wolfman, Frankenstein, the Creature from the Black Lagoon, or any of the other 'stars' who happen to be wandering about on the Entertainment Center level,
and *maybe that two-day pass becomes an even better idea.*

> The Burbank Studios, 4000 Warner Boulevard, Burbank, ph (818) 954 1744, home of Warner Bros and Columbia Pictures, offer personalised VIP tours which include live shooting whenever possible. Shows that may be in production include *Designing Women*, *Murphy Brown*, *Growing Pains* and *Night Court*, but if all the shows are in recess you will only get to see sets, the wardrobe department, and maybe where they make the sets.
>
> Tour hours are Mon-Fri 10am and 2pm, with additional tours in the summer. Adults $22, no children under 10 admitted, and reservations must be made in advance, as numbers have to be kept small.

If you are not really interested in seeing behind the scenes, but would like to be part of a studio audience, write to *Audiences Unlimited*, 100 Universal City Plaza, Bldg 153, Universal City, CA 91608, enclosing a stamped self-adressed envelope and mentioning what programs you would like to see. It is best to do this before you leave home. Alternatively, when you arrive in LA you can keep your fingers crossed and contact them by phone, (818) 506 0043, or pop into their ticket office at Fox TV Center, 5746 Sunset Boulevard, Hollywood. Another company that may be able to accommodate you is *Audience Associates*, ph (213) 467 4697.

Continuing our tour of Hollywood, we have to leave the Tinsel Town parts and come back to earth, literally.

Forest Lawn, 1712 South Glendale Avenue, at Los Feliz Road, Glendale, ph (213) 254 3131, is one of five Forest Lawns Cemeteries in LA, but is undoubtedly the most famous (but not necessarily the most tacky). At the Information Booth you can pick up a copy of a map, which will also give details of anything special that is on that day.

Famous residents include Jean Harlow, Clark Gable, Walt Disney, W.C. Fields and Humphrey Bogart *(not Rudolf Valentino, he's at the Hollywood Memorial Cemetery on Santa Monica Boulevard, with many other movie stars)*, but the reason that Forest Lawn is included here is that its museum is home to two paintings - *The Crucifixion*, painted by Jan Styka, conceived by Paderewski, which got a rave review from Pope John Paul II; and *The Resurrection*, painted by Robert Clark, conceived by Dr Eaton. Other exhibits include reproductions of Michelangelo's *Sotterraneo* and Ghiberti's *Paradise Doors*.

Griffith Park is in the Santa Monica Mountains, and has an area of 1663ha (4,107 acres), and 85km (53 miles) of bridle and hiking trails. Horses can be hired from Los Angeles Equestrian Center, 480 Riverside Drive (in the Park), ph (213) 840 9063, open Tues-Sun 8am-4pm. The main entrances to the Park are at Western Avenue and Los Feliz Boulevard; Vermont Avenue and Los Feliz Boulevard; and Riverside Drive and Los Feliz Boulevard. There are golf courses, a bird sanctuary, tennis courts, restaurants, very large picnic areas, a merry-go-round, miniature train rides and a large wilderness area. The Park Ranger Visitor Center, 4730 Crystal Springs Drive, ph (213) 665 5188, can provide all park information.
The golf courses are: Coolidge Golf Course, ph (213) 661 3408; and Griffith Park Golf Course, ph (213) 633 2555; and Harding Municipal Golf Course, ph (213) 663 2555. The Griffith Park Tennis Courts' phone number is (213) 665 5188.

Los Angeles Zoo, 5333 Zoo Drive (in Griffith Park), ph (213) 666 4090, features more than 2000 birds, reptiles and mammals from around the world. There are regularly scheduled animal shows, plus a new children's zoo, Adventure Island. The Zoo is open daily 10am-6pm, mid-June through August; 10am-5pm, September through mid-June, and **admission is: adults, 13 and over, $8, and children, 2 to 12, $3.00.**

Gene Autry Western Heritage Museum, 4700 Zoo Drive (in Griffith Park), ph (213) 667 2000, is a mission-style complex entered through a Hollywood-style arch, and the first thing you see is a life-size bronze statue of 'the singing cowboy' himself and Champion, his horse (who I always thought was the better actor of the two). Off the courtyard are entrances to the museum and the theatre, and straight ahead is the information centre, where you can hire an audio tour narrated by Willie Nelson for $3.

Even if you are not into museums as such, this is one that you should not miss. **It is virtually a monument to the Wild, Wild West,** the people who helped settle it, and those who took part of it to the East in the various forms of showbiz. There are over 16,000 artifacts and art works, including one hundred of Gene Autry's personal treasures, like *The Bronc Buster* and *The Cheyenne,* bronze sculptures by Frederic Remington.

The kids are not forgotten here, either, as there are plenty of hands-on exhibits, and a stagecoach that they can climb all over, or maybe hold up.

The section of the museum devoted to the entertainment sphere includes memorabilia from Buffalo Bill's Wild West Show and performances by Annie Oakley; clips from silent movies and TV western series; and videos of the backbones of action movies, the stuntmen.

Needless to say, there is a souvenir shop, and it is overflowing with western gear, posters and silver and turquoise jewellery. There is also a cafeteria, appropriately called the Golden Spur Cafe. The museum is open Tues-Sun 10am-5pm, and **admission is adults $6.00, students 13 to 18 $4.50, and children 2 to 12 $2.50.**

Griffith Observatory and Planetarium, in Griffith Park, north end of Vermont Avenue, ph (213) 664 1191 (recorded information) has solar telescopes operating during the day, and the Zeiss Refractor views the moon and planets at night. There are very interesting shows, lasting about one hour, daily in summer, Tues-Sun in winter, both during the day and at night. **Admission is adults $3.50, children 5 to 15 $2,** with a special show on Saturday at 1.30pm for the under 5s (they are not admitted to the other shows). If you are a James Dean fan, you will remember this complex from *Rebel Without a Cause.*

The Greek Theatre, 2700 North Vermont Avenue (in Griffith Park), ph (213) 410 1062, is a 6187-seat outdoor amphitheatre, which has top-name entertainers during the season, May through October. All the big names perform here and have the shows recorded, but the one that always sticks in my mind is Neil Diamond's *Hot August Night*.

The Hollywood Bowl, 2301 North Highland Avenue, ph (213) 850 2000 - see the Entertainment section for details.

Hollywood Studio Museum, 2100 North Highland Avenue, ph (213) 874 2276, is located in the DeMille-Lasky barn where Hollywood's first feature-length film, *The Squaw Man*, was filmed in 1913. The museum has cameras, costumes, props and photos from the early days of Hollywood, and an excellent video on the history of the area, and motion picture pioneer Cecil B. DeMille. It is open Sat and Sun, 10am-4pm.

Max Factor Museum, 1666 North Highland Avenue, ph (213) 463 6668, has exhibits including makeup from each decade of the century, and wigs, such as that worn by Bille Burke in *The Wizard of OZ*. This is really only for those interested in theatrical and film makeup.

Melrose Avenue, between Robertson Boulevard and La Brea Avenue, West Hollywood, is one of LA's most trendy streets. It is a youthful mecca of thrift shops, art galleries, boutiques, theatres, comedy clubs and restaurants.

Wilshire Boulevard is actually the main street in Los Angeles, and the famous *Miracle Mile* is the section between Highland and Fairfax. In the 30s, the Mile was **the** place to do your shopping and spend your money, but now it is attractive only to those who are into art deco. Richard Harris' favourite MacArthur Park is also on Wilshire, at Hoover Avenue, but the most important park on the street is Hancock Park, because of the following.

Rancho La Brea Tar Pits and George C. Page Museum, Hancock Park, 5801 Wilshire Boulevard, ph (213) 936 2230 or 857 6311. The tar pits date back to about 40,000 years ago, and are **the richest fossil site from the Ice Age**. Back in those days they apparently looked like a good place to quench a thirst, and unsuspecting animals ventured too close and became stuck. Predators tried to take advantage of their trapped state, and suffered the same fate. Even humans were not spared by the malevolent mud.

The existence of the pits was recorded in the 18th century, but it wasn't until 1906 that scientists turned their attention to them, and began to remove and classify the fossils. Over one hundred excavations have been made, with over three million specimens being removed, including mastodons, camels, saber-toothed cats, vultures, prehistoric versions of bears, lizards and birds, and a Native American thought to have lived about 9000 years ago.

The George C. Page Museum of La Brea Discoveries is at the east end of Hancock Park, and has more than twenty of the recovered specimens. There are also replicas of trapped animals and birds standing in their original setting, to give a good idea of how the area would have looked way back then. A 15-minute documentary film and slides about the pits will also put you in the picture.

Free guided tours of the museum and the tar pits are conducted Wed-Fri, 1-4pm, ph (213) 857 6306 for full information. The museum is open Tues-Sun 10am-5pm, and the Page Museum Shop is open Tues-Sun 10am-4.45pm, ph (213) 931 5273 for shop information.

Los Angeles County Museum of Art is adjacent to the George C. Page Museum, and is open Tues-Fri 10am-4.30pm, Sat-Sun 10am-5.30pm. This museum has special exhibitions, film series and lectures, and for free guided tours, ph (213) 857 6108. In the museum there is also a shop and the indoor-outdoor Plaza Cafe, which has the same hours as the museum.

Beverly Hills Golden Triangle is bounded by Canon Drive, Wilshire Boulevard and Little Santa Monica Boulevard, and has at its heart the famous Rodeo Drive. As mentioned in the Shopping section, this is the in place for the rich and famous.

WESTSIDE

Westwood Village is bounded by Gayley, Le Conte and Hilgard Avenues and Wilshire Boulevard, and is tucked in between Bel Air, Beverly Hills and Century City. It is a busy shopping and entertainment area and has a shuttle bus service to nearby *UCLA* (University of California at Los Angeles).

The University is best visited in vacation time, although there will still be many students in residence. The 170ha (419 acres) campus has the Museum of Cultural History, Pauley Pavilion, the Wight Art Gallery, the Mathias Botanical Gardens, the Japanese Garden and Sculpture Garden.

There is a visitor centre at 10886 Le Conte Avenue, ph (213) 8147, and the Contempo Westwood Centre, ph (213) 208 4107, on Le Conte Avenue is home to the Westwood Playhouse.

Another 'attraction' in the area is Westwood Memorial Park, 1218 Glendon Avenue, where Marilyn Monroe and Natalie Wood are endeavouring to rest in peace.

SPORT AND RECREATION

Golf

There are fifty golf courses in the Los Angeles area, and some have been mentioned in the Sightseeing section. The helpful people at the Los Angeles Visitor Information Center, ph (213) 689 8822, will be able to advise you of the closest one to where you are.

The following have been rated by *Golf Digest* as among the top 25 public courses in the nation:

Brookside Golf Course, 1133 Rosemont Avenue, Pasadena, ph (818) 796 0177. Two 18-hole courses (par 70, 5800 yds, 66.3 rating; par 72, 6600 yds, 71.6 rating) adjacent to the Rose Bowl, 15 minutes north of Downtown.

Griffith Park Golf Course, 4730 Crystal Springs Drive, LA, ph (818) 663 2555. Two WPA courses, the Harding Course (par 72, 6536 yds, 70.4 rating) and the Wilson Course (par 72, 6942 yds, 72.7 rating).

Tennis

Many hotels have tennis courts, but here are a few clubs and public courts:

Arcadia Park Tennis Club, 405 South Santa Anita, Arcadia, ph (818) 447 4441.
Gerrish Swim & Tennis Club, 2713 New York Drive, Pasadena, ph (818) 798 1313.
Griffith Park, 3401 Riverside Drive, LA, ph (213) 665 5188.
La Cienega Park, 311 South La Cienega Boulevard, LA, ph (213) 550 4864.
Mountain Gate Tennis Club, 2205 North Sepulveda Boulevard, LA, ph (213) 476 2291.
Penthouse Racquet Club, 2020 Avenue of the Stars, LA, ph (213) 553 6672.
Roxbury Park, 471 South Roxbury Drive, Beverly Hills, ph (213) 550 4761.

Tennis Village of Santa Monica, 2751 Ocean Park, Santa Monica, ph (213) 396 3130.

Horse-riding

Griffith Park has 85km (53 miles) of bridle paths, and within the park, the Los Angeles Equestrian Center, ph (818) 840 9063, holds polo matches, jumping shows and competitions that are open to the public. Generally, **horses can be rented for about $15 to $18 an hour,** and a deposit is sometimes required (in case you decide to take the horse back home with you).

The following stables service Griffith Park, and it is best to call ahead for additional information:

Circle K Stable, 914 Mariposa Street, Burbank,
ph (818) 843 9890.
Griffith Park Livery Stable, 480 Riverside Drive, Burbank,
ph (818) 840 8401.
Sunset Hollywood Stables, 3400 North Beachwood Canyon Drive, Hollywood, ph (213) 469 5450.

Bicycling

The South Bay Bicycle Trail winds for nearly 32km (20 miles) from Santa Monica to Torrance, and connects with a network of paths from inland areas.

Across from the Santa Monica Pier on the boardwalk *Sea Mist Rental*, 1619 Ocean Front, ph (213) 395 7076, rents bicycles, roller skates and boggie boards.

Spokes 'n Stuff, 3001 Ocean Front Walk, Marina del Rey, ph (213) 306 3332, and the *Venice Pier Bike Shop*, 21 Washington Street, Venice, ph (213) 823 1528, have bicycles for rent in two of the area's most ridable locations.

Boating

Boating and sportsfishing charters are available from the following:

Captain Medina's Yacht Chartering and Marine Services, Marina del Rey, ph (213) 823 1019.
Marina del Rey Sportfishing, ph (213) 822 3625.

Malibu Pier Sportfishing, ph (213) 456 8030.

Bowling

Active West, 2050 South Bundy Drive, LA, ph (213) 879 5791, operates 21 ultra-modern bowling centres throughout Southern California. All centres have restaurants, cocktail lounges, supervised children's playrooms, game rooms, and many have automatic scoring equipment. Phone the above number for locations.

Rollerskating

Beachfront skating is popular in Santa Monica and Venice, where skate rental shops are easily found. The coastal paths in Venice are particularly popular for this sport.

Shooting

L.A. Gun Club, 1375 East Sixth Street, LA, ph (213) 612 0931, has a 50-foot indoor range with 15 individual booths and spectator viewing area. Free safety instruction in English, Japanese, Korean and Spanish. Fire arms are available for rent and sale. Open Mon-Thurs 3-11pm, Fri-Sun 11am-11pm.

SPECTATOR SPORTS

Baseball

The Los Angeles Dodgers, Dodger Stadium, ph (213) 224 1421 - regular season is April-September.

Basketball

The Los Angeles Clippers, Los Angeles Sports Arena, ph (213) 748 0500 - regular season is November-April.

The Los Angeles Lakers, The Great Western Forum, ph (310) 419 3220 - regular season is November-April.

Football

The Los Angeles Raiders, Los Angeles Memorial Coliseum, ph (213) 322 5901 - regular season is August-December.

Hockey

The Los Angeles Kings, The Great Western Forum, ph (310) 673 6003 - regular season is November-March.

Horseracing

Fairplex Park/LA County Fair Grounds, Pomona, ph (909) 623 3111 - regular season is September-October.
Hollywood Park, Inglewood, ph (310) 419 1529 - regular seasons are April-July and November-December.
Santa Anita Park, Arcadia, ph (818) 574 6400 - regular seasons are July-September and December-April.

Tennis

The Los Angeles Strings, The Great Western Forum, ph (310) 419 3257 - regular season is July-August.

TOURS

There are many tours on offer from different companies, and the LA Visitor Information Centre, ph (213) 689 8822, has all the details. The Bell Captain in your hotel, or tour desk, can also arrange tours for you, and the tours he arranges will have arrangements for pick-up from your hotel.
Here are samples of the tours available.

Oskar J's Sightseeing Tours, **4334 Woodman Avenue, Sherman Oaks, ph (818) 501 2217, or outside LA 1-800-458-2388, has the following itineraries:**

Tour 1 - LA At Night - four hours, includes dinner.
Tour 2 - Universal Studios - eleven hours.
Tour 3 - Disneyland - all day, including admission to the park.
Tour 4 - Los Angeles - five hours, including Hollywood, Beverly Hills, Stars' Homes, Melrose Avenue, Farmer's Market, Rodeo Drive, Century City, Westwood Village.

Tour 5 -	Combination of 2 and 4 - all day.
Tour 6 -	J. Paul Getty Museum - eight hours, including Venice Beach, Santa Monica Beach, Marina del Rey, Fisherman's Village and a Harbour Cruise.
Tour 7 -	Catalina Island - ten and a half hours.
Tour 8 -	Movie Stars' Homes - two hours.
Tour 9 -	Comination of 2 and 8 - eleven hours.
Tour 10 -	LA by Helicopter - two hours - not always available.
Tour 11 -	LA by Helicopter & Universal Studios - fourteen hours
Tour 12 -	San Diego & Tijuana - 2 days/1 night.
Tour 13A -	Grand Canyon - all day.
Tour 13B -	Las Vegas Overnight - 2 days/1 night.
Tour 13C -	Combination of 13A and B - 2 days/1 night.

Similar tours are offered by *Magic Line Sightseeing Tours*, 5322 Wilshire Boulevard, LA, ph (213) 653 1090, and many other tour companies.

The tours seem to be quite expensive when you first see the prices (which are subject to change at a minute's notice, so I have not included them) but when you take into account the distances travelled, and the excellent service, they are value for money.

Tip

Some can also be used to your advantage. For example, last time I was staying in Beverly Hills and wanted to go to Anaheim, it worked out cheaper to take a Disneyland Tour, and take my luggage with me, than to arrange to go by shuttle or taxi.

> *Even the tip I gave the bus driver to drop me of at my Anaheim hotel, did not bring what I had outlayed up to the price of the alternative transport.*
> *After checking into the hotel and dropping off my luggage, I took the free shuttle back to Disneyland and used the entry ticket that was part of the tour.*

West Coast Tours, ph (213) 549 4401 for reservations, offe dinner tours, nightclub tours, golf tours, shopping tours and special arrangements for concerts and sports events.

NOTES

LOS ANGELES COAST

The beaches are some of Los Angeles' biggest attractions, and the weather does its best to fit in with their use. Lifeguards are on duty year round at county beach facilities, and for weather and surfing conditions you can phone (213) 451 8761. The stretch of coastline detailed here begins at Malibu and continues down to Long Beach.

MALIBU

Situated north-west of Santa Monica, and only 40km (25 miles) from Los Angeles Civic Center, Malibu is actually the strip of shoreline from Topanga Canyon west to the Ventura County line.
The area has four main beaches:
Malibu Pier, which offers swimming, surfing, diving and volleyball, and from where sportfishing boats depart twice daily;

Surfrider Beach, just north of the pier and the best surfing spot, is adjacent to a wildlife/marine reserve with tidepools and hiking trails;

Corral State Beach, 6km (4 miles) north of the pier, is good for diving and fishing, but surfing is not allowed;

Zuma Beach, 13km (8 miles) north of the pier, is great for bodysurfing, and has showers, volleyball courts and a playground. Lifeguards are on duty year round at county beach facilities.

Notorious in the 1920s for its hell-raising beach parties, and famous in the 1950s and 60s for its use in many squeaky-clean beach movies, Malibu has mellowed over the years. It is still home to many top-paid movie stars, but they are rather paranoid about their privacy, which is fair enough, and your chance of spotting one on the beach is practically nil. You could, although, run across a couple in the shopping malls on Pacific Coast Highway.

The J. Paul Getty Museum, 17985 Pacific Coast Highway, between Sunset and Topanga Canyon Boulevards, is the world's wealthiest museum, and one of seven programmes of the J. Paul Getty Trust, a private operating foundation devoted to the visual arts. Mr Getty, who was born in Minneapolis, Minnesota, in 1892, was an oil multi-millionaire with a penchant for ancient history and culture. He travelled the world collecting rare Roman and Greek treasures, which he installed in his ranch house in Malibu, and opened it to the public. By the mid-1960s, the house could no longer accommodate the rapidly growing collections, so Mr Getty decided to commission a new building.

Construction on the present museum began in 1971, and it was opened to the public in January 1974. The building is a recreation of an ancient Roman country house, the Villa dei Papiri, which stood outside the city of Herculaneum, overlooking the Bay of Naples. The Villa was completely buried by the eruption of Mount Vesuvius in 79AD, and rediscovered in the 18th century by archaeologists using a system of underground tunnels. They made comprehensive notes and drew a floor plan, before re-sealing the villa and leaving it sixty feet below the ground.

The museum's gardens are completely in character, with trees, flowers, shrubs and herbs that would have been found in the original Villa, and bronze statues that are modern casts of those unearthed by the archaeologists in the 18th century. The originals are in the archaeological musem in Naples.

The collection comprises antiquities, decorative arts, drawings, maiolica and glass objects, manuscripts, paintings, sculpture and photographs, and ranges from the early days of Rome, through to modern European masters.

It really is incredible. The information booklet suggests that a visit should take from two to three hours, but I think that you really need more time to absorb the magnificent array of exhibits, especially if you make use of the videos of medieval and Renaissance manuscripts.

The Garden Tea Room serves sandwiches, salads and snacks, and lunch is 10.30am-2.30pm, light refreshments 2.30-4.30pm. **The museum is open Tues-Sun 10am-5pm, except for New Year's Day, Independence Day, Thanksgiving and Christmas Day. Admission is free, but there are certain restrictions.**

The local homeowners have apparently kicked up a fuss in the past about people parking in the streets around the museum, so **pedestrians are not allowed entry.**

You have a few choices for getting there, though.

You can arrive by taxi, which will drop you off at the entrance;
by RTD bus 434, if you get an admission pass from the driver (ph (800) 252 7433 for more information);
be dropped off by a private car, but check in with the officer at the Front Gate Guardhouse before getting out of the car;
ride a bicycle - there are racks for the bikes, although there is no designated bicycle path along Pacific Coast Highway;
come by motorcycle, then you will be directed to designated parking spaces;
or drive yourself after making a reservation to park in the museum's limited parking area, which should be done seven to ten days before you visit by calling the Reservations Office, ph (213) 458 2003 between 9am-5pm, seven days a week.

Sounds crazy, doesn't it, but it is worth the hassle to see one of the most interesting museums in the world.

SANTA MONICA

Wilshire, Sunset, Olympic, Pico and Santa Monica Boulevards, the streets that you have been following through LA, all end when they meet Ocean Avenue in Santa Monica.

Main Street, between Ocean Park Boulevard and Marine, is a pedestrian shopping area with lots of restaurants and cafes, and Third Street, between Broadway and California, is another pedestrian mall with fashionable boutiques, a movie theatre, and more restaurants and coffee houses.

Santa Monica Pier, at the foot of Colorado Avenue, ph (213) 458 8900, was built in 1908 and is the last of the great pleasure piers. Games, rides, an historic carousel, shops, cafes and restaurants with full bars await you, in a unique setting with panoramic views of the ocean and the Santa Monica Mountains. **The pier is open year-round,** and you should allow about three hours for a visit. Several movies have used the pier as a location, including *The Sting* and *Funny Girl*.

Adjacent to the pier is the Santa Monica Beach, one of the Southland's most popular, although not necessarily for swimming.

The Museum of Flying at Santa Monica Airport, 2772 Donald Douglas Loop North, ph (310) 392 8822, has a good collection of historic and vintage aircraft, including the Douglas World Cruiser, which, in 1924, was the first plane to circle the globe. **The museum is open Tues-Sun (in summer) 10am-6pm.**

Angels Attic, 516 Colorado Avenue, ph (213) 394 8331, is a restored Victorian house with displays of antique dolls' houses, miniatures, dolls and toys.

VENICE

It is possible to get a bus from Santa Monica to Venice, but then you would miss the lovely walk along the beachfront, which only takes about 40 minutes at a leisurely stroll.

Tobacco magnate Abbot Kinney designed his dream community here at the turn of the century, inspired by that other Venice in Italy, and of the original twelve canals, three still remain.

The nearby *Venice Boardwalk*, along a three-mile stretch of beach is a popular spot for people-watching, and there are always street performers and stalls selling dubious goods.

Next to Venice City Beach is the it-could-only-happen-in-America *Muscle Beach*. There is actually a wired-off outdoor gymnasium, in which sweating individuals work on their biceps, triceps and quadriceps, for the benefit of an admiring audience of 'seven-stone weaklings' who are probably used to getting sand kicked in their faces. Call me a cynic if you will, but I think that these oh-so-serious ape-men probably have bigger muscles between their ears.

MARINA DEL REY

Marina del Rey is the world's largest man-made harbour, and caters in a big way for boating, sailing, fishing, cruises and watersports.

Fisherman's Village, 13763 Fiji Way, ph (310) 823 5411, is on the marina, and less than a kilometre from Lincoln Boulevard. **It is open daily 10am-9pm (winter) and 10am-10pm (summer)**, and apart from water-based attractions, has art and craft shops, fashion boutiques, and restaurants and boardwalk cafes.

SAN PEDRO

Situated 34km (21 miles) from Downtown LA, and 29km (18 miles) from LAX, San Pedro nestles on the slopes of the Palos Verdes Peninsula, and is the Port of Los Angeles. The town's history dates from 1542 when Juan Rogriguez Cabrillo landed and claimed the land for Spain. Commerce began with the founding of the Franciscan missions in 1769, San Pedro was incorporated in 1888, and it was annexed by Los Angeles in 1909 to manage the port. Now *Worldport LA* is the nation's busiest harbour, and the busiest passenger port of call in the West.

One of the main industries is fishing, and most of the fish sold in the Los Angeles area comes from the vessels docked at San Pedro's Fishermen's Wharf.

The downtown area, *Old San Pedro*, has many good restaurants and pubs, unique gift shops, antique stores, galleries and boutiques. The historic *Arcade Building*, in the Italian Renaissance style, has specialty shops and offices.

Sixth and Beacon Streets are known as *Sportswalk*, and have sidewalk plaques honouring professional and Olympic athletes. At the end of Sixth Street is the *LA Maritime Museum*, the largest maritime museum in California. **It is open Tues-Sun 10am-5pm**, ph (310) 548 7618.

Ports O'Call, at the end of the Harbor Freeway, is 6ha (15 acres) of authentic New England seaside village, with 75 specialty shops, 15 international restaurants, harbour/dinner cruises, charter cruises, and a great atmosphere. The village is open every day 11.00am-9pm, and for more information, ph (310) 831 0287.

Cabrillo Marina, next to Ports O'Call, is home to 1500 boats, a hotel, and several good restaurants. It also has scenic cycling and walking paths through the complex, and next to it is the Cabrillo Beach Youth Waterfront Sports Center, which is mainly for youth groups, but available to all.

Beyond the marina is *Cabrillo Beach*, which is actually two beaches: the one outside the breakwater has ocean surf; the one inside the harbour is perfect for families with children. The *Cabrillo Marine Museum* is part of the beach, and has aquaria, touchtanks, and displays on the California Gray Whale and other local marine life. Admission is free.

The land rises dramatically once past the breakwater and heading towards Point Fermin, making for some great views. The *Point Fermin Lighthouse* guided ships from 1874 until it was replaced by Angels Gate Lighthouse in 1913.

Above Point Fermin is *Angels Gate Park*, in which you will find the Korean Friendship Bell, Angels Gate Cultural Center, LA's Youth Hostel, and the Fort MacArthur Military Museum. The museum was once an operation post for the giant guns that defended the harbour against enemy attack.

Pride of Los Angeles is LA's main harbour cruise ship, and offers daily lunch, brunch, and dinner cruises, as well as weekend moonlight cruises. The food's good, as is the bar service, and there are live dance bands, and a show put on by the waiting staff, ph (310) 519 2999.

LONG BEACH

The sixth-largest city in California, with a 9km (5.5 miles) beach, Long Beach can be reached by driving over the Vincent Thomas Bridge from San Pedro, or by following the Long Beach Freeway from the Santa Ana Freeway turnoff. It is home to a unique attraction - The *Queen Mary*.

The Queen Mary arrived in Long Beach at 10am on December 9, 1967, and became a hotel. She is still beautiful, but has become quasi-English, in other words, she has been turned into what the American public probably expect of a grand old British ship, instead of being left with her own personality. All the old fittings are there, and the shops on the Promenade Deck, in a section called Piccadilly Circus, all have an English flavour to them, but I'm sure that the Queen feels a little embarrassed at her present state.

The *Queen Mary* was launched on Sepember 26, 1934, and sailed on her maiden voyage on May 27, 1936. During her cruising days she carried the royal, the rich and the famous, and many of her passengers are documented in photos liberally sprinkled on the Promenade Deck. During the second world war, she saw duty as a troop ship, and due to her new grey paint job, was dubbed the *Grey Ghost*. She transported more than 750,000 troops over 600,000 miles, and Adolf Hitler offered a $250,000 reward and the *Iron Cross* to anyone who could sink or destroy her.

Now she sits stately at the dock and hundreds of people prowl through every inch of her, looking for dark secrets and haunted passages.

A free souvenir guide map lets you wander around on your own, or you can hire an Audio Tour (in English, Spanish, German or Japanese) for $4 per unit. To find out absolutely everything, you can book a Captains Tour, at the desk located on the starboard (right) side of the Promenade Deck, near Piccadilly Circus, $4 adults, $3 children.

The ship is open to the general public daily 10am-6pm, and admission is $7 adults, $4 children 4-11.

The elegant restaurant on board is *Sir Winston's*, which is open for lunch and dinner, or you can have a drink in Sir Winston's Piano Bar, with entertainment nightly. Entrance to these is on the Sun Deck at the stern of the ship on the starboard side. Another good place for a drink is the *Observation Bar*, the original First Class lounge.

Back on dry land there is Londontowne, a village consisting of a souvenir shop, a wine tasting room, glass blowers, a video game arcade, a bakery, an ice cream parlour and a Mexican restaurant - all very English!

CATALINA ISLAND

Santa Catalina, called 'the island of romance' in the song, is 35km (22 miles) from San Pedro, and can be reached by Catalina Express, fast passenger boats that have frequent daily departures from San Pedro and Long Beach (take Downtown exit, not Port of Long Beach-Queen Mary exit), and seasonally from Redondo Beach. They arrive at *Avalon*, the only city on the island, or *Two Harbors*, and for details and reservations, ph (310) 519 1212.

Catalina is so different from Los Angeles that it is hard to believe that it was once joined to the mainland, even if it was over half a million years ago. Archaeologists have discovered that the island was once populated by a race of giants, and a Stone Age people lived here as late as the 1600s, when Spanish explorers visited.

Russian fur hunters were based on the island for a while in the early 1800s, but after wiping out the sea otter population, and along with it, the local Indian population, they vamoosed. The island then became home to pirates and anyone else who did not want to be found, until a mini-gold rush in the 1860s, which was brought to an end during the Civil War.

Catalina was bought and sold a few times until it was purchased by William Wrigley Jr in 1915. Spending more of his chewing gum money, he purchased the Chicago Cubs during the 1920s, and took them to the island for spring training. The inevitable camp followers, the sports journos, wrote home about more than the team training sessions, and a tourist boom followed until Catalina became an important military base during World War II.

Now the island is very popular for water sports, hiking, golf, tennis and horse-riding, to the extent that accommodation has to be booked well in advance. The *Wrigley Memorial and Botanical Gardens* are worth a visit, but your first stop will be the *Green Pleasure Pier* in Avalon, where the boat pulls in, and the Catalina Island Chamber of Commerce and Visitors Bureau, ph (310) 510 1520, for maps, information and brochures.

There is also a Visitors Information and Services Centre on Crescent Avenue (across from the Pier), ph (310) 510 2000, that has everything you need to know about tours.

THE VALLEYS

SAN FERNANDO VALLEY

It lies to the north of Los Angeles and is known locally as "The Valley". It is home to over 1 million people, and has an area of 570 sq km (220 sq miles).

The most scenic way to begin a tour of The Valley is to take legendary *Mulholland Drive* which runs west from the Hollywood Freeway to Topanga Canyon Boulevard. The drive takes about one hour, and rises above the LA basin to the south and San Fernando Valley to the north, allowing great views of both, and ensuring a scenic trip day or night.

The Sepulveda Dam Recreational Facility is bounded by the Ventura and San Diego Freeways, and has a 13km (8 miles) jogging and bicycle path, archery facilities and a grassy picnic area.

Six Flags Magic Mountain, north of The Valley in Valencia, is a 105ha (260 acres) amusement park that has the world's largest looping roller-coaster, the Viper, and its newest roller-coaster Psyclone, which first drops 29m (95 ft), then whips through ten more drops with five fan banked turns, then goes through a 56m (184 ft) tunnel, all at the speed of 80km/ph (50mph). The park is about 25 minutes north of Hollywood, in Magic Mountain Parkway, off the Golden State Freeway, ph (805) 255 4111 for opening hours, which vary.

The roller-coasters aren't the only rides that will test your ability to hang onto your last meal, there is also a Tidal Wave that will plunge you in a wall of water; Revolution, with its 44m (144 ft) tunnel and 360-degree loop; and Roaring Rapids, a white-water rafting adventure par excellence; in fact there are over 100 rides and attractions.

For the littlies, the park has Bugs Bunny World, where they can meet that 'wascally wabbit' and his friends, and next door is Wile E. Coyote Critter Canyon.

The park also has dolphin shows, high divers, and in summer the fireworks spectacular is a nightly event. There are plenty of places to grab a bite to eat, or you can take a picnic lunch, but make sure that you allow plenty of time for a visit.

Admission is adults $28, children under 48 inches $17, which includes all rides.

SAN GABRIEL VALLEY

This valley is east of Los Angeles, and the best-known city in the area is **Pasadena**, where the annual New Year's Day Tournament of Roses parade and Rose Bowl game are held. Pasadena has some of Southern California's most beautiful historic homes.

The *Gamble House*, 4 Westmoreland Place, ph (818) 793 3334, is one of the finest examples of the native California craftsmen home, and tours are offered on the quarter hour from noon to 3pm, Thurs-Sun.

Fenyes Mansion, 470 West Walnut Street, ph (818) 577 1660, was built in 1905, and one-hour tours of the house, research library and grounds are held from 1pm to 4pm on Tues, Thurs, and the first, second and last Sunday of the month.

The *Tournament House*, 391 South Orange Grove Boulevard, ph (818) 449 7673, was once owned by William Wrigley, Jr, the chewing gum magnate, and is now headquarters of the Tournament of Roses. Tours of the house are available 2-4pm each Wed from early-February through late-September.

The famous *Pasadena Playhouse* is at 39 South El Molino Avenue, ph (818) 356 7529.

Old Town Pasadena is bordered by Pasadena Avenue, Walnut, Holly and Green Streets, and has been recently restored. It features a variety of antique shops, boutiques, cafes and restaurants in turn-of-the-century brick buildings.

Pacific Asia Museum, 46 North Los Robles Avenue, ph (818) 449 2742, has a vast collection of artifacts and art of the Orient, Afghanistan, the Pacific Islands and the West Coast of North America.

Rose Bowl, Brookside Park, between Linda Vista and Arroyo Boulevards, ph (818) 577 3106, is where the New Year's Day Rose Bowl game is held, and it also hosts UCLA's home games. A giant swap meet is held on the second Sunday of each month.

Arcadia is east of Pasadena, near the base of the San Gabriel Mountains, and here you find the *Los Angeles State and County Arboretum*. The gardens cover 51ha (127 acres) and contain 5000 species and varieties of plants, a lagoon and the Lucky Baldwin House, which was featured in the opening scene of the television series *Fantasy Island*.

Santa Anita Park, one of the most beautiful and famous racetracks in the world, is also situated in Arcadia, at 285 West Huntingdon Drive, ph (818) 574 7223. Races are held from October through mid-November, and December through late April. **Morning workouts are held 7.30-9.30am, and the public is invited to watch on weekdays.**

NOTES

DISNEYLAND

Disneyland is probably the reason you are visiting this neck of the woods, so let's start with it before giving the general information on the area.

Disneyland is situated in Anaheim, the largest of twenty-eight cities of Orange County, south-east of Los Angeles. It's address is 1313 Harbor Boulevard, off the Santa Ana Freeway, but you will see it before you actually come to it. For information on How To Get There, see the following chapter - Orange County.

The Magic Kingdom opened on July 17, 1955 with eighteen attractions - today there are over sixty, and who knows how many will be added in the future? The first thing you will come into contact with is the car park. Even if you arrive by bus, it will enter through the toll gates of the car park. If you come by car, you will pay your parking fee ($5) here, and be directed to your parking spot. **The car park** is divided into sections with appropriate names, eg *Winnie The Pooh, Tinker Bell, Pinocchio,* and you should make a note of the name to make it easy for you to find your car later on.

There are several different passports (tickets) to ***Disneyland:***
1 Day - adult $30.00, child (3-11) $24.00
2 Days - adult $55.00, child $44.00
3 Days - adult $75.00, child $60.00

If you only have limited time, you can take a guided tour that lasts from 3.5 to 4 hours and costs adult $42, child $33.50, including one-day admission.

ORIENTATION

Having paid the entrance fee, and picked up your Souvenir Guide and a copy of Disneyland Today (which gives the times of current changing shows throughout the park), you can enter the Magic Kingdom and **everything is paid for**, except in the Video Game Arcades and, naturally enough, food and drinks.

Years ago the different attractions were categorised A, B, C, etc, and the passport you bought then might have entitled you to, say, four E rides, which were the best, five D rides, through to some number of A rides. **Now your passport entitles you to do and see whatever you like, with only a few provisos.**

Splash Mountain,
Space Mountain,
Star Tours,
Matterhorn Bobsleds,
Big Thunder Mountain Railroad
and Autopia
have some restrictions such as:
People wishing to take these rides should be in good health and free from heart, back or neck problems, and should not be affected by motion sickness. Children under 3 and expectant mothers should not take these rides.

There are special services throughout the park for disabled visitors, and a booklet entitled *Disabled Guest Guide* can be obtained from Carefree Corner, on Main Street, near the Central Plaza. Wheelchairs and strollers can be hired for a nominal charge, plus a refundable deposit, from just inside the main entrance, on the right-hand side. Some rides, however, require that people be able to leave their wheelchairs, and have someone with them to assist.

In the interests of safety, shoes and shirts must be worn at all times, and no smoking is permitted in any attraction or waiting area.

A First Aid station is located on the east side of Main Street, next to the Lost Children Center. Also near here is the Baby Center, which has facilities for preparing formulas, warming bottles, changing diapers, etc.

INSIDE THE ENTRANCE is **Town Square** and **Main Street U.S.A.**, and some people start here and work their way in a circle around the park. Others rush in hell for leather, see their favourites, or the ones they have been told about, first, then leisurely take in whatever else they see that catches their fancy.

There are no hard and fast rules about which way is the best, but one thing that you should keep in mind is that if you are going to systematically go into every shop and every attraction, you are going to take days to finish, and may end up running out of time before you get to one of the feature rides.

It can be a good idea to hop a ride on the Disneyland Railroad, which makes a complete circuit of the park, stopping at New Orleans Square, Videopolis, (the gateway to Fantasyland) and Tomorrowland, visiting the Grand Canyon and Primeval World on the way. This helps you to get your bearings, and some idea of the layout of the various lands.

The best advice:
- **Start early in the morning.**
- **Do not eat at the restaurants and cafes during normal meal hours.**
- **If an attraction does not turn you on, forget it and move onto the next.**
- **Do not be put off by long queues outside an attraction.** Everyone is in a holiday mood, people chat to strangers, and the lines of people move quite quickly.
- **If you can, it is a good idea to avoid visiting on the weekends.**

> If this is your first trip in years, do not take the attitude that you saw, for example, *Pirates of the Caribbean* last time, so **won't worry about it this time, or you will be sadly disappointed.** *The rides are changed periodically, and while some elements will be the same as on your last visit, others will be bigger and better, and when someone is discussing it back at your hotel, you will kick yourself.*
> **Always pretend that this is your first trip.**
> And last, but not least, don't think for one moment that Disneyland is for kids. It is for everyone who has not really grown up, and that includes most of us.

Disneyland is divided into different lands:

MAIN STREET USA

As already mentioned, Main Street begins at the park entrance, and represents the main thoroughfare of any small town in America at the turn of the century.

Attractions include:
Horse-drawn Street Cars, a **Horseless Carriage** and an **Omnibus** of the double-decker variety, which take passengers down the street and around the Central Plaza.

Disneyland Railway, an old-fashioned steam train that travels a circular route around the park, stopping at New Orleans Square, Videopolis and Tomorrowland, and visits the Grand Canyon and Primeval World.

The Walt Disney Story, a walk-through exhibit honouring the man whose dreams created Disneyland, that leads to a theatre presenting **Great Moments with Mr Lincoln**, a tribute to the 16th President of the United States. There is also an explanation of what makes Mr Lincoln 'work'. When I originally saw this exhibit, Mr Lincoln sat through the performance, and I was amazed at his life-like appearance and voice, but now he even stands and gesticulates, all through the

Little Tokyo is bounded by Los Angeles, Temple, 3rd and Alameda Streets, and dominated by the Japanese American Cultural and Community Center, home to the Japan American Theatre which stages musical, dance and dramatic performances. The Center also has a gallery, a library, and the Garden of the Clear Stream, a typical Japanese garden. The area also has the Nishi Hongwangi Buddhist Temple, off Central Street, the Little Tokyo Tower, the Union Church, and shopping plazas and restaurants.

The Biltmore Hotel, 515 South Olive Street, ph (213) 624 1011, is opposite Pershing Square, an inner-city park that has had much restoration work done. The Biltmore was designed by the same architects that worked on the Waldorf Astoria in New York, and opened in 1923. Although it is in the vicinity of the Jewellery District, an area where it is wise to keep an eye out for muggers, The Biltmore is an elegant hotel in the grand old tradition. In 1927, its Crystal Ballroom was the birthplace of the Academy of Motion Picture Arts and Sciences, and it was there that the design of the Oscar statuette was devised by MGM art director Cedric Gibbons.

The Financial District is bounded by 3rd and Olive Streets, Wilshire Boulevard and Figueroa Street. The *Central Library*, 5th Street and Grand Avenue, was built in 1925, and its art deco structure stands out among the surrounding glass and steel of more modern edifices.

Nearby is the recently completed *First Interstate World Center*, on 5th and Hope Streets, the tallest building on the West Coast; the *ARCO/Bank of America* twin towers complex, 515 South Flower Street, with its underground shopping plaza; and the ultra-modern *Bonaventure Hotel*, 404 South Figueroa Street, that is used in many TV shows and movies.

You can get a good view of the Financial District from the *Security Pacific Plaza*, **333 South Hope Street**, where a 1.5ha (3.5 acres) park surrounds the 55-storey building. Adjacent to the Plaza is the *Wells Fargo Center*, 333 South Grand Avenue, which has the *Wells Fargo History Museum* on the atrium level (open Mon-Fri 9am-5pm); and nearby, at 250 South Grand Avenue, is the $1.2 billion *California Plaza* complex, which houses the *Museum of Contemporary Art*.

Exposition Park is between Exposition Boulevard and Figueroa Street, south of the University of Southern California, and a fair step from the Financial District. The park has quite an outstanding collection of cultural attractions: the *Los Angeles Memorial Coliseum*, 3911 South Figueroa Street, ph (213) 747 7111; the *Los Angeles Sports Arena*, 3939 South Figueroa Street, ph (213) 748 6131; the *California Museum of Science and Industry*, 700 State Drive, ph (213) 744 7400, which has permanent and changing exhibits, including a simulated earthquake, and screens science-related films in the five-storey Mitsubishi IMAX Theater; the *Natural History Museum of Los Angeles County*, 900 Exposition Boulevard, ph (213) 744 3466, has permanent exhibits that include the skeletons of two dinosaurs, fossils, and many items devoted to early American and Californian history.

While you are still in the Downtown area, there are a couple of places worth visiting, but I have left them to last because they are on the way to Hollywood.

Chinatown is within walking distance of Union Station and Olvera Street, to the north-east. Situated between Hill Street and North Broadway (north of Sunset Boulevard), Chinatown is pretty much like any other Chinese district in any other city - hundreds of shops featuring Asian products, and dozens of restaurants offering *dim sum* and other Chinese delicacies.

Dodger Stadium is on Elysian Park Avenue, to the west of Chinatown, and is the home of the Los Angeles Dodgers, who were originally the Brooklyn Dodgers. If you are in LA between April and September, and a visit to a baseball game is on your agenda, phone (213) 224 1400 for tickets. The stadium is enormous and overlooks the skyline of Downtown from Chavez Ravine, in *Elysian Park*. The park is the second largest

Big Thunder Mountain Railroad takes you on a runaway mine train ride through a deserted 1870s mine, where you will be threatened by swarming bats, experience an earthquake, ride through rushing water, etc, etc.
Frontierland Shootin' Arcade, where you can discover how long you would have lasted in the old West.

New to this land is *FANTASMIC*, a night-time battle when Mickey's imagination runs wild with huge monsters and heroes. (This attraction is subject to seasonal demands, so check your program.)

FANTASYLAND

The most-loved ride in this land has to be **It's a Small World**, a cruise around the world with thousands of dolls, dressed in national costumes, singing and dancing to the title theme. All the little 'people' have big smiles on their faces but, for some reason, the experience brings tears to your eyes. Maybe we're all softies at heart.
Many of the other attractions in Fantasyland have a storybook theme. There's
Snow White's Scary Adventures,
Sleeping Beauty Castle,
Pinocchio's Daring Journey,
Alice in Wonderland,
Mad Tea Party,
Peter Pan's Flight, etc.

Then there are the **Matterhorn Bobsleds**, a roller-coaster ride that travels past waterfalls, through caverns, and ends with a big splash into lakes at the bottom of the mountain. On the way there is an icy encounter with the Abominable Snowman.

At the outdoor amphitheatre, **Videopolis**, there are changing shows, so check what is on offer in your *Disneyland Today* pamphlet.

From Fantasyland, you can take the **Skyway to Tomorrowland**, or you can head for Disneyland's new land, **Mickey's Toontown**.

TOONTOWN

Home to all the favourite cartoon characters, Toontown is the first new 'land' at Disneyland for over 20 years. Here you can visit Mickey in his own home, drop in on Minnie and admire her decor, or climb aboard Donald's boat. There's also **Mickey's Movie Barn** set, **Goofy's Bounce House** and **Chip 'N Dale's Treehouse**. Rides include **Gadget's Go Coaster** and **Roger Rabbit's Car Toon Spin**.

Themed shops and eateries abound, and it is obvious that this new attraction is sure to become a real favourite with everyone.

TOMORROWLAND

As the name suggests, this land has attractions with a futuristic theme, and some of them are the most spectacular in the whole of Disneyland.

Space Mountain is a thrilling voyage through the far reaches of the universe; **Rocket Jets** take you on a soaring adventure high above Tomorrowland; **Mission to Mars** has people taking off for the mysterious red planet; and **Star Tours**, which combines the creative forces of Disney and George Lucas, leaves for a mission to the Moon of Endor, and it is not plain flying.

When you enter the **Tomorrowland Spaceport**, keep an eye out for two old friends, C-3PO and R2-D2 from *Star Wars*.

The **Magic Eye Theater** shows the incredible 3-D musical motion picture starring **Michael Jackson**, *Captain EO*. Michael wrote the musical score, and the 3-D effects make it seem as if he is leaping off the screen and into the audience. His supporting cast are a bunch of fabulous space characters. *Don't miss out on this one.*

After you have explored the wonders of the universe, why not take a ride on a submarine and experience the wonders of the deep offered by **Submarine Voyage**. While you are waiting to board this ride you will notice that the water is not very deep, and the submarine is not really completely submerged, but that will be forgotten once you have 'dived'.

The *other must-see* in Tomorrowland is **Circle-Vision**. You stand in the middle of the theatre with the screen all around you. The effect is incredible as you actually become part of the show. As you leave Circle-Vision you can cast your vote for the person you think had the greatest impact on the 20th century. The winner of this 10-year poll will be announced on January 1, 2000.

DISNEYLAND HOTEL

The hotel is definitely part of Disneyland, and you can board the **Disneyland Monorail** in Tomorrowland and be transported there in minutes.

> You do have to get your hand stamped for re-entry to the park, but that is really to stop people trying to get into Disneyland from the hotel without paying.

You can even book a room, or a table at a restaurant from within Disneyland, at City Hall, Carefree Corner or the Main Street locker area, and the number for room reservations is (714) 778 6600.

Apart from being a great place to have a cool drink away from the madding crowd, the hotel has a few attractions of its own. There's the **Dancing Waters Show**, featuring fountains, lights and Disney music; **Off-Road Raceway**, with remote-controlled mini-racers zooming around quite a challenging course; two-seater **Pedal Boats** on the Marina; and **Sgt Preston's Yukon Follies Revue**, held twice-nightly Tues-Sun. Also, people staying at the Disneyland Hotel now get the opportunity to enter Disneyland one hour before it opens to miss the crowds.

PARADES

In summer, when *Disneyland* is open 8am-1am, there are two day-time **parades,** currently at **2pm and 4.30pm**. With a cast of hundreds, including, of course, Mickey and Minnie and their friends, the parades are great entertainment, and a lot of fun. There are lots of music, dancers, jugglers, great costumes, everything.

From Thanksgiving Day to New Year's Week the **Very Merry Christmas Parade** features dancing snow-people, Disney characters and, of course, Santa himself.

Then, again in summer, there are two night-time parades, **8.45pm and 11pm,** called **The Main Street Electrical Parades**, which have to be seen to be believed. Every float has hundreds of lights, and all your favourites from the Disney film classics turn Disneyland into Fairyland. Then, at the completion of the earlier parade, *Tinker Bell* flies across the sky to signal the beginning of the **Fantasy in the Sky** fireworks display. If the kids are too tired to stay for the night parade, it is worth coming back for a second visit.

During the off season, the park's open hours are reduced, and some of the shops and restaurants may not operate. Some of the attractions may also be closed, for maintenance, etc. For information on hours, events and current prices, write or phone Disneyland Guest Relations, PO Box 3232, Anaheim, CA 92803, ph (714) 999 4565.

SHOPS

Each land has a number of shops that offer items appropriate to the theme of the land, and every one of them does a roaring trade. *Disneyland* even has its own currency, available in $1, $5 and $10 denominations at a one-for-one exchange rate with

US currency. **Disney Dollars** can be purchased at all ticket booths, the Main Street Penny Arcade, Tomorrowland Starcade, City Hall, the Newsstand, The Disneyland Hotel Monorail Station, and at the front desk of the Disneyland Hotel.

RESTAURANTS AND REFRESHMENTS

No one has to go hungry in *Disneyland*. There are restaurants, cafes and fast-foot outlets every way you turn, with something to suit everyone's budget.

You are not allowed to take your own food into the park, but there is a picnic area on the left-hand side of the Main Entrance.

All of the above is really just the tip of the iceberg. There is so much to see and do in *Disneyland* that every time you visit, you will come across something that you did not happen upon before. It matters not if you are eight or eighty, *Disneyland* is indeed **The Magic Kingdom**.

NOTES

120 CALIFORNIA AT COST

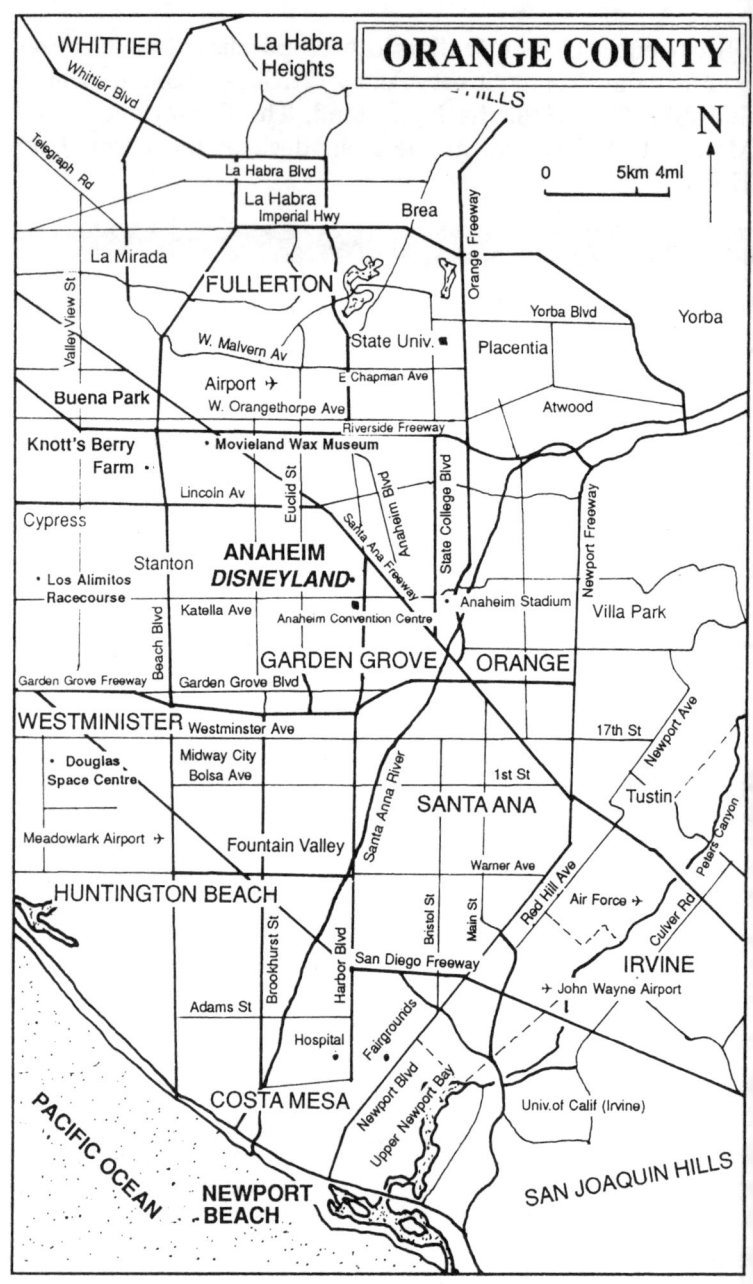

ORANGE COUNTY

Orange County has a population of 2 million, 65km (40 miles) of coastline, and attracts more than 35 million visitors every year.

The largest city is Anaheim, home of Disneyland, and other cities include Buena Park, Newport Beach, Balboa, Laguna Beach, Irvine and Costa Mesa.

ANAHEIM

Originally a small town in the Valencia orange grove area, Anaheim is now high on the list of the world's tourist venues, and all because of that one attraction, Disneyland.

HOW TO GET THERE

By Shuttle from LAX

If you are not staying in Los Angeles, you can get a shuttle direct from the airport to Anaheim. See the "Local Transport" section in the Los Angeles chapter.

A taxi from LAX to Anaheim costs around $55.

By Bus

If you are travelling from LA to spend the day at Disneyland, bus 460 leaves from the RTD terminal, 6th and Los Angeles Streets, Downtown, and the fare is about $2.50 each way. Getting there is easy enough, but getting home would be a bit of a problem, especially when you are worn out after a day at Disneyland. In fact, just finding the right bus to take would be a hassle.

By Car

From LA, take the Santa Ana Freeway and turn off at Harbor Boulevard.

By Tour

Most tour companies offer one-day tours to Disneyland from Downtown, Hollywood and Beverly Hills, for reasonable rates.

By Air

If you are travelling from other parts of the States, the John Wayne Airport is the closest to Anaheim, and there are the usual shuttle services. A taxi from the airport to Anaheim costs around $25.

> The best advice I can give you is to stay in Anaheim for as long as you can afford.
> You need at least *two days* to see most of **Disneyland**, then *a day* to go to nearby Buena Park for **Knott's Berry Farm** and the **Movieland Wax Museum**.
>
> *Add a day* to visit the enormous **South Coast Plaza** shopping centre in **Santa Ana/Costa Mesa**, (4 days total).

If you haven't hired a car, Anaheim is a good place to pick up tours to San Diego and Tijuana.

Actually, it is becoming more common for visitors to stay for longer periods in Anaheim and take tours to Los Angeles and its attractions, rather than staying in LA itself.

ACCOMMODATION

Anaheim seems to be a city of hotels, but even so, it is imperative that you book in advance, due to the incredible amount of visitors to the city each year. Most that are not in walking distance of Disneyland offer free **shuttle buses** that leave every hour from the hotel and from Disneyland. This is really a better option than being within walking distance, because just walking through the car park can require a rest break.

Here is a selection, with prices for a double room per night in US Dollars, which should be used as a guide only. **The telephone area code is 714.**

Disneyland Hotel, 1150 West Cerritos Avenue, ph 778 6600 - 1132 rooms, restaurants, cocktail lounges, swimming pool, tennis, airport bus service - $150-230.

Sheraton-Anaheim Hotel, 1015 West Ball Road, ph 778 1700 - 500 rooms, restaurant, cocktail lounge, swimming pool, airport bus service - $110-145.

Howard Johnson's Hotel, 1380 South Harbor Boulevard, ph 776 6120 - 318 rooms, restaurant, cocktail lounge, swimming pool, airport bus service - $90-99.

Granada Inn of Anaheim, 2375 West Lincoln Avenue, ph 774 7370 - 80 suites, restaurant, swimming pool, continental breakfast included - $75-85.

Ramada Inn Garden Grove, 10022 Garden Grove Boulevard, Garden Grove, ph 534 1818 - 116 rooms, restaurant, cocktail lounge, swimming pool - close to Disneyland - $75-85.

Best Western Courtesy Inn, 1200 South West Street, Anaheim, ph 722 2470 - 35 rooms, swimming pool - $52-80.

Anaheim Angel Inn, 1800 East Katella Avenue, ph 634 9121 - 61 rooms, restaurants, cocktail lounges, swimming pool, airport bus service - $49-79.

Anaheim Park Motor Inn, 915 South West Street, ph 778 0350 - swimming pool, includes Continental breakfast - $49-66.

Anaheim Cavalier Inn, 11811 South Harbor Boulevard, ph 750 1000 - 60 rooms, swimming pool, airport bus service - $46-69.

Anaheim Super 8, 415 West Katella Avenue, Anaheim, ph 778 6900 - 175 rooms, swimming pool - $54-64.

LOCAL TRANSPORT

Orange County Transit Authority (OCTA) provides a scheduled bus service throughout the County, ph (714) 636-RIDE for routes and fares, but I have never used it. There are the free shuttle buses that run from hotels to Disneyland, and others that charge a minimal amount to take you to Santa Ana shopping centres, Knott's Berry Farm, and just about anywhere else you want to go.

These buses do not stop at every hotel, but there will be a hotel within walking distance of yours where the buses do stop.

If the shuttle has just left, and you can't wait for the next one, grab a cab. But they are a little on the expensive side.

EATING OUT

Anaheim is not renowned for its fine dining experiences. Most of the hotels have restaurants and cocktail bars, or for something different, you could try the following:

King Henry's Feast, 1856 Manchester Avenue, Anaheim, ph 937 2969. A new restaurant offering family-style dining, and entertainment by jugglers, magicians, sword swallowers and more. Show times are Mon-Thurs 7.30pm, Fri 6.30 and 9pm, Sat 4pm, 6.30pm and 9pm, Sun 1.30pm, 4pm and 6.30pm - Moderate - Amex, DC, MC, V.

Benihana of Tokyo, 2100 East Ball Road, Anaheim, ph 774 4940 - Japanese meals prepared at the table - open Mon-Fri 11.30am-2pm, Mon-Thurs 5-10pm, Fri Sat 5-11pm, Sun 4.30-9.30pm - Moderate - Amex, DC, MC, V.

However, if you just walk down the street, say Katella Ave or Harbor Boulevard, there are plenty of quick serve diners that serve copious amount of food, though the quality is indifferent. Even the Chinese restaurants do not provide you with chopsticks, only a fork and spoon.

SHOPPING

Anaheim Plaza Shopping Centre, 500 North Euclid, Anaheim, ph 635 3431, is the closest centre to Disneyland, and is open Mon-Fri 10am-9pm, Sat 10am-6pm, Sun noon-5pm, and a shuttle bus service is available.

Minutes from Anaheim is *The City Shopping Center*, 20 City Boulevard East, #149, Orange, ph 634 8734, which has J.C. Penney and Robinsons-May Department Stores, and over a hundred specialty stores and services, including sixteen food outlets. There are also banking and financial services, foreign currency exchange and a nightclub.

Shopping hours are Mon-Fri 10am-9pm, Sat 10am-6pm, Sun noon-5pm, with varied hours for the department stores.

Transport to the centre is by The City Shopper shuttle buses, which pick up at major hotels and operate between Mon-Fri 9am-9pm, Sat 9am-6pm, Sun 11.30am-5pm, except on major holidays. The fare is $2, children 5 and under free, ph 535 2211.

In nearby Santa Ana there are two shopping experiences - Main Place and South Coast Plaza, both with shuttle services from Anaheim.

Main Place, 2800 North Main Street, ph (714) 547 7000, has 190 specialty stores, Bullock's, May-Robinson's and Nordstrom Department Stores, six theatres and seventeen international cafes.

South Coast Plaza is actually three centres -
South Coast Plaza, 3333 Bristol Street, Costa Mesa, ph (714) 435 2000; *Crystal Court*, 3333 Bear Street, Costa Mesa; *South Coast Plaza Village*, Sunflower and Bear Streets, Santa Ana. The Plaza and the Plaza Village, although in different cities, are across the road from each other.

The three combine to form a mind-boggling shopping complex, one of the biggest in the country.

South Coast Plaza has Bullock's, May-Robinson, Nordstrom, Saks Fifth Avenue and Sears Department Stores, and the fashion stores include names like Benetton, Chanel, Esprit, Giorgio, Bucci, Laura Ashley, Liz Claiborne, Yves Saint Laurent - the list goes on. Shoe shops include Bruno Magli, Charles Jourdan, Sacha London and The Shoe Box.

At 1641 West Sunflower, across from Nordstroms and South Coast Plaza is the restaurant and entertainment complex *Planet Hollywood*, ph 434 7827, with loads of memorabilia from television and movies. It is open daily from 11am.

Crystal Court has The Broadway and May-Robinson Department Stores, and a comparable range of fashion shops.

The smaller Village has Barker Bros, a gallery, antique shop, a tailor, and eight restaurants.

In the Town Center, across Bristol Street from the Plaza, are six more restaurants, Edwards Theatres, two cinema complexes, Orange County Performing Arts Center, South Coast Repertory Theatre, branches of ten banks, and the Westin South Coast Plaza Hotel.

Take a whole day, take your money, and shop till you drop.

SIGHTSEEING

Disneyland is the *raison d'etre* for the town, but there are a couple of other things worth seeing.

The Crystal Cathedral, 12141 Lewis Street, Garden Grove, ph 971 4000. This is a multimillion-dollar glass church with more than 10,000 windows of silver-coloured tempered glass, held in place by a framework of 16,000 white steel trusses. It seats 2,890 people, and has one of the largest pipe organs in the world. It is open to visitors daily 9am-4.30pm, and The City Shopper shuttles provide transport, ph 971 4063. The pastor has a Sunday broadcast from the Cathedral on TV.

Anaheim Convention Centre, 800 West Katella Avenue, ph 999 8900, has a 16ha (40 acres) exhibition area, in which all kinds of shows from rock concerts to antique fairs are held. It is worth phoning to see what is on when you are there. The visitor information service is here as well.

Anaheim Stadium, on State College Boulevard, has one of the biggest scoreboards in the country, and is home to baseball's California Angels and football's Los Angeles Rams. It has a 36.5m (120 ft) pole surmounted by a halo that lights up for home runs, but apparently it doesn't get much use.
To check on tickets for games - phone for baseball (April-September) (714) 634 2000; for football (August-December) ph (213) 277 4748.

BUENA PARK

Buena Park is only 8km (5 miles) from Anaheim, and has several major attractions:
Knott's Berry Farm,
Movieland Wax Museum,
Medieval Times and
Ripley's Believe It or Not! Museum.

Pacific Coast Sightseeing Tours, ph 978 8855, pick up and drop off at most hotels in Anaheim, and the return fares range from $3 to $6 (children $2 to $4), depending on the distance travelled. They also offer a round trip, plus admission to Knott's for a very competitive price.

KNOTT'S BERRY FARM

8039 Beach Boulevard, Buena Park, ph (714) 220 5147, is the third most popular family entertainment centre in the States (only Disneyland and Disney World have more visitors).

The Berry Farm started as just that - a farm for growing berries, mostly boysenberries, but the proprietors, Walter and Cordelia Knott, fell on hard times, and Cordelia started a roadside stall selling preserves and pies. Then she hit the jackpot when she started offering home-cooked chicken dinners, and Walter built an Old West Ghost Town to keep people occupied while they waited for a table. Now the famous Chicken Dinner Restaurant cooks over a million chickens every year, and the Ghost Town has become a 61ha (150 acres) theme park.

The park is divided into areas:
Old West Ghost Town is a collection of authentic buildings of the Old West which have been relocated here and renovated. In this section you can pan for gold, ride on a stagecoach or an old train, get held up by outlaws, or visit the Birdcage Theatre and cheer the hero and hiss the villain.

Fiesta Village has a 'south of the border down Mexico way' atmosphere, and the famous Montezooma's Revenge, a roller-coaster ride that travels upside down and backwards.

Roaring 20s Amusement Area has the Parachute Sky Jump, which drops you twenty storeys, the Sky Cabin, the Whirlpool, the Kingdom of the Dinosaurs, and the Good Time Theatre.

Wild Water Wilderness is a turn of the century California wilderness with the very wet Bigfoot Rapids ride.

Mystery Lodge is the latest addition to the Farm, and it involves a multi-sensory journey deep into the Native American West. The most technically advanced project ever accomplished at Knott's, it an advanced version of Spirit Lodge which was a huge success at the 1986 World's Fair in Vancouver.

Camp Snoopy is a fun place for the littlies, where they can chat to, and have their photos taken with, Snoopy, Charlie Brown and Lucy.

Knott's Berry Farm is open
Sun-Thurs 9am-11pm, Fri-Sat 9am-midnight (summer);
Mon-Fri 10am-6pm, Sat 10am-10pm, Sun 10am-7pm (winter).
Admission is
adults **$26.95**, children 3-11 **$15.95**,
seniors (60+), the handicapped, and expectant mothers **$17.95** (obviously because they would not be able to take part in most of the rides).

Outside the Farm, to the south past the entrance gates, is the marketplace, which has the best range of clothing I've seen in this type of situation, and the famous Chicken Dinner Restaurant. There is even a shop where you can still buy Cordelia's preserves, but I'll bet she doesn't make them herself anymore.

After doing your shopping, take the underpass to the car park and you will discover another type of attraction - a replica of the Philadelphia Independence Hall, complete with the Liberty Bell. There is a very unusual presentation of the signatories to the Declaration of Independence discussing the document, but there are no people! Flickering candles show that people are walking past them, the voices come from different parts of the room, and it is all really well done.

MOVIELAND WAX MUSEUM

7711 Beach Boulevard, Buena Park, ph (714) 522 1155, is one block north of Knott's Berry Farm, and claims to have the "biggest gathering of stars in the world".

When you arrive you will be forced to have your photo taken with George Burns (they may change the star, so don't hold me to that), which, of course, will be printed by the time you are ready to leave, but there is no pressure put on you to buy.

Then you can spend as long as you like with your favourite stars, some of whom are in group sets, such as *Dr Zhivago, The Poseidon Adventure, The Wizard of Oz* and *Gone With The Wind*; others are in costumes from movies, eg Paul Newman and Robert Redford are dressed as for *Butch Cassidy and The Sundance Kid*, Sylvester Stallone is *Rocky*, Marilyn Monroe is in a costume from *Gentlemen Prefer Blondes* and Superman is, well, *Superman*; and some are in typical clothing - Michael Jackson, Bette Davis, Carole Burnett, etc. There are so many it's hard to think who has not been 'waxed'.

Most of the figures are so life-like that you think they'd get tired being in the one position, others are not so good. I can't imagine that Elizabeth Taylor was particularly thrilled with her Cleo cleavage, and it is a wonder that Richard Burton didn't sue.

There is a **refreshment stop** roughly in the middle of the exhibition, then the Chamber of Horrors section, which is all to do with movies and special effects, then it's back to the 'real' people.

The Museum is definitely worth a visit, open
every day, including holidays, 9am-7pm
Admission is adults **$12.95**, children **$6.95**.
Or, you can get a **combined ticket** for entry to this and Ripley's for adults $19.90.

> And, don't forget your camera, there is no restriction on photography.
> Almost forgot to say that there was a shop, but you guessed that, didn't you?

RIPLEY'S BELIEVE IT OR NOT!

This establishment is between the Wax Museum and Knott's, on the other side of the road, at 7850 Beach Boulevard. It's the newest addition to Buena Park, and is a collection of unique and bizarre artifacts collected by Robert Ripley from around the world.

It is **open** daily 9am-10.30pm(summer), 10am-9.30pm(winter). **Admission** is adults **$8.95,** children $5.25. Or, you can get the offer of a **ticket combined** with admission to the Wax Museum for $19.90.

I don't quite understand these museums. There is another in San Francisco, and there may be others elsewhere, so are some of the exhibits copies? I'm afraid this is not my style.

The other two attractions in Buena Park are theatre restaurants.

Wild Bill's Dinner Extravaganza, 7600 Beach Boulevard, Buena Park, ph 522 6414, is a re-created wild west emporium, and an all-American four-course meal with unlimited beer, wine and Coke is offered with lots of audience participation, hootin', hollerin' and shootin'.

Show times are Mon-Thurs 7.30pm; Fri 6pm and 9.15pm; Sat 3pm, 6pm and 9.15pm; Sun 1.30pm, 4.30pm and 7.30pm Reservations are required at least 24 hours in advance, and admission **is adults $29.95 Mon-Thurs; $31.95 Fri-Sun; $26.95 Sat-Sun matinees; child (3-11) any day $19.50.**

Medieval Times Dinner & Tournament, 7662 Beach Boulevard, Buena Park, ph 521, 4740 is the same type of thing, but the entertainment here includes equestrian drills, swordplay, sorcery and romance.

Advance reservations are required, and admission **costs adults $35.75 Sat evening; $31.75 other evenings; $30.75 Sun matinee; child $19.95 evenings; $18.95 Sun matinee.**

IRVINE

Irvine is home to one of the newest family parks in Orange County, and is about a 30-minute drive from Disneyland.

Wild Rivers Waterpark, 8770 Irvine Center Drive, ph (714) 768 9453, has over forty water rides and attractions for all ages. You can go white water tubing, be fired from the Bombay Blaster, surf in Hurricane Harbor or Thunder Cove, or if you have little kids with you, visit Explorer's Island, where everywhere is scaled down to their size.

The park has changing opening hours, but in summer it is usually open 10am-5pm, phone for current times.

Admission is adults $18, children $14.

NEWPORT BEACH

The closest thing America has to the Riviera, Newport Beach is a busy harbour that encompasses the pretty town of Balboa. The harbour can be reached from LA via the Pacific Coast Highway, or from Anaheim by taking Harbor Boulevard to Newport Boulevard.

Other beaches in the area are Huntington Beach, Balboa, Corona del Mar, Laguna, Dana Point, San Juan Capistrano and San Clemente.

If you are a beach person, you might consider staying at Newport, and taking tours to the other attractions in Orange County. Your hotel will have all the necessary information, or you can contact the Newport Beach Chamber of Commerce, 1470 Jamboree Road, Newport Beach, ph (714) 644 8211.

ACCOMMODATION

There has been a lot of building activity over the last few years, and supply is keeping up with demand in the accommodation department, but it is still wise to book ahead. The following is a selection, with prices for a double room per night in US Dollars, which should be used as a guide only. **The telephone area code is 714.**

Newport Beach Marriott Hotel and Tennis Club, 900 Newport Center Drive, Newport Beach, ph 640 4000 - 400 rooms, restaurants, cocktail lounge, swimming pools, tennis courts - $195+.

Newporter Resort, 1107 Jamboree Road, Newport Beach, ph 644 1700 - across the road from the Newport Beach Country Club, and guests can use the facilities there - 414 rooms, restaurants, cocktail lounge, swimming pools - $175+.

The Sheraton Newport, 4545 MacArthur Boulevard, Newport Beach, ph 833 0570 - 342 rooms, restaurants, cocktail lounge, swimming pools, tennis courts - $155+.

The Ritz-Carlton, Laguna Niguel, 33533 Ritz-Carlton Drive, Laguna Niguel, ph 240 2000 - 362 rooms, ocean frontage, restaurant, cocktail lounge, swimming pool, tennis courts - $175-310.

Seacliff Motel, 1661 South Coast Highway, Laguna Beach, ph 494 9717 - 25 rooms, swimming pool - $45-85.

EATING OUT

The Cannery Restaurant, 3010 Lafayette Avenue, Newport Beach, ph 675 5777, is an historic landmark - a refurbished 1934 cannery that once handled 5000 cases of swordfish and mackerel a day. It is a favourite, and is open Mon-Sat 11.30am-3pm, Sun 10am-2.30pm, nightly 5-10pm.

Charley Brown's, 151 East Pacific Coast Highway, ph 675 5910, is an authentic paddlewheeler turned restaurant with a varied menu. Weeknight Happy Hours feature complimentary goodies from the 25' buffet table. Open Mon-Thurs 11am-10pm, Fri-Sat 11am-11pm, Sun 10am-3pm.

SIGHTSEEING

First and foremost, the beach is the main attraction, but there are a few others.

The Balboa Pavilion, 400 Main Street, is the hub of the district, and was originally a bathhouse. It has shops and restaurants, and is the departure point for harbour cruises and trips to Balboa Island and Catalina Island. Whalewatching cruises also leave from here January-April.

Fashion Island is Orange County's only open-air regional shopping center, and it has 200 stores and services, more than 40 eateries (including the Hard Rock Cafe), and plenty of entertainment options. It is open Mon-Fri 10am-9pm, Sat 10am-6pm and Sun noon-5pm.

Newport Harbor Art Museum, 850 San Clemente Road, adjacent to Fashion Island, ph 759 1122, has varied exhibitions of 20th century art. It is open Tues-Sun 10am-5pm.

Corona del Mar is south-east of Newport Harbor off the Pacific Coast Highway. Known as the "Crown of the Sea", this area has some of the most scenic beaches in Southern California. The town still has a small-town atmosphere, with narrow streets named after flowers, and antique shops and galleries, plus over 24 eateries to cater for every taste and budget. Also here is the Sherman Library and Gardens, a 0.8ha (2 acres) garden with a Japanese koi pond, fountains, driftwood sculptures and a tropical conservatory.

South of Corona del Mar is Pelican Hill Golf Club at Newport Coast, and its par three 12th hole is one of the most scenically beautiful in the country.

CRUISES

Catalina Passenger Service, ph 673 5245, has daily departures from Newport Beach/Balboa Pavilion to Catalina Island. They also offer daily harbour cruises, brunch cruise, and whalewatching cruises (January-April).

Hornblower Yachts, ph 646 0155, offer dining cruises,

champagne brunch and dinner dance cruises year-round from Newport Beach. Whalewatching cruises are held from January through April.

Catalina Channel Express, ph (213) 519 1212, have frequent daily departures from San Pedro to Catalina Island (Avalon and Two Harbors).

Catalina Cruises, ph 740 2000, offer regular trips from Long Beach and San Pedro to Catalina Island. They also have whalewatching cruises during December-March.

SPORT AND RECREATION

Golf
Anaheim Hills Public Country Club, 6501 East Nohl Ranch Road, Anaheim, ph 637 7311. An 18-hole course in the Santa Ana Canyons - par 71, SCGA rated at 70.5-6180 yards.

Anaheim Municipal Golf Course, 430 North Gilbert Street, ph 991 5530. An 18-hole course played year round from dawn to dusk daily. Reservations are recommended. There is also a restaurant and a cocktail lounge.

Horse Racing
Los Alamitos Race Course, 4961 Katella Avenue, Los Alamitos, ph 995 1234. Situated 15 minutes west of Disneyland, quarterhorse race meetings are held mid-November through January, and May through mid-August. Harness racing is conducted from end of February through April.

Tennis
Disneyland Hotel Tennisland, 1330 South Walnut Street, Anaheim, ph 535 4851. Ten championship courts one block from Disneyland, available for day and night play. Full service pro shop on premises.

Fishing
Davey's Locker, Balboa Pavilion, 400 Main Street, Balboa, ph 673 1434, has 14 ft boats with outboard motors and full galley facilities for full or half day rental.

SAN DIEGO

The County of San Diego covers 10,363 sq km (4000 sq miles), which includes 113km (70 miles) of sunny beaches; colourful desert areas; and the mountains of the Cleveland National Forest. The city of San Diego is America's sixth largest.

In 1542, Juan Rodriguez Cabrillo landed at Point Loma, and in 1769, Fr Junipero Serra established the first of the missions in San Diego, so the city has two reasons to boast that it is the birthplace of California. The Spanish period is beautifully preserved in the Old Town, a reconstruction of the first settlement, and modern magnets include Sea World and San Diego Wild Animal Park, but probably the main attractions the area has to offer are the beautiful beaches and the weather.

The average January temperatures range from a high of 18C (65F) to a low of 7C (46F), and those for August from 25C (77F) to 18C (66F). San Diego has been voted by meteorologists as the "only area in the United States with perfect weather", but best news of all, there is no smog. But, if you are visiting San Diego to swim, pack your wetsuit - the average water temperature is 17C (62F).

HOW TO GET THERE

By Air
See the Travel Information chapter for details of flights.

San Diego International Airport (Lindbergh Field) is 5km (3 miles) north-west of downtown San Diego, and there is a bus service connecting the two.

Many hotels also offer an airport transfer service, or you can contact the following shuttle services.

Coronado Livery, Inc, PO Box 180179, Coronado, CA, 92178-0179, ph (619) 435 6310.

Production Transport, Inc, 6033 West Century Boulevard, no 1200, Los Angeles, ph (310) 412 8456.

SuperShuttle, 4229 Ponderosa Avenue, San Diego, ph (619) 278 8877.

By Rail

The local Amtrak office is on Kettner & Broadway, San Diego, ph (800) USA RAIL US.

The service from LA to San Diego stops at Fullerton, Anaheim, Santa Ana, San Juan Capistrano, San Clemente, Oceanside and Del Mar. The service does not continue on to the Tijuana border.

Rail time from LA is 2 hours 45 minutes, from Anaheim, 2 hours.

By Bus

Greyhound Lines have several daily express services between LA and San Diego, all of which continue onto, or begin at, Tijuana, Mexico. For information on schedules contact Greyhound - LA, ph (213) 620 1200; San Diego, ph (619) 239 9171.

By Car

San Diego is 201km (125 miles) from LA; 145km (92 miles) from Anaheim on Interstate Highway 5. Incidentally, Interstate Highway 5 is sometimes called the 'BC Highway' because it travels all the way from British Columbia to Baja California.

TOURIST INFORMATION

The International Visitor Information Center, 11 Horton Plaza, ph (619 236 1212) is **open Mon-Sat 8.30am-5pm, Sun 11am-5pm June-August**, and has information on everything you need to know, plus a multilingual staff.

The Visitor Information Center, 2688 East Mission Bay Drive, ph (619) 276 8200, is also very helpful. They are **open Mon-Sat 9am-6pm, Sun 9am-4.30pm.**

ACCOMMODATION

San Diego is becoming more of a destination for visitors from overseas, probably because of the publicity caused by the America's Cup, and brochures advise that there are more than 42,000 hotel rooms available in the county. **It is still advisable to book ahead, though.**

The following is a selection of hotels, with prices for a double room per night in US Dollars, which should be used as a guide only. The **Telephone Area Code is 619.**

DOWNTOWN/BALBOA PARK

San Diego Marriott Hotel & Marina, 333 West Harbor Drive, ph 234 1500 - 1355 rooms, restaurant, cocktail lounge, swimming pool, tennis, walking distance to shops, shuttle service to shops and attractions, airport transfer service - $155-200.

Pan Pacific Hotel, San Diego, 400 West Broadway, ph 239 4500 - 436 rooms, restaurant, cocktail lounge, swimming pool, walking distance to shops, shuttle service to shops and attractions, airport transfer service - $150-190.

Embassy Suites Hotel-San Diego Bay, 601 Pacific Highway, ph 239 2400 - 337 rooms, restaurant, cocktail lounge, pool, walking distance to shops, airport transfer service - $134-189.

Horton Grand Hotel, 311 Island Avenue, ph 544 1886 - 134 rooms, restaurant, cocktail lounge, walking distance to shops, airport transfer service - $109-169.

Holiday Inn on the Bay, 1355 North Harbor Drive, ph 232 3861 - 600 rooms, restaurant, cocktail lounge, swimming pool, walking distance to shops, shuttle service to shops and attractions - $121-146.

Best Western Bayside Inn, 555 West Ash Street, ph 233 7500 - 122 rooms, restaurant, cocktail lounge, swimming pool, walking distance to shops, airport transfer service - $100.

Radisson Hotel Harbor View, 1646 Front Street, ph 239 6800 - 333 rooms, restaurant, cocktail lounge, swimming pool golf, walking distance to shops, shuttle service to shops and attractions, airport transfer service - $89.

Howard Johnson Hotel-Harborview, 1430 7th Avenue, ph 696 0911 - 136 rooms, restaurant, cocktail lounge, swimming pool, walking distance to shops, airport transfer service - $59-79.

Rodeway Inn-Downtown-Balboa Park, 833 Ash Street, ph 239 2285 - 45 rooms, walking distance to shops, airport transfer service - $54-69.

Comfort Inn-Downtown, 719 Ash Street, ph 232 2525 - 67 rooms, walking distance to shops, shuttle service to attractions and shops, airport transfer service - $46-66.

La Pensione Hotel, 1654 Columbia Street, ph 232 3400 - 56 rooms, walking distance to shops - $44-69.

Travelodge-Balboa Park, 840 Ash Street, ph 234 8277 - 28 rooms, restaurant, cocktail lounge, swimming pool, walking distance to shops - $58.

Pickwick Hotel, 132 West Broadway, ph 234 0141 - 250 rooms, restaurant, walking distance to shops - $38.

AIRPORT/HARBOR ISLAND

Sheraton Harbor Island East & West Towers, 1380 Harbor Island Drive, ph 291 2900 - 1050 rooms, restaurant, cocktail lounge, swimming pool, tennis, airport bus service - $150-170.

Forte Travelodge Hotel-Harbor Island, 1960 Harbor Island Drive, ph 291 6700 - 208 rooms, restaurant, cocktail lounge, swimming pool, shuttle to shops and attractions, airport transfer service - $89+.

HILLCREST/NORTH PARK

Sommerset Suites Hotel., 606 Washington Street, ph 692 5200 - 80 rooms, swimming pool, shuttle to shops and attractions, airport transfer service - $90.

Embassy Hotel, 3645 Park Boulevard, ph 296 3141 - 80 rooms, restaurant, walking distance to ships - $35.

POINT LOMA/SHELTER ISLAND/SPORTS ARENA

Humphrey's Half Moon Inn, 2303 Shelter Island Drive, ph 224 3411 - 182 rooms, restaurant, cocktail lounge, swimming pool, walking distance to shops, shuttle to shops and attractions, airport transfer service - $95-165.

Bay Club Hotel & Marina, 2131 Shelter Island Drive, ph 224 3888 - 105 rooms, restaurant, cocktail lounge, swimming pool, walking distance to shops, airport transfer service - $112-150.

Kona Kai Resort, 1551 Shelter Island Drive, ph 222 1191 - 170 rooms, restaurant, cocktail lounge, swimming pool, tennis airport transfer service - $95.

Best Western Shelter Island Marina Inn, 2051 Shelter Island Drive, ph 222 0561 - 97 rooms, restaurant, cocktail lounge, swimming pool, walking distance to shops, airport transfer service - $80-165.

Airport West, Point Loma Travelodge, 5102 North Harbor Drive, ph 223 8171 - 45 rooms, swimming pool, walking distance to shops, airport transfer service - $58-79.

The Grosvenor Inn, 3145 Sports Arena Boulevard, ph 225 9999 - 206 rooms, restaurant, cocktail lounge, swimming pool, walking distance to shops, shuttle to shops and attractions, airport transfer service - $64-68.

Loma Lodge Motel, 3202 Rosecrans Street, ph 222 0511 - 43 rooms, swimming pool, walking distance to shops - $39-47.

HOTEL CIRCLE/MISSION VALLEY/OLD TOWN

San Diego Mission Valley Hilton, 901 Camino Del Rio South, ph 543 9000 - 350 rooms, restaurant, cocktail lounge, swimming pool, walking distance to shops, shuttle to shops and attractions - $69-140.

Hacienda Hotel-Old Town, 4041 Harney Street, ph 298 4707 - 150 rooms, restaurant, swimming pool, walking distance to shops, shuttle to shops and attractions, airport transfer service - $95-135.

Radisson Hotel San Diego, 1433 Camino del Rio South, ph 260

0111 - 260 rooms, restaurant, cocktail lounge, swimming pool, walking distance to shops, shuttle to shops and attractions, airport transfer service - $65-125.

Hanalei Hotel, 2270 Hotel Circle North, ph 297 1101 - 424 rooms, restaurant, cocktail lounge, swimming pool, shuttle to shops and attractions, airport transfer service - $85-95.

Best Western-Seven Seas Lodge, 411 Hotel Circle South, ph 291 1300 - 309 rooms, restaurant, cocktail lounge, swimming pool, walking distance to shops, shuttle to shops and attractions, airport transfer service - $69-85.

Ramada Inn, 2151 Hotel Circle South, ph 291 6500 - 183 rooms, restaurant, cocktail lounge, swimming pool, walking distance to shops, shuttle to shops and attractions, airport transfer service - $62-82.

The Kings Inn, 1333 Hotel Circle South, ph 297 2231 - 140 rooms, restaurant, swimming pool, walking distance to shops, shuttle to shops and attractions - $67.

Holiday Inn-Mission Valley, 595 Hotel Circle South, ph 291 5720 - 322 rooms, restaurant, swimming pool, walking distance to shops, shuttle to shops and attractions, airport transfer service - $54-70.

Howard Johnson Hotel Circle, 1631 Hotel Circle South, ph 293 7792 - 81 rooms, restaurant, cocktail lounge, swimming pool, walking distance to shops, airport transfer service - $49-99.

PACIFIC BEACH/MISSION BAY/MISSION BEACH

Hilton Beach & Tennis Resort, 1775 East Mission Bay Drive, ph 276 4010 - 354 rooms, restaurant, cocktail lounge, swimming pool, tennis, walking distance to shops, shuttle to shops and attractions, airport transfer service - $145-250.

Bahia Resort Hotel, 998 West Mission Bay Drive, ph 488 0551 - 322 rooms, restaurant, cocktail lounge, swimming pool, tennis, walking distance to shops - $120-250.

Dana Inn & Marina, 1710 West Mission Bay Drive, ph 222 6440 - 196 rooms, restaurant, cocktail lounge, swimming pool, tennis, walking distance to shops, shuttle to shops and attractions, airport transfer service - $70-130.

Beach Haven Inn, 4740 Mission Boulevard, ph 272 3812 - 23 rooms, swimming pool, walking distance to shops - $70-105.

Mission Bay Motel, 4221 Mission Boulevard, ph 483 6440 - 50 rooms, swimming pool, walking distance to shops - $65-90.

Super 8 Motel-Mission Bay, 4540 Mission Bay Drive, ph 274 7888 - 117 rooms, swimming pool, walking distance to shops, shuttle to shops and attractions - $44-62.

CORONADO

Hotel del Coronado, 1500 Orange Avenue, Coronado, ph 435 5611 - 690 rooms - $145-1250.

This national historic landmark has every facility, and then some. It was built in 1888 and has had amongst its guests: twelve US Presidents; the entire cast of *Some Like It Hot* (this is where that 'all girl' band performed); and thousands of celebrities. And, there are those in the know who say that this is where Prince Edward met Wallis Simpson. Even if staying here is not in your price range, it is worth a visit and maybe a bite to eat in the Del Deli, or a magnificent dining experience in the Crown Room.

LOCAL TRANSPORT

The Metropolitan Transit System (MTS), 1225 Imperial Avenue, Suite 1000, offers more than ninety bus and trolley routes throughout San Diego County. Bus fares range from $1.50 to $2.25, and Trolley fares range from $1.00 to $1.75, depending on distance travelled. **One-Day ($4) and Four-Day ($12) Tripper passes** can be bought at the Convention Center, The Transit Store, 449 Broadway, ph 234 1060, Cruise San Diego, 1050 North Harbor Drive, and other selected locations.

Bus

MTS San Diego Transit (ph 231 1466 for customer service, or ph 233 3004 for regional information) runs a metropolitan bus service with routes to the International Airport at Lindbergh

Field, regional shopping centres, Balboa Park, San Diego Zoo, Old Town, all beaches, and major hotels and visitor attractions.

Trolley

San Diego Trolley, Suite 900, 1255 Imperial Avenue (ph 233 3004 for regional information, or ph 231 8549 for recorded trolley information) offers quick travel between the San Diego Convention Center and Centre City. It also travels south to the Mexican border and east to the cities of Lemon Grove, La Mesa and El Cajon.

The Trolley runs every fifteen minutes from 5am until 8pm, and every thirty minutes until after midnight. Before boarding you have to have either a Day Tripper pass, or a ticket from one of the vending machines located at each of the 37 stations throughout the system. **Trolleys are equipped with wheelchair lifts.**

Taxi

Getting around San Diego and to the various attractions necessitates fairly long trips, so travelling by taxi is an expensive alternative. For example, **the rate for all taxi companies from San Diego International Airport is $1.50 flag fall, $1.70 per mile and $13.00 per hour waiting time/traffic delay.**

For other trips, including travelling to the airport, the fares differ from company to company, but the maximum is $1.50 flag fall, $1.90 per mile, and $14.00 per hour waiting time/traffic delay. As you can see, if you get in a traffic jam, it becomes a very expensive exercise.

Car

For the same reasons mentioned above, if you decide to hire a car, it is best to look around for an unlimited mileage deal. Probably the bigger rental companies are your best bet:
Avis Rent A Car Systems, 3875 North Harbor Drive, San Diego,

ph 231 7171;
Budget Rent A Car, 2535 Pacific Highway, San Diego,
ph 279 2900;
Hertz Rent A Car, 3871 North Harbor Drive, San Diego,
ph 231 7000;
Thrifty Car Rental, 2100 Kettner Boulevard, San Diego,
ph 239 2281.

EATING OUT

San Diego boasts a large number of restaurants offering every imaginable type of cuisine. A dining guide with listings of restaurants by cuisine is available from the Convention and Visitors Bureau, or you can contact the Restaurant Information Line, 1010 Turquoise Street #350, San Diego, ph 488 3480.

As with any seaside city, dinner cruises are very popular, and the following companies are recommended.
Hornblower Dining Yachts/Invader Cruises, 2825 5th Avenue, San Diego, ph 686 8700.
San Diego Harbor Excursion, 1050 North Harbor Drive, ph 234 4111.

ENTERTAINMENT

The morning newspapers the *San Diego Union* and the *San Diego Tribune* have details of what is on in the city, but more information is given in the weekly *Reader* which comes out each Thursday. It is a free paper, and can be obtained at convenience, liquor and stationery stores, and at delicatessens. For information on art and entertainment, ph 234-ARTS.

Theatres

Old Globe Theatre in Balboa Park is the oldest professional theatre in the United States and presents Shakespearean plays as well as old and modern classics. For information on current shows, contact the box office, ph 239 2255, and for information on tours of the theatre, ph 231 1941.

San Diego Repertory Theatre, ph 235 8025 (box office) or 231 3586 (administration), presents eight productions October-May at the Lyceum Theatre complex in Horton Plaza.

San Diego Opera Association, ph 232 7636, presents operas in their original languages (English text projections accompany all performances) at the Civic Theater, Third and B Streets. Tickets may be purchased at the Center Box Office, 202 C Street, ph 236 6510. The Association also arranges recitals at different venues throughout the year, so telephone for current programmes.

San Diego Symphony Orchestra, 1245 Seventh Avenue, ph 699 4200, has weekly schedules of classical and popular programmes. The Winter season concerts (October-May) are held at the Copley Symphony Hall; the Summer (June-September) outdoors next to the Convention Center.

San Diego Theatre League, Inc, 701 B Street, #225, ph 238 0700, is an organisation that sponsors over 60 performing arts groups in the county, and runs the Times Arts Tix half price ticket booth at Horton Plaza and the Convention Center, ph 238 3810.

Starlight Musical Theatre, ph 544 7827, presents Broadway quality musicals nightly at the Starlight Bowl in Balboa Park, and in the Civic Theatre.

The Comedy Store, 916 Pearl Street, La Jolla, ph 454 9176, has amateur nights on Monday and Tuesday, and nationally known stand-up comedians Wed-Sun, when the admission is $6-10.

SHOPPING

Shops in San Diego are usually open Mon-Sat 10am-6pm, most until 9pm Thurs. Generally, they are closed on Sunday.

Horton Plaza, ph 239 8180, offers seven city blocks of shopping, dining and entertainment, plus great views of the city. Department stores in this area are Nordstrom, Robinsons-May, The Broadway and Mervyns. This is the downtown area.

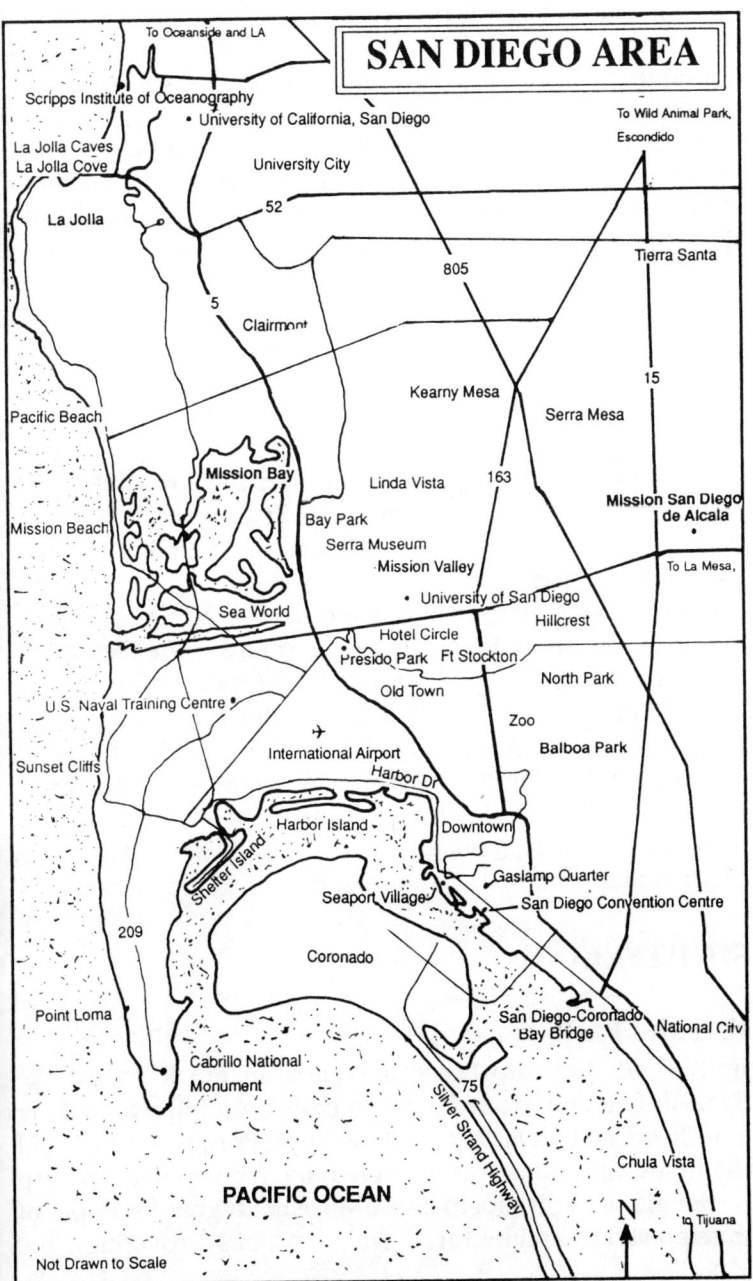

Gaslamp Quarter, 410 Island Avenue, ph 233 5227, is bounded by Broadway, Harbor, 4th, 5th and 6th Avenues, and features boutiques, art galleries and restaurants, all housed in historic buildings.

Olde Cracker Factory Antique Shopping Center, 448 West Market Street, ph 233 1699, has three floors of antique and specialty shops, and easy access to Seaport Village, Horton Plaza, and the Convention Center. Open Tues-Sun 11am-5pm.

Seaport Village Ltd, 849 West Harbor Drive, #D, ph 235 4013 for information. A complex consisting of acres of shopping, dining and entertainment outlets on San Diego Bay near the Convention Center. There is a boardwalk and a carousel, and the complex is open daily.

Fashion Valley Shopping Center, 452 Fashion Valley Road, ph 297 3381, is an open air centre with over 140 specialty shops, restaurants and theatres, and the Broadway, I. Magnin, Neiman-Marcus, Nordstrom, JC Penny and Robinsons-May department stores.

Mission Valley Center, 1640 Camino del Rio North, #1290, ph 296 6375, is an outdoor shopping centre with Saks Fifth Avenue, Robinsons-May, Bullock's, Montgomery Ward, Brooks Brothers and over 150 specialty shops.

Belmont Park, 3126 Mission Boulevard, #H, ph 488 0668, is the site of the Giant Dipper roller-coaster, many specialty shops, eateries, family amusements and restaurants. The location is at the corner of Mission Boulevard and West Mission Bay Drive, Mission Beach.

SIGHTSEEING

Presidio Park

In 1769, Fr Junipero Serra, a Franciscan monk, raised the Spanish flag and erected a crude cross on a hill overlooking San Diego, and it was here that the Royal Presidio, or fort, and the first Californian mission were built. Now perched on top of the hill is the Junipero Serra Museum, a good example of mission-style architecture with exhibits covering the pre-American era of San Diego history. The museum is open Tues-Sat 10am-4.30pm, Sun noon-4.30pm, and admission is $3. For more information contact San Diego Historical Society, ph 297 3258.

Old Town

The Royal Presidio became overcrowded with the influx of settlers, and by 1821, houses and gardens were established at the foot of the hill in what became Old Town, the first European settlement in California. It was abandoned over a century ago, but in 1967, the state provided $2.5 million to buy six blocks in the heart of Old Town, and many of its old buildings have been restored.

Bounded by Congress, Twiggs, Juan and Wallace Streets, the historic park contains souvenir and specialty shops and restaurants serving mainly Mexican food. Walking tours are offered by the state park and the Old Town Historical Society, and depart at 2pm daily from park headquarters on the north side of the plaza. For more information contact the Old Town Chamber of Commerce, 2461 San Diego Avenue, ph 291 4903.

Balboa Park

Situated in the heart of the city, Balboa Park has an area of 435ha (1074 acres) and contains museums, art galleries, theatres, sporting facilities, one of the world's largest zoos, as well as the usual grass and trees.

San Diego Zoo, ph 557 3966, takes up about 40ha (100 acres) of the park and has over 3900 animals from 800 species, living in close-to-nature accommodations. Its newest feature is an African rainforest complete with colourful birds, waterfalls, and six lowland gorillas.

Other popular attractions are the Children's Zoo and the Skyfari aerial tram ride, which crosses the zoo grounds 52m (170 ft) above the ground. Forty-minute guided bus tours travel a three-mile safari through 80% of the zoo's canyons and mesas.

Open every day of the year, the hours are 9am-5pm

(March-October), 9am-4pm (November-February).

Deluxe admission, which includes the aerial tram ride and bus tour, is $16.00 adults, $7.50 children.

Reuben H. Fleet Space Theater and Science Center, ph 238 1233, had the world's first OMNIMAX theatre when it opened in March 1973, and it is still worth a visit for its 23m (76 ft) surrounding screen that makes you part of the action. Every evening the theatre has a Laserium laser-light concert in which dancing laser beams are choreographed to music, creating a high-tech audio-visual blend that is mind-blowing to say the least. For recorded show information, ph 238 1168.

The Science Center, in the same building, has more than 60 'hands-on' exhibits demonstrating various principles of the physical sciences.

The complex is open daily 9.45am-9.30pm, and admission is $5.50 adults, $3.00 children (5-15).

S.D. Hall of Champions Sports Museum, 1649 El Prado, Balboa Park, ph 234 4542, is open daily 10am-4.30pm, and has twenty-five exhibits recognising forty sports, plus the Breitbard Hall of Fame. There is also a gift shop and a theatre. **Admission is $4 adults, $1 children.**

San Diego Aerospace Museum, 2001 Pan American Plaza, Balboa Park, has a collection of over seventy aircraft, spacecraft and artifacts, and portrays the history of aviation through its great men and women. **Open daily 10am-4.30pm.**

Museum of Man, Balboa Park, ph 239 2001, is the only anthropological museum in San Diego, and is located in the historic California Tower building. The museum has changing and permanent exhibits. **Admission is $5 adults, $1.50 children.**

Natural History Museum, Balboa Park, ph 232 3821, is the second oldest scientific institution in the western United States, and also has changing and permanent exhibits on the natural history of the south-west region. **Admission is $5 adults, $2 children.**

San Diego Museum of Art, Balboa Park, ph 232 7931, has a permanent collection of European, American, Asian, Indian and contemporary Californian art, including works by Giorgione, Cotan, Toulouse-Lautrec, Georgia O'Keefe, and Calder. There are also regular special exhibitions. **Admission is $5 adults, $2.50 children.** The Sculpture Garden Cafe offers reasonably-priced fare, and the Museum Shop has a wide selection of art publications, gifts and jewellery.

Timken Art Gallery, Balboa Park, ph 239 5548, has works by the European Old Masters 1300-1900, 19th century American paintings, Russian icons, a gift shop, and is **free to the public.**

Gaslamp Quarter

This historic area has many restored buildings and all the atmosphere of a waterfront town of the 1890s. Walking tours ($5 donation) are available every Saturday at 11am, leaving from the William Heath Davis House, 410 Island Avenue, ph 233 5227, which is home to the Gaslamp Quarter Foundation. **The house itself is open Mon-Sat 11am-2pm.**
The Foundation can supply you with a brochure on the area.

Cabrillo National Monument

The monument consists of a statue of Juan Rodriguez Cabrillo, an exhibit room, and audio-visual programs from 10am-4pm (on the hour) Thur-Tues, on the tip of Point Loma. The park is open daily 9am-5.15pm, later in summer, and admission is $4 per vehicle, or $2 for hikers, bus and bike riders. The restored Old Point Loma Lighthouse is nearby, and from the tower you can get a great view of the entire area.

There is also a free whale-watching station - a glassed-in observatory where you can look out for whales (mid-December to mid-February), look at whale exhibits, or listen to a taped description of the whales' habits.

Mission Bay

It is hard to imagine, but when Cabrillo arrived in 1542, the 1862ha (4600 acres) aquatic playground called Mission Bay Park was a desolate marshland. The park is the largest facility of its kind in the world for boating, fishing, water skiing, swimming and recreation. There are many marinas where you can rent or charter a wide range of craft; 43km (27 miles) of sun-drenched beaches with nine designated swimming areas that are off limits to boats; and acres of grassland for picnicking, kite flying, or just getting away from it all. Then, there is Sea World.

Sea World

A 55ha (135 acres) marine zoological park that offers loads of entertainment for people of all ages, ph 226 3845. There is so much to see that it is best to get an early start (opens 9am), and be prepared to stay till the end, which in summer is around 11pm. In winter, Sea World closes at dusk.

When you enter the park and collect a map and a show schedule, it is best to spend some time planning your day, and organising a spot for people to head for if they get separated from your group. The skytower is probably the best place as it is visible from all parts of the park. There is an information centre on the right side of the entrance that also doubles as a lost children's center and first aid area. The map contains some helpful information on camera rental, disabled services, etc, but if you are travelling with children, take particular notice of the advice on sea gulls. They are enormous! I have never seen such big gulls, and a small child on its own holding food of any kind would not stand a chance against one of them. **Sea World** is trying very hard to discourage the birds, and will replace free of charge any food they steal. Needless to say, they request people not to feed the critters.

The main attractions are the shows:

Shamu Stadium features performing killer whales, gigantic creatures who do high jumps and back flips, and seem to thoroughly enjoy themselves, particularly when they practically drench the people sitting in the first few rows of the stadium. The show is entertaining, and the commentary is very interesting, especially when you realise that the park's facilities are not there simply to amuse humans, they also allow a lot of valuable research to be done on the creatures of the deep.

Dolphin Stadium has the "One World" Dolphin and Whale show, which features different types of dolphins and small whales performing all kinds of jumps and dives.

Marooned! has some human actors who are completely upstaged by Clyde and Seamore, a couple of sea lions, and a very cheeky otter.

City Streets takes visitors away from the water theme and presents dancing, singing, BMX bikes and skateboards.

Beach Blanket Ski Party is held on the Water Ski Lagoon and features world-class skiers in a 60s style show.

Window to the Sea takes you on a video voyage to rarely seen wonders of the sea.

Ice Show is held in the Nautilus Amphitheater in the evenings only, from June to September, and features top professional skaters.

Then for the kids there is ***Cap'n Kids World*, a playground with a nautical theme.**

Sea World also offers two rides:

The Bayside Skyride, a six-minute ride above Mission Bay; and *Skytower Ride*, an 80m (265 ft) spiral ride for the best views of Sea World. The two rides cost $1.50 each, or you can get a combination ticket for $2.

Add to all that, the Freshwater Aquarium, Marine Aquarium, Shark Exhibit, World of the Sea Aquarium; exhibits of otters, beached animals, penguins, sea turtles, walruses, bat ray shallows and moray eel caverns; dozens of snack bars and cafes; and twenty-one shops selling gifts and souvenirs. You really have to spend at least eight hours at this destination.

Entry to Sea World is $27.95 adults, $19.95 children 3-11.

La Jolla

Situated north-west of San Diego, La Jolla (pronounced La Hoya) is a residential area where wealthy families have been building retirement homes for over fifty years. Prospect Avenue, which runs parallel with the seaside has blocks of boutiques, restaurants, cafes and art galleries.

La Jolla is also home to a new facility, the *Stephen Birch Aquarium-Museum*, 2300 Expedition Way, ph 534 4086. The museum is part of the Scripps Institution of Oceanography, a world renowned research organisation, and visitors can see twenty-two marine life tanks, and learn heaps about the research the institution is undertaking.

The aquarium is open daily 9am-5pm, and admission is $6.50 adults, $3.50 children.

San Diego Wild Animal Park

The famous Wild Animal Park is 48km (30 miles) north of downtown San Diego, via Interstate Highway 15/Highway 163, and has an area of 850ha (2100 acres). It has gained a worldwide reputation for its animal preservation efforts. You can hop aboard the Wgasa Bush Line monorail and take a 50-minute safari through parts of Africa and Asia, with guides pointing out many of the 2500 animals roaming in surroundings similar to their native homelands. Or, you can explore the African-inspired Nairobi Village with its impressive animal shows, Kilimanjaro Trail, and Tropical Asia. And visit the Australian Rain Forest, Kupanda Falls and Botanical Center, the petting kraal, the animal care centre, or some of the park's shops and restaurants.

The park is open daily 9am-6pm in summer, and 9am-4pm in winter. Admission is $17.45 adults, $10.45 children 3-11.

Mission San Diego de Alcala

The "Mother of Missions", 10818 San Diego Mission Road, ph 281 8449, now surrounded by shopping centres and suburban homes, still retains its white adobe facade, topped by a striking campanile. The nearby museum has mission records in Fr Serra's handwriting, and an imposing courtyard with olive trees. It is open daily 9am-5pm, admission is by donation.

SPORT AND RECREATION

With so much water around, it is not surprising that swimming is high on the sporting scene, but if you don't fancy the ocean, Belmont Park, 3126 Mission Boulevard, ph 488 3110, has Southern California's largest indoor swimming pool - The Plunge.

Sailing and Boating

Boats can be chartered or rented from the following organisations.
Bahia Resort Hotel, 998 West Mission Bay Drive, ph 488 0551.
Club Nautico of San Diego, 333 West Harbor Drive, ph 233 9311.
H & M Landing, 2803 Emerson Street, ph 222 1144.
San Diego Yacht Charters, 1880 Harbor Island Drive,
ph 297 4555.
Seaforth Boat Rental, 1641 Quivira Road, ph 223 1681.

Diving

The clearest waters on the California coast are in La Jolla Cove in the San Diego-La Jolla Underwater Park, part of which is an ecological preserve. You can take sea life from other areas, such as Tourmaline Canyon and Sunset Cliffs, but you have to have a fishing licence. For information on ocean diving charters, contact one of the following.
Buhrow Into Surf & Dive, 1536 Sweetwater Road, #B, National City, ph 477 5946.

SeaJet Cruise Lines, 980 F Street, Chula Vista, ph 691 1033.

Sportfishing

Fisherman's Landing, 2838 Garrison Street, ph 222 0391.
Lee Palm Sportfishers, 2801 Emerson Street, ph 224 3857.
Point Loma Sportfishing, 1403 Scott Street, ph 223 1627.
San Diego Sportfishing Council, PO Box 86039, San Diego, CA 92138-6039, ph 294 7912.

Golf

Stand By Golf, 68-703 Perex Road, Suite 25A, Cathedral City, ph 327 2665, is a golf course booking service that specialises in standby tee times at low cost pricing for San Diego and Palm Springs.

Carmel Highland Golf & Tennis Resort, 14455 Penasquitos Drive, ph 672 9100.

Carmel Mountain Ranch Country Club, 14050 Carmel Ridge Road, ph 487 9224.

Eastlake Country Club, 2375 Clubhouse Drive, Chula Vista, ph 482 5757.

Lake San Marcos Country Club, 1750 San Pablo Drive, Lake San Marcos, ph 744 0120.

Meadowlake Country Club, 10333 Meadow Lake Way, East Escondido, ph 749 1620.

Mt Woodson Country Club, 16422 North Woodson Drive, Ramona, ph 788 3555.

Pala Mesa Resort Hotel & Golf Course, 2001 South Highway 395, Fallbrook, ph 728 5881.

Rancho Bernardo Inn, 17550 Bernardo Oaks Drive, ph 487 0700.
Singing Hills Golf Club, 3007 Dehesa Road, El Cajon,
ph 442 3425.

Tennis

Carmel Highland Golf & Tennis Resort, 14455 Penasquitos Drive, ph 672 9100.

Four Seasons Resort Aviara, 7447 Batiquitos Drive, Carlsbad,

ph 438 4801.
Handlery Hotel & Country Club, 950 Hotel Circle North,
ph 298 0511.
San Diego Hilton Beach & Tennis Resort, 1775 East Mission Bay Drive, ph 276 4010.
Hotel del Coronado, 1500 Orange Avenue, Coronado,
ph 435 6611.
Hyatt Regency La Jolla at Aventine, 3777 La Jolla Village Drive, ph 552 1234.
Kona Kai Resort, 1551 Shelter Island Drive, ph 222 1191.
Le Meridien San Diego at Coronado, 2000 Second Street, Coronado, ph 435 3000.
San Diego Marriott Hotel & Marina, 333 West Harbor Drive,
ph 234 1500.
San Diego Princess Resort, 1404 West Vacation Road,
ph 274 4630.
Sea Lodge, 8110 Camino del Oro, La Jolla, ph 459 8271.
Sheraton Harbor Island-East & West Towers, 1380 Harbor Island Drive, ph 291 2900.

Spectator Sports

Del Mar Thoroughbred Club, ph 755 1141. The horseracing season is from late July through September, and attracts leading thoroughbreds and jockeys from all over the country. The track was founded by Bing Crosby in 1937, and is known as 'the track where the turf meets the surf'. **Grandstand - $3; Clubhouse $6; Reserved Seats $3.50 and $4.**

TOURS

Baja California Tours Inc, 6986 La Jolla Boulevard #204, La Jolla, ph 454 7166. Coach tours to Baja California with daily departures, 3day/2 night tours to Baja's Gold Coast between Rosarito Beach and Ensenada, and to San Felipe on the Sea of Cortez.
Cinderella Carriage Co, 801 West Market Street, San Diego, ph 239 8080. Horse drawn carriage service tours along Gaslamp Quarter, Embarcadero or city tour via Horton Plaza.

Gray Line Tours, 3855 Rosecrans Street, San Diego, ph 491 0011. Scheduled tours to Mexico and major attractions.

Old Town Trolley Tours of San Diego, Inc, 2115 Kurtz Street, San Diego, ph 298 8687. Professionally narrated historical tour covering over 100 points of interest with reboarding privileges.

San Diego Express, Inc, PO Box 13159, San Diego, CA 92170-0159, ph 233 1292, have minibus tours in San Diego area and southern California.

San Diego Mini Tours, 1726 Wilson Avenue, National City, ph 477 8687, have fully narrated city tours, Zoo, Sea World, harbour tours, Disneyland, Universal Studios, Tijuana hourly, Ensenada, San Felipe and other destinations.

Tour Du Jour, PO Box 711322, San Diego, CA 92171-1322, ph 560 6545, offer single and multiple-day tours of San Diego, Tijuana, Ensenada, and Southern California attractions.

NOTES

THE DESERT

The California desert is roughly divided into two areas, the high desert and the low. The **high** is the Mojave Desert, which lies between the Sonoran Desert to the south, San Bernardino and the San Joaquin Valley to the west, the Sierra Nevada to the north, and Death Valley to the east; the **low** is the Sonoran Desert in the south-east of the State, and stretching from the Mexican border north to the town of Needles, and west to the Borrego Desert.

The low desert is hot and dry, but the Coachella Valley, where attractions include the desert resorts of Palm Springs, Cathedral City, Indian Wells, Indio, La Quinta, Palm Desert and Rancho Mirage, is irrigated from the Colorado River, and agriculture is an important industry.

The high desert, although cooler, is not as popular with travellers as a destination, but many travel through the main centre of Barstow on their way from the coast to Las Vegas.

Death Valley consists of areas of both high and low desert, and contains the lowest point in the United States - 86m (282 ft) below sea level - near Dantes View.

If you intend to drive through the desert, make sure you carry plenty of water for drinking and the car radiator. Check that your car has a good spare tyre and the necessary tools.

Tip

In the event of the car breaking down, always stay with it, do not start wandering off into the desert. A car is a lot easier to spot from the air than people are. Do not drive off the main roads, or you could easily become bogged in the sand, and seek advice at every town you come to about the next petrol outlet. It is very unwise, in fact downright stupid, to consider hiking or even hitch-hiking through the desert.

PALM SPRINGS

Originally the home of the Agua Caliente (Hot Water) Indians, Palm Springs became a mecca for the rich and famous in the 1930s, when film stars Charles Farrell and Ralph Bellamy bought 81ha (200 acres) and started the Palm Springs Racquet Club. The Agua Caliente are one of the richest tribes in the country because they still own about 12,146ha (30,000 acres) of Palm Springs desert.

Nestling in the shelter of Mt San Jacinto, its natural beauty, glorious weather (sunshine on 350 days a year!), and sensible building restrictions (no building over 10m high), make Palm Springs as popular as ever. The elected mayor of Palm Springs is Lloyd Maryanov, but the honorary mayor is Bob Hope.

HOW TO GET THERE

By Air
Palm Springs Regional Airport is one mile from downtown, and is serviced by most major carriers, including Delta, USAir, Continental, United and American Airlines.

By Road
Palm Springs is 164km (102 miles) from Los Angeles via Interstate Highway 10; and 224km (139 miles) from San Diego via Interstate Highway 15, State Highway 215, then linking up with Interstate Highway 10.

As you enter the resort town you will see hundreds of windmills. These were erected to make use of the very strong winds, but many locals would like to see them demolished because they ruin the resort's 'image'.

TOURIST INFORMATION
Palm Springs Visitors Information Center, 2781 North Palm Canyon Drive, ph (619)778 8418, is open daily.

Historic Plaza Theatre District Tourist Information Center, 132 South Palm Canyon Drive, ph (619) 778 7654.

ACCOMMODATION

There are more than 160 hotels, from bed-and-breakfasts to full-service luxury resorts. All are close to attractions, shopping, dining and sporting facilities. Palm Springs also has a free hotel reservation service, and the telephone number is 1-800-347-7746.

Here is a selection of accommodation, with prices for a double room per night in US dollars, which should be used as a guide only. The prices stated are for the high (winter) season. Rates for the summer (June-September) could be up to 50% cheaper.

The telephone area code is 619.

Palm Springs Hilton Resort & Racquet Club, 400 East Tahquitz Way, ph 320 6868 - 259 rooms, restaurants, cocktail lounge, swimming pool, tennis, spa, jacuzzi - $200-280.

Ingleside Inn, 200 West Ramon Road, ph 325 0046 - 29 rooms, restaurant, cocktail lounge, pool, jacuzzi - $150-500.

Spa Hotel & Mineral Springs, 100 North Indian Avenue, ph 325 1461 - 230 rooms, restaurant, cocktail lounge, swimming pool, swirlpool tubs, tennis - $150-230.

Villa Royale, 1620 South Indian Trail, ph 327 2314 - 34 rooms, restaurant, cocktail lounge, swimming pool - $90-230 (includes continental breakfast).

Courtyard by Marriott, 1300 Tahquitz Canyon Way, ph 322 6100 - 149 rooms, restaurant, swimming pool - $70-100.

Westward Ho Seven Seas Hotel, 701 East Palm Canyon Drive, ph 320 2700 - 209 rooms, restaurant, cocktail lounge, swimming pool - $50-70.

Motel 6, 660 South Palm Canyon Drive, ph 327 4200 - 149 rooms, swimming pool - $50.

LOCAL TRANSPORT

Bus

SunBus has regular services from Desert Hot Springs to Coachella, travelling through the Coachella Valley, ph 343 3451 for route and timetable information.

The same company also operates the Sun Trolley, which plies up and down Palm Canyon Drive in the peak season from 9am-7.30pm. The trolley fare is 50c.

Taxi

Airport Taxi, ph 861 0365; Desert Cab, ph 325 2868.

Car

The most convenient way to get around is in your own car, and if you didn't bring one with you, the following companies have agencies in Palm Springs:
Avis, ph 325 1331;
Budget, ph 327 1404;
Hertz, ph 778 5100;
National, ph 327 4100.

EATING OUT

The hotels have some of the best, and best-known, restaurants in Palm Springs, eg Melvyn's at the Ingleside Inn, which *Lifestyles of the Rich and Famous* rates in the top ten, but here are a few that are not connected to hotels, and are worth trying, with an idea of prices for a main course, excluding drinks, as follows:
Expensive - $20+;
Moderate - $10-20;
Reasonable - under $10.
NB: Some restaurants close during the off-season.
Le Vallauris, 385 West Tahquitz, ph 325 5059 - French cuisine, formal atmosphere, jacket and tie required - Expensive - Amex, DC, MC, V.

Banducci's Bit of Italy, 1260 South Palm Canyon Dr, ph 325 2537 - piano bar, casual dress, dinner only - **Moderate/Expensive** - Amex, MC, V.

Bono, 1700 North Indian Avenue, ph 322 6200 - owned by Sonny Bono, southern Italian cuisine, casual dress, dinner only - **Moderate** - Amex, MC, V.

Cafe St James, 254 North Palm Canyon Drive, ph 320 8041 - menu changes weekly, casual dress, lunch and dinner Tues-Sun - **Moderate** - Amex, DC, MC, V.

Flower Drum, 424 South Indian Avenue, ph 323 3020 - Chinese cuisines, open lunch and dinner, casual dress - **Moderate** - Amex, MC, V.

Louise's Pantry, 124 South Palm Canyon Drive, ph 325 5124 - real home-cooking, local landmark, casual dress, open daily 7am-9.45pm - **Reasonable** - no credit cards.

ENTERTAINMENT

The local newspaper, the *Desert Sun*, and a free monthly magazine called *Guide* have all the current entertainment attractions.

Many of the hotels have piano bars, or you can party the night away at *Moody's Supper Club*, 1480 South Palm Canyon Drive, ph 323 1806.

The most popular discos in town are probably:
Cecil's, 1775 East Palm Canyon Drive, ph 320 4202; and
Zelda's, 169 North Indian Canyon Drive, ph 325 2375.

For stand-up comedy, there are two venues: *The Comedy Haven*, Desert Fashion Plaza, ph 320 7855; and *The Laff Stop*, cnr Tahquitz & Caballeros, ph 327 8889.

If you are after **something more classical,** ask your hotel for a copy of *Palm Springs Life* magazine or the *Desert Guide*.

The McCallum Theatre in the Bob Hope Cultural Center is the main venue for performing artists and regularly presents overseas artists.

The Annenberg Theatre in the Palm Springs Desert Museum is the other major arts venue.

The Valley Players Guild regularly presents plays in the *VPG Theatre*, 225 South El Cielo Road, ph 320 9898.

Then there is the reason for the town's existence - the Springs. *The Palm Springs Spa Hotel*, 100 North Indian Avenue, ph 325 1461, has mineral baths and an inhalation room, and offers massage and facials, starting from around $25. Open daily 10am-5pm.

SHOPPING

Fine boutiques, exclusive department stores and elegant art galleries - what more could any shopper want?

SHOPPING DISTRICTS

Palm Canyon Drive, from Alejo Road in the north to Ramon Road in the south, is the main shopping area and has plenty to tempt shoppers, though don't expect to pick up many bargains. Apart from specialty shops, the hub is the *Desert Fashion Plaza*, with stores such as Saks Fifth Avenue, I. Magnin, and Gucci.

The Courtyard, at the Bank of Palm Springs Center, presents Yves St Laurent and Rodier fashion outlets, and a six-theatre cinema.

El Paseo Village, 73-111 El Paseo Drive, Palm Desert, ph 340 1414, is a Spanish-styled shopping centre offering fashions for men and women. It is often compared to LA's Rodeo Drive.

The Palm Desert Town Center has five major department stores, a seven-theatre movie complex, and a skating rink.

Rancho las Palmas, cnr Highway 111 and Bob Hope Drive, Rancho Mirage, has antiques and several good restaurants.

SIGHTSEEING

The best way to get your bearings, and a good overall view of the desert, is to ride on the **Palm Springs Aerial Tramway**, *which* travels 4km (2.5 miles) up the slopes of Mount San Jacinto to an elevation of 2596m (8516 ft).

The trip takes less than twenty minutes, and is its most dramatic in winter when you travel from the warm desert to snowdrifts. The end of the ride is the beginning of 87km (54 miles) of hiking tracks, the Alpine Restaurant, a cocktail lounge, gift shops, picnic areas, and a great view. The Nordic Ski Center is also found here, and is open (depending on the availability of snow) from mid-November to mid-April for cross-country skiing.

You board the tram in Tramway Drive, Chino Canyon, off State Highway 111 north, and it is open Mon-Fri from 10am, Sat-Sun from 8am. The last train up is at 8pm, last one down at 9.45pm; May-September (Labor Day) last train up is at 9pm, last one down is at 10.45pm.

Return fare is $16 adults, $10 children, or you can get a ride'n'dine ticket for $20 adults, $15 children. The combination tickets are only available after 2.30pm, and there are no reservations.

The Desert Museum

This interesting museum is on Museum Drive, north of Tahquitz Way, ph 325 7186, and has natural history and science exhibits of the surrounding desert, and displays of the art of the south-west, including Native American and contemporary artists. The late actor William Holden's collection of Asian and African art is on permanent display, and the museum also has changing exhibitions loaned from other museums and galleries.

Admission is $5 adults, $2 children under 17, and opening hours are Tues-Fri 10am-4pm, Sat-Sun 10am-5pm, closed Mondays and June 5-September 22.

The Annenberg Theatre, located in the museum, has concerts featuring artists such as Liza Minnelli and Frank Sinatra.

The Village Green Heritage Center

The Center consists of two 19th-century pioneer homes, situated at 221 and 223 South Palm Canyon Drive. The adobe house was built by John McCallum, a San Francisco lawyer, in 1885, and next door was built for Cornelia White in 1894, from railroad sleepers. The houses now contain most of the collection of the Palm Springs Historical Society, and are open Wed-Sun noon-3pm, Thurs-Sat 10am-4pm, closed June to mid-October. **There is a small admission fee.**

Moorten's Botanical Garden

Situated at 1701 South Palm Canyon Drive, ph 327 6555, the garden is open daily 9am-4.30pm, and has over 2000 varieties of plants in a 1.6ha (4 acres) site. There are also exhibits of Indian artifacts.

The Indian Canyons

The Canyons begin at the end of South Palm Canyon Drive, about 8km (5 miles) south of downtown. You step back in history when you visit this Indian-owned sanctuary, with hundreds of ancient relics, herds of ponies roaming free, freezing mountain streams, rock caves, desert wildlife, and stands of towering trees. Every movie you have seen about Indians will come flashing back. **The canyons are open daily, September-June, 8am-5pm, and admission is $3.50 adults, $1 children, ph 325 5673.**

Living Desert Reserve

The reserve is in Palm Desert, at 47-900 Portola Avenue, and has a walk-through aviary, a reptile exhibit, a coyote grotto, a six mile nature walk, and animal shows. It also has roaming herds of bighorn sheep and slender-horned gazelles, which are endangered species. The reserve is open daily 9am-5pm, except from mid-June to August. **Admission is $7 adults, $3.50 children 3-12.**

Joshua Tree National Monument

The Monument is about one hour's drive from Palm Springs, and marks the meeting place of the low Sonoran Desert and the high Mojave Desert, resulting in a variety of scenery. The tree that gives the place its name has strangely shaped limbs that sometimes reach 15m (50 ft) in height, and forests of them range for miles in the central and eastern sections of the Monument. The trees were named by Mormons who passed this way in the nineteenth century, because the branches reminded them of the arms of Joshua leading them to the promised land. The local Indians, although not having the benefit of Christianity, found the trees a godsend and used different parts for laxatives, shampoo, sandals, hunting nets, and food.

It is possible to make a round trip from Palm Springs by taking Highway 62 from Indian Avenue to Twentynine Palms and the Oasis Visitor Center, 74485 National Monument Drive, then driving through the Monument to the Cottonwood Visitor Center at the southern gateway, then taking Interstate Highway 10 back to Palm Springs. The entry fee to the Monument is $5 per vehicle.

> The Oasis Visitor Center is the best place to enter the park as they have loads of information on the area, and a wide selection of maps and brochures.

At the Center is the Oasis of Mara, which was first inhabited by Indians, then prospectors and ranchers, but is now a wildlife refuge, and nearby are camping grounds, restrooms and picnic areas.

Other attractions in the Monument are Hidden Valley, Lost Horse Mine and Keys View, and the Visitor Center can point you in the right directions.

TOURS

Palm Springs Celebrity Tours, 174 North Palm Canyon Drive, ph 325 2682, offer one-hour and two-hour tours of the homes and playgrounds of the rich and famous.

The one-hour version leaves from the above address and costs **$10 adults, $5 children;**

the two-hour will pick up from Palm Springs hotels and costs **$14 adults, $7 children.**

Reservations are necessary, and should be made a couple of days ahead.

Carriage Trade, ph 327 3214, offer narrated rides through the city streets in horse-drawn carriages, starting at the Hyatt Regency Hotel in North Palm Canyon Drive. **Costs are $20 for one to four people.**

Gray Line Tours, ph 325 0974, have a variety of tours in Palm Springs itself, and to the other desert resorts.

American Balloon Society, ph 568 6700; *Fantasy Balloon Flights*, ph 568 0997; and *Sunrise Balloons*, ph 346 7591, can arrange for flights over the desert of varying lengths and prices.

SPORT

The brochures advertise that the area has "nearly 10,000 swimming pools, over 80 golf courses, and 500 tennis courts", and this is probably true, but not all are open to the public.
The following venues are.

Swimming

Palm Springs Swim Center, Sunrise Park, Sunrise Way and Ramon Road, ph 323 8278.

Golf

Palm Springs Municipal Golf Course, 1885 Golf Club Drive, ph 328 1005.
Tommy Jacobs' Bel Air Greens, 1001 El Cielo Road, ph 322 6062.

Tennis

Palm Springs Tennis Center, 1300 Baristo Road, ph 320 0020.
Demuth Park, 4375 Mesquite Avenue, ph 323 8272.

Bicycling

With so many miles of bike trails and several mapped city

tours, hiring bikes almost becomes a necessity. Maps are available at the Palm Springs Recreation Department, 401 South Pavilion, ph 323 8276, or
from the following rental shops:
Bicycle Barn, 429 South Sunrise Way at Ramon Rd,
ph 325 7844.
Canyon Bicycle Rentals & Tours, 305 East Arenas Road,
ph 327 7688.
Palm Springs Cyclery, 661 South Palm Canyon Drive,
ph 325 9319.

Spectator Sports

Palm Springs Angels Stadium, east of Sunrise Way, is the venue for exhibition games during March and early April, and is the spring training ground for the California Angels.
The Bob Hope Desert Classic in January and the *Nabisco Dinah Shore Invitational* (March/April) are only two of the many **golf championships** played in Palm Springs. Check with the Convention and Visitors Bureau.

The *Newsweek Champions Cup* **tennis tournament** is held at the Hyatt Grand Champions Resort in Indian Wells and attracts top seeded players. Again, check with the Convention and Visitors Bureau for dates.

MOJAVE DESERT

The only good reason I can think of for visiting the Mojave Desert and its main town of Barstow is if you are passing through to get to some amazing attraction, such as Las Vegas.

The best way to travel through this area is by Greyhound (letting someone else do the driving and the worrying about water, etc), and they have regular services between LA and Las

Vegas that pass this way. Still, there is no accounting for taste, and some people just have to drive themselves, maybe thinking they will need a car in Vegas, which is definitely not the case.

I have travelled in a few deserts in different countries, but this is the only place where I have actually seen a mirage. In the middle of dry nothingness I could see two men in a boat - fishing. The other people in my party could see them too, and I hasten to add, none of us had been tippling.

Anyway, if you find yourself in the vicinity of Barstow, there is one place that is worth visiting:

Calico Ghost Town

The town is 16km (10 miles) north of Barstow sitting high in the multi-coloured hills, and had its heyday between 1881 and 1896. It died in 1907 after giving up $86 million in silver and $9 million in borax. Once home to 4000 people, with eight saloons in the main drag, it became a ghost town, then along came Walter Knott, of Knott's Berry Farm fame, and the town became a sightseeing attraction.

Now you can walk down the wooden sidewalks of Main Street, shop for western souvenirs, eat at any of the restaurants, visit the playhouse, roam though the tunnels of Maggie's Mine, or board a railroad car for old workings to the north. You can even stay at the 110-unit camping ground with modern conveniences.

You will hear a lot about the outlaws of the 'bad old days', but from my experience, don't take what you are told as gospel. I'm sure they have invented many of the meetings of famous baddies that supposedly took place in the area.

Still, it is a lot of fun, and the town is open daily, except Christmas, from 7am until dusk. **The shops are open 9am-5pm. Parking is provided and costs $5 per car.** For information on prices of tours, the vaudeville show, or for camping reservations, ph (619) 254 2122.

THE CENTRAL COAST

San Francisco is 672 km (418 miles) north-west of Los Angeles, and the majority of visitors travel the stretch between San Luis Obispo and San Francisco on State Highway 1, which literally hugs the shoreline, and passes through the beautiful towns of Carmel and Monterey.

Depending on the time of the year, this trip can be one of incredible scenic beauty, with whales frolicking in the bays, or one of can't-see-the-car-in-front fog. During the rainy season there is also the possibility of dirt or mud slides, so during that time it is safer to take US 101 all the way, or maybe only to Salinas where State Highway 68 branches off for Monterey.

Unfortunately, because of lack of time, many visitors decide to fly between LA and San Fran, but I am sure they regret their decision when they speak to people who made the trip by road. Many three day coach tours are available, travelling in both directions, and usually offering accommodation in Solvang and Monterey. Some of these tours also add an extra day and take in Yosemite National Park. Brochures are available in hotels in Los Angeles and San Francisco, or arrangements can be made before you leave home.

OXNARD

The largest city in Ventura County, Oxnard is the gateway to Channel Islands National Park. It is 97km (60 miles) north-west of LA city centre, and about 11km (7 miles) from the ocean.

HOW TO GET THERE

By Air

The Ventura County Airport is in Oxnard, and is serviced by three airlines:
United Express, ph (800) 241 6522, have flights to/from San Francisco and LA.
American Eagle, ph (800) 433 7300, have flights to/from LA.
California Air Shuttle, ph (800) 759 2359, have flights to/from Las Vegas, San Francisco, San Jose and Sacramento.

By Rail

Amtrak have several services that stop at Oxnard, and for information on timetables, etc, ph 1-800-872-7245.

By Bus

The following companies provide buses and/or charters from LAX: *California Limousine Service*, ph (818) 345 1780;
Antelope Valley Bus, ph (805) 483 6737;
The Run Around, ph (805) 659 5077;
Great American Stageline, ph (805) 375 1361;
and *Lambert's Tours & Travel*, ph (805) 653 1911.

By Car

Oxnard is 97km (60 miles) north-west of LA, and can be reached by taking State Highway 1, or US Highway 101. Oxnard has a $7.5 million Transportation Center that provides a transport hub for rail, bus, car rental, taxi and air connections.

TOURIST INFORMATION

The Oxnard Convention & Visitors Bureau is at 400 East Esplanade Drive, ph (805) 485 8833.

ACCOMMODATION

Accommodation in Oxnard ranges from major hotels at and near Channel Islands Harbor to camping at the 121ha (300 acres) McGrath State Beach. Here is a selection with prices for a double room per night in US dollars, which should be used as a guide only.

The telephone area code is 805.

Embassy Suites, Mandalay Beach Resort, 2101 Mandalay Beach Road, ph 984 2500 - 250 rooms, restaurant, cocktail lounge, swimming pool, tennis courts - $145-210.

Casa Sirena, 3605 Peninsula Road, ph 985 6311 - 273 rooms, restaurant, cocktail lounge, swimming pool, tennis courts - $70-225.

Radisson Suite Hotel, 2101 Vineyard Avenue, ph 988 0130 - 253 rooms - restaurant, cocktail lounge, swimming pool, tennis courts - $85-125.

The Country Inn at Port Hueneme, 350 East Hueneme Road, ph 986 5353 - 135 rooms, swimming pool - $78-135.

Financial Plaza Hilton, 600 Esplanade Drive, ph 485 9666 - 160 rooms, restaurant, cocktail lounge, swimming pool, tennis courts - $65-103.

Channel Islands Motel, 1001 East Channel Islands Boulevard, ph 487 7755 - 91 rooms, restaurant, cocktail lounge, swimming pool - $43-80.

Vagabond Inn, 1245 North Oxnard Boulevard, ph 983 0251 - swimming pool - $40-43.

Oxnard Lodge Motel, 1156 South Oxnard Boulevard, ph 483 9581 - 106 rooms, cocktail lounge, swimming pool - $38-75.

Wagon Wheel Motor Inn, 2751 Wagon Wheel Road, ph 485 3131 - 83 rooms, tennis courts - $29-39.

EATING OUT

The Visitors Bureau has a restaurant guide that sets out all the venues in and around Oxnard, and those featuring seafood menus, and offering harbour views, are top of the list.

SIGHTSEEING

The Visitors Bureau should be your first stop for a complete list of attractions, but here are a few to whet your appetite.
Heritage Square has some of Oxnard's finest vintage buildings, which are being restored to active use.

PORT HUENEME

It is the only deep-water port between LA and San Francisco, has a good historical museum with exhibits of the history of the port's early days.

THE CHANNEL ISLANDS

They are a group of eight volcanic islands in the Santa Barbara Channel with the closest 18km (11 miles) and the furthest 64km (40 miles) off the coast. Five of them - Anacapa, Santa Cruz, Santa Rosa, San Miguel and Santa Barbara - make up Channel Islands National Park, and the surrounding waters are a marine sanctuary. Accommodation on, and air travel to Santa Cruz and Santa Rosa Islands can be arranged through Channel Islands Adventures, ph 987 1678.

It is thought that the islands were formed about 14 million years ago, and archaeological findings support the theory that they are among the oldest sites of human habitation in the continent. In 1542, when Juan Cabrillo was in the area, the islands were occupied by the Chumash Indians, but they have long since been removed and the islands are largely uninhabited. Wildlife is prolific, and the islands have been likened to the Galapagos as many unique life forms have evolved here, including the island fox [as big as a house cat).

The Channel Islands National Park Visitor Centre, which is on the mainland at 1901 Spinnaker Drive, Ventura, ph 644 8262, has museum displays and a very good 25 minute film about all aspects of the park. Next door is Island Packers, ph 642 7688, who run narrated boat cruises to the islands.

VENTURA

This village is roughly 32km (20 miles) north-west of Oxnard, right on the coast, and the Harbor Village has lots of unique shops and restaurants. The Ventura Visitors & Convention Bureau, 89-C South California Street, ph 648 2075, has a complete list of attractions, which include the *Mission San Buenaventura*, and the *Olivas Adobe*, built in 1847 for one of California's early Spanish Dons. Both places offer tours.

The *Buenaventura Trolley* links the historic downtown area with Ventura Harbor and many hotels along the coast.

OJAI

Ojai is 23km (14 miles) north-east of Ventura, and the name meant 'the nest' to the Chumash Indians. Today, the town is an artist colony, a mecca for health freaks because of its spas and hot springs, and a centre for several religious sects.

The Ojai valley with its wildflowers, and the surrounding mountains, evoke a sense of tranquility, and were used as the set for Shangri-La in the 1937 film *Lost Horizon*. It is not surprising that mystics are attracted to the area.

The Ojai Valley Chamber of Commerce, 338 East Ojai Avenue, ph 646 8126, has maps and information on the area, including the Grand Avenue loop, which travels past orange orchards and horse ranches. On Krotona Hill, overlooking the valley, is the Krotona Institute of Theosophy, ph 646 2653, a 48ha (118 acres) estate, where visitors are welcome to tour the library and enjoy the beautifully landscaped grounds. On the other side of town is the Krishnamurti Foundation, 1130 McAndrew Road, ph 646 4948, which also welcomes visitors to its library.

SPORT & RECREATION

Oxnard's River Ridge Golf Course is a PGA-designed 18-hole, par 72 course, and there are nine courses within twenty miles.

Boat charters and tours can be arranged through any of the following:
  Harbor Hopper, ph 984 1366;
  Holly Tours, ph 644 7482;
  Captain Daves, ph 647 3161;
  Island Packers, ph 642 7688;
  Mantra Charters, ph 644 6212;
  John Bamford Ocean Chartering, ph 984 6752;
  Channel Islands Adventures, ph 987 1678.
Then there are the miles and miles of beaches.

SANTA BARBARA

Undisputedly one of the prettiest places in California, Santa Barbara owes its Mediterranean ambience to an earthquake. The Spanish who settled the area called it 'la tierra adorada' (the beloved land) and established a mission here in 1786. It became an important centre of Spanish culture, but when the Americans took charge of California in the 19th century, they built anything that took their fancy, and the town became a hotchpotch of architectural styles. Then in 1925 an earthquake that measured 6.3 on the Richter scale, destroyed the entire business district, and enabled the town to start again from scratch. Fortunately an Architectural Board of Review was formed very quickly to guide the rebuilding, and it laid down strict laws that are still in effect. All new buildings had to be in similar style, basically California adobe with light-coloured, stucco walls, and low sloping terracotta-tile roofs.

HOW TO GET THERE
Several airlines have services from Los Angeles and San Francisco to Santa Barbara, as does Amtrak and Greyhound bus lines.

By Car
Santa Barbara is 148km (92 miles) north-west of Los Angeles,

and 534km (332 miles) south east of San Francisco, and is reached by State Highway 1 or US Highway 101.

TOURIST INFORMATION

The town has two information centres. The Santa Barbara Visitor Information Center, 1 Santa Barbara Street at Cabrillo Boulevard near Stearns Wharf, ph (805) 965 3021, is open Mon-Sat 9am-5pm, Sun 10am-5pm (May-Sept), Mon-Sat 9am-4pm, Sun 10am-4pm (Oct-April).

The Downtown Organization Visitor Information Center is in Old Town at 504 State Street, and it is open Mon-Fri 9am-5pm all year.

Both offices have loads of information on the district, including a scenic drive that takes in fifteen major points of interest, and a walking tour of the city's historical landmarks.

ACCOMMODATION

There is a wide range of accommodation near the beach and in the town centre, but Santa Barbara is such a popular holiday centre that it is also wise to book well in advance. Here is a selection, with prices for a double room per night in US dollars, which should be used as a guide only.
The telephone area code is 805.

Four Seasons Biltmore, 1260 Channel Drive, ph 969 2261 - 234 rooms, restaurant, cocktail lounge, swimming pool - $225-325.
San Ysidro Ranch, 900 San Ysidro Lane (off US 101), ph 969 5040 - 44 cottages, restaurants, cocktail lounge, swimming pool, tennis, stables - $200-270.
The Franciscan Inn, 109 Bath Street (corner of Mason), ph 963 8845 - 53 rooms, snackbar, swimming pools, one block from the beach - $150-320 (includes continental breakfast).
The Upham, 1404 De la Vina Street, ph 962 0058 - 49 rooms, restaurant, restaurant - $100-175 (including continental breakfast).
Miramar Hotel-Resort, 1555 South Jameson Lane, Montecito, ph 969 2203 - 212 units, restaurant, cocktail lounge, swimming

pools, tennis, right on the beach - $95-135.

King's Inn, 128 Castillo Street, ph 963 4471 - 45 rooms, swimming pool - $99-114.

Tropicana Inn, 223 Castillo Street, ph 966 2219 - 30 units, swimming pool, no smoking on premises - $80-95 (includes continental breakfast).

Motel 6, 443 Corona del Mar, ph 564 1392, and at 3505 State Street, ph 687 5400 - swimming pools - $55.

EATING OUT

Visitors certainly do not have to go hungry in Santa Barbara, and every style of cuisine is available.

Here are few restaurants that are recommended, rated
Expensive - $20+,
Moderate - $10-20;
Reasonable - under $10 for a main course.

Brophy Brothers Restaurant & Clam Bar, 119 Harbor Way, ph 966 4418 - great seafood - open Sun-Thurs 11am-10pm, Fri-Sat 11am-11pm - **Moderate.**

Joe's Cafe, 536 State Street, ph 966 4638 - home cooked steak/seafood - open Mon-Thurs 11am-11.30pm, Fri-Sat 11am-12.30am, Sun 4-11.30pm - **Reasonable.**

Mousse Odile, 18 East Cota Street, ph 962 5393 - French - open Mon-Sat 8-11am, 11.30am-3pm, 6-9pm - **Moderate.**

The Stonehouse Restaurant, San Ysidro Ranch, 900 San Ysidro Lane, Montecito, ph 969 5046 - varied menu - open for lunch dinner and Sunday brunch - **Expensive.**

Hola! Amigos, 29 East Cabrillo Blvd, ph 963 1968 - extensive menu - open Mon-Thurs 11am-10pm, Fri 11am-11pm, Fri-Sat 11am-11pm, Sun 10am-9.30pm - **Moderate.**

ENTERTAINMENT

Apart from the restaurants and hotels, where evening entertainment is often provided, there are a couple of places that offer entertainment, and you should check to see what's on offer when you are there.

The Lobero Theater, 33 East Canon Perdido Street, ph 963 0761, has a wide variety of productions throughout the year including concerts, recitals, operas, dance, plays, films and lectures. The theatre had many famous actors tread its boards, eg Edward G. Robinson, Robert Young, and Clark Gable.

Arlington Theatre, 1317 State Street, ph 966 9382, has concerts ranging from performers like Ray Charles, to the Los Angeles Philharmonic.

SHOPPING

The main shopping area is on State Street:

El Paseo, near De La Guerra Street, ph 963 8741, is an historic adobe house which, combined with the surrounding buildings, offers some of the best designer label boutiques, art galleries and jewellery stores in the city.

La Arcada Court, 1100 block, east side, ph 966 6634, is a Spanish-style mall with very stylish and up-market shops.

Paseo Neuvo is bordered by State and Chapala Streets, and Ortega and Canon Perdido, and is home to Nordstrom and The Broadway as well as many boutiques, restaurants and galleries.

The Galleria, cnr of State Street and La Cumbre Road, is one of Santa Barbara's newest and most attractive shopping experiences.

La Cumbre Plaza is on the 3800 block of State Street, and has over fifty specialty shops and six food outlets, as well as Robinson's and Sears Department Stores. The Plaza is open Mon-Fri 10am-9pm, Sat 10am-6pm, Sun 11am-6pm, ph 687 6458.

> If you are into antiques, head for Brinkerhoff Avenue, a residential street with several interesting outlets.

Every Sunday and holiday there is an Arts & Crafts Show in East Cabrillo Boulevard, and the local artists and craftspeople offer their work for sale. The market opens at 10am, and the crafts represented include macrame, stained glass, woodwork and jewellery.

SIGHTSEEING

Red Tile Walking Tour

The walking tour takes visitors to fifteen major points within the city, and included here are the major attractions. The tour begins at the **Santa Barbara County Courthouse**, 1100 Anacapa Street, ph 962 6464 (between Figueroa and Anapamu Streets), a fine example of Santa Barbara nouveau-Spanish architecture, although it was built in 1929. The courthouse is a must for any visitor and is open Mon-Fri 8am-5pm, Sat-Sun 9am-5pm, with free guided tours on Wed and Fri at 10.30am and Mon-Sat at 2pm.

The beautiful murals that depict incidents in the history of the city were done by Dan Sayre Groesbeck, and it is interesting to note that they are on cloth so that they can be removed in the event of a severe earthquake. For a great view of the city take the elevator up to El Mirador, the 26m high deck of the clock tower.

Santa Barbara Museum of Art, 1130 State Street, cnr Anapamu Street, ph 963 4364, has a collection of art spanning forty-one centuries, from an Egyptian New Kingdom relief to *Bruges II*, 1981, by Al Held, an acrylic on canvas. Artists represented from the intervening period include Monet, Daumier, Grandma Moses, Kandinksy, Chagall, Picasso, and Matisse, to name a few.

The museum is open Tues-Sat 11am-5pm (Thurs till 9pm), Sun noon-5pm, and admission is $3 adults, $1.50 children 6-16. Tours are available Tues-Sun at 2pm. Admission is $3 adults, $1.50 children 6-16.

Hill Carrillo Adobe, 11 East Carrillo Street, is an 1826 home that was built by a settler from Massachusetts for his bride. The house is now furnished with period pieces.

Casa de Covarrubias, 715 Santa Barbara Street, is an L-shaped house dating from 1817. It is thought to be the site of the last Mexican assembly, in 1846. Next door is the **Historic Fremont Adobe** which was the headquarters for Colonel John C. Fremont after the Americans captured Santa Barbara in 1846.

Santa Barbara Historical Society Museum, 136 East de la Guerra Street, cnr Santa Barbara Street, ph 966 1601, has displays of fine arts and sections depicting the different periods of the city's history - Spanish, Mexican and early American. Featured are memorabilia from the visits of Richard Henry Dana, author of *Two Years Before the Mast*.

The museum is heavily into the restoration and preservation of two important 19th century homes - the **Trussell-Winchester Adobe**, 414 West Montecito Street, built by Captain Horatio Gates Trussell when he married Ramona Earys Burke, a granddaughter of one of the *Bounty* mutineers; and **Fernald House**, built by Judge Charles Fernald in the early 1860s.

The museum is open Tues-Sat 10am-5pm, Sun noon-5pm;
the Gledhill Library for historical research, within the museum, is open Tues-Sat 10am-4pm, and the two houses are open Sun 2-4pm.

El Presidio de Santa Barbara State Historic Park, 123 East Canon Perdido Street, ph 966 9719, has two original buildings from the town's 1782 garrison - El Cuartel, the guards' house, and La Canedo Adobe, a military residence. Probably more interesting in this complex though, is the Santa Barbara Presidio Chapel, a re-created Spanish church.

Scenic Drive

The 48km (30 miles) drive takes in some of the attractions included in the walking tour, but here are the major sites that are a bit further afield.

Andree Clark Bird Refuge, 1400 East Cabrillo Boulevard, is a lagoon set in gardens with many varieties of freshwater fowl.

There are walking and bike tracks around the lake.

Santa Barbara Zoological Gardens, 500 Ninos Drive, ph 962 5339, is an open range zoo with picnic grounds and playground, a scenic railroad, bird refuge and all the animals that are usually locked in these establishments. It is open every day 9am-5pm in summer, 10am-5pm in winter. **Admission is $5 adults, $3 children 2-12.**

Stearns Wharf at the end of State Street was completed in 1872, and was for a time the longest deep-water pier on the coast between LA and San Francisco. Named for its builder, John P. Stearns, the wharf was originally constructed for passengers and freight, and served the shipping needs of the community until the early 1900s. When the railroad reached Santa Barbara in 1901, the demand for an ocean transport terminal diminished. An attempt to link Stearns Wharf to the expanding railroad system was unsuccessful, and left the pier with the dog-leg shape that still remains. The Harbor Restaurant was built on the wharf in 1941, marking the end of the shipping era, and proved to be the economic backbone of the wharf. The restaurant is open for breakfast, lunch and dinner, and prices are reasonable.

The wharf also has arts & crafts shops, boutiques, souvenir shops, an art gallery, and complimentary wine tasting from the local Santa Ynez Winery.

The Santa Barbara Trolley, ph 962 0209, leaves from the wharf and travels along the waterfront, through the downtown area, and to the mission.

Santa Barbara is very proud of its **Moreton Bay Fig Tree** on the corner of Chapala and Moreton Streets. OK, it's around a hundred-years-old, its branches spread 49m (160 feet), and it is the oldest of its kind in the United States, but to most Aussies, it is just your everyday Moreton Bay Fig Tree.

Mission Santa Barbara is at the end of Laguna Street, ph 682 4713. Called the 'Queen of the Missions' because of its beauty, it is surrounded by lush green lawn, flowering trees and shrubs, with a Moorish fountain in the front, and is the only mission with twin bell towers. The church is still used today by the parish of Santa Barbara.

The mission has a museum with displays of typical mission furniture and artifacts of the Chumash people, and the **entry fee is $2 adults, no charge for children under 16**.
It is open daily 9am-5pm.

Santa Barbara Museum of Natural History, 2559 Puesta del Sol Road, ph 682 4711, has the usual displays of marine, plant and insect life, but it is worth visiting for its exhibits of Indian tribes from throughout the United States. It is open Mon-Sat 9am-5pm, Sun 10am-5pm, and **admission is $3 adults, $2 teens 13-17, $1 children**.

SPORT & RECREATION

Beaches

Carpinteria State Beach, at the end of Palm Avenue in Carpinteria, is locally known as 'the world's safest beach', and has a lagoon and breakwater reef. Good for swimming and snorkelling.

East Beach and *West Beach* are either side of Stearns Wharf, and have grassy areas, palm trees, and all facilities.

Arroyo Burro County Park, at 2981 Cliff Drive, is a 2.5ha (6 acres) park with a sandy beach and surrounding hills.

El Capitan State Beach is a 68ha (168 acres) park with 1km of shoreline. There is also a nature trail, and seals and sea lions are often seen offshore. The beach is about 32km (20 miles) north of Santa Barbara at Goleta.

Refugio State Beach is a 16ha (39 acres) park with 2km of shoreline, located about 37km (23 miles) north of Santa Barbara, off Route 101 in Goleta.

Gaviota State Park, about 53km (33 miles) north of Santa Barbara, is on both sides of Route 101 and covers 1124ha (2776 acres). The beach section is in a sandy cove between sedimentary rock formations. The inland side of the park has a hiking trail that leads up to Gaviota Hot Springs, and into Los Padres National Forest.

Golf

Santa Barbara Community Course, 3500 McCaw Avenue, ph 687 7087, is an 18-hole, 5495m (6009 yds) course with a driving range. Visitors are welcome.

Sandpiper, 7925 Hollister Avenue, Goleta, ph 968 1541, is an 18-hole, 6035m (6099 yds) course with a driving range and pro shop.

Ocean Meadows, 6925 Whittier Drive, Goleta, ph 968 6814, is a 9-hole 2733m (3033 yds) course.

Twin Lakes, 6034 Hollister Avenue, Goleta, ph 964 1414, is a 9-hole, 1326m (1450 yds) course.

Tennis

For some strange reason, you need a tennis permit to play on the following public courts. It is available from the Recreation Department, 620 Laguna Street, ph 564 5428, and sometimes from the courts themselves.

Municipal Courts, near the corner of Salinas Street and US 101.
Pershing Park, cnr Castillo Street and West Cabrillo Boulevard.
Las Positas Courts, 1002 Las Positas Road.

Boating & Fishing

All types of boats can be rented in Santa Barbara for fishing, diving, sailing, etc. Two companies are:

Sea Landing, at the end of Bath Street and Cabrillo Boulevard, ph 963 3564.

Sailing Center of Santa Barbara, Santa Barbara Breakwater, ph 962 2826.

Bicycling

Beach Rentals, 8 West Cabrillo Boulevard, ph 963 2524, rents out bikes and roller skates, and offers bicycle tours.

Horseback Riding

San Ysidro Ranch Stables, 900 San Ysidro Lane, ph 969 5046, have one-hour guided trail rides, and can organise private lessons.

Hiking

The Sierra Club, ph 966 6622, do not have an office, but a phone call will give you information on the many trails in the Los Padres National Forest and other scenic parts of the area.

SANTA YNEZ VALLEY

Continuing on the journey to San Francisco, US101 travels west to Gaviola then leaves the coast and continues north through the Santa Ynez Valley, a prime winegrowing region.

There are several dozen wineries scattered in the valley, including:

Santa Ynez Valley Winery, 343 North Refugio Road, Santa Ynez, ph (805) 688 8381.
Firestone Vineyard, 5017 Zaca Station Road, Los Olivos, ph (805) 688 3940.
Zaca Mesa Winery, Foxen Canyon Road, Los Olivos, ph (805) 688 3310.

The Visitors Bureau in Solvang can advise on tasting hours, etc, or contact the Santa Barbara County Vintners' Association, PO Box 1558, Santa Ynez, CA 93460, ph 688 0881.

There are only five small towns in the valley - Buellton, Santa Ynez, Los Olivos, Ballard, and **Solvang**, the main attraction.

SOLVANG

Driving into Solvang for the first time is like stumbling on a town in the wrong place. It was established by a group of Danish emigrants in 1911, and they built themselves a Danish town, complete with cobblestone walks, gaslights and stained-glass windows, and named it 'sunny valley'.

The Solvang Visitors Bureau, 1571 Mission Drive, ph (805) 688 6144, has all the necessary information on the town, or there is a Visitor Information Booth on Copenhagen Drive next to the Mid-State Bank. The Center is open daily 9am-5pm, and the Booth is open Mon-Fri 10am-4pm, Sat-Sun 10am-5pm.

There's not a great deal to choose from as far as accommodation is concerned, but you can't go past the *Sheraton Royal Scandinavian Inn*, 400 Alisal Road, ph (805) 688 8000, with its 135 rooms, restaurant, cocktail lounge, and swimming pool for US$76-116 per double per night.

> One word of warning about Solvang: do not consider a visit if you are on a diet. The town is full of bakeries and restaurants offering the most mouth-watering Danish pastries and pretzels, and enormous meals featuring such things as meatballs and stuffed cabbage leaves, scrumptious little sausages and potatoes in all types of sauces. Solvang is truly a gastronomic delight!

And when you have finished eating, you can stroll down Copenhagen Drive and shop for all sorts of things imported from northern Europe, from handknitted sweaters to cuckoo clocks, all sorts of toys, fantastic children's gear, and unusual crystal jewellery.

The only real sightseeing venue in the town is the *Mission Santa Ines*, 1760 Mission Drive, built in 1804, and the only non-Danish building in the town. It has a small museum, and is open Mon-Sat 9am-5pm, Sun noon-5pm in summer, with shorter hours in winter.

Mission La Purisima Concepcion in Purisima Road, Lompoc, ph (805) 733 3713, is north-west of Solvang, and is the best preserved of all the missions. The entire complex is open to visitors. The city of Lompoc is set in thousands of hectares of flowers, and is ablaze with colour throughout the year.

SAN LUIS OBISPO

The pretty town of San Luis Obispo is situated 19km (12 miles) from the coast in the centre of an agricultural area. The town was built around the Mission San Luis Obispo de Tolosa, and the people in the street include cowboys from the outlying ranches and students from the nearby California Polytechnic State University.

HOW TO GET THERE
San Luis Obispo is roughly half-way between Los Angeles and San Francisco, on US Highway 101.

TOURIST INFORMATION
The San Luis Obispo Chamber of Commerce Visitors Center, 1039 Chorro Street, ph (805) 543 1323, is open Tues-Fri 8am-5pm, Sat-Mon 9am-5pm.

ACCOMMODATION
As San Luis Obispo is only 68km (42 miles) south of San Simeon, it is a good base to use for visits to Hearst Castle.

Here is a selection of accommodation, with prices for a double room in US dollars, which should be used as a guide only.
The telephone area code is 805.

Madonna Inn, 100 Madonna Road, ph 543 3000 - 109 rooms, restaurant, coffee shop, cocktail lounges - $80-140.

Apple Farm Inn, 2015 Monterey Street, ph 544 2040 - 68 rooms, restaurant next door - $60-160.

The Motel Inn, 2223 Monterey Street, ph 543 4000 - this is where the word 'motel' was coined in 1925 - $40-70.

Lamp Lighter Motel, 1604 Monterey Street, ph 543 3709 - 42 rooms, swimming pool - $34-54.

The Allstar Inn, 1625 Calle Joaquin, ph 541 6992 - 30 rooms, swimming pool - $38.

EATING OUT

While not the gourmet capital of the world, San Luis Obispo has several restaurants in and around the town that offer good meals in pleasant surroundings, with friendly service.

A few examples:

F. McLintock's Saloon & Dining House, 750 Mattie Road, Shell Beach, ph 773 1892 - ranch house style meals - open Mon-Fri 11.30am-10.30pm, Sat 8-11.30am, 2-4pm, Sun 9am-1.30pm, 2-4pm. **Moderate.**

McLintock's Saloon, 686 Higuera Street, ph 541 0686, has the same type of menu and is open Mon-Fri 6.30am-8.30pm, Sat 8.30am-8.30pm, Sun 8.30am-4pm, Mon-Sat 9pm-midnight. Prices for a main meal rated **Moderate.**

The Apple Farm, 2015 Monterey Street, ph 544 6100 - home-style food - open daily 7am-9pm - **Moderate.**

1865, 1865 Monterey Street, ph 544 1865 - steak/seafood - open Mon-Fri 11am-2.30pm, Mon-Thurs and Sun 5-10pm, Sat 5-11pm. **Moderate.**

ENTERTAINMENT

For something a bit out of the ordinary, try *The Rose and Crown*, 1000 Higuera Street, ph 541 1911, an English pub offering drinks and dance from Thursday to Saturday.

A bit more up-market is the piano bar at *The Inn at Morro Bay*, 19 Country Club Drive, Morro Bay, ph 772 5651.

SIGHTSEEING

The Chamber of Commerce has marked out a walking tour that begins at the Mission and visits twenty historic landmarks. So get your map, and follow the green line.

The main attractions are:

Mission San Luis Obispo de Tolosa

Situated at Chorro Street and Mission Plaza, ph 543 6850, the mission was built of adobe bricks by the Chumash Indians, and was the first to adopt the red roof tiles in place of the thatched roofs which caught fire so easily. Founded in 1772, the buildings were completed in 1776. Today the mission has been reconstructed, and is one of the most interesting in the chain. The Mission Museum has a large display of artifacts, both to do with the mission itself, and the Native Americans who lived in the area.

The mission is open daily from 7am Mass, the museum is open daily (except Christmas, New Year's Day, Easter Sunday and Thanksgiving) 9am-5pm. Normally a donation of $2 is given.

Mission Plaza has several shops, restaurants and boutiques, as well as the Network shopping complex.

San Luis Obispo County Historical Museum, 696 Monterey Street, ph 543 0638, has an extensive research library, many historical photographs, and artifacts of the Chumash Indians and the early settlers.

St Stephen's Episcopal Church, Nipomo and Pismo Streets, was built in 1867 and was one of the first Episcopal churches to be built in California.

The Ah Louis Store, 800 Palm Street, ph 543 4332, opened in 1874, and is still run by the original Cantonese family. Ah Louis came to California in the 1856 gold rush to seek his fortune, but was unsuccessful. He moved to San Luis and got a job as a cook, but soon began a labour contracting business, hiring Chinese crews to work on the railroad. In addition to his store, he had several other lucrative businesses. His son,

Howard, now operates the store, which is open Mon-Sat, but the hours change with his moods.

California Polytechnic State University can be reached by bus from City Hall to the administration building, where you can get a map of a self-guided tour. The 2093ha (5169 acres) campus is mainly devoted to agricultural studies, and you can visit 'fascinating' places such as the feed mill, meat-processing plant, barns and chicken coops. Anyway, the kids might like it. There is also some experimental architecture on show, and in fact the university has the largest architecture school in the country.

Beaches

If you are a water-baby, for goodness sake grab a swim around here. It's the last place on your trip north that is warm enough for swimming.

Pismo Beach is a 15-minute drive south of San Luis Obispo, and has 37km (23 miles) of wide, sandy beach, with a million-dollar pier slap bang in the middle. The Pismo Beach Chamber of Commerce, 581 Dolliver Street, ph 773 4382, is open Mon-Fri 9.30am-5pm, Sat 10am-4pm, and they can tell you about the other local attractions. The town has a large calendar of festivals and special shows.

The strange name, by the way, is 'known' by the natives to be from the Spanish 'pismo' which translates as 'a place to fish'. Some carpers like to point out that the Chumash Indian word 'pismu' means 'the place where blobs of tar wash up on the beach'.

Avila Beach, a 10-minute drive south of San Luis Obispo, is probably the best swimming beach in the area, and the village also offers chartered deep-sea fishing and pleasure cruises from the Port St Luis Marina. There are picnic and barbecue facilities at the beach.

Morro Bay, is a 15-minute drive north of San Luis Obispo, on California 1. In the bay is Morro Rock, the last of a chain of extinct volcanoes, and a sanctuary for thousands of birds. The Morro Bay Chamber of Commerce, 895 Napa Street, ph 772 4467, is open Mon-Fri 8am-5pm, Sat 9am-5pm, and can head you in the right direction with regard to restaurants, fishing facilities, shops and art galleries in the centre of the community, the Embarcadero.

PASO ROBLES

Situated on Highway 101, 43km (27 miles) north of San Luis Obispo, Paso Robles is the centre of a grape growing and winemaking area which had its beginnings in 1797 at the nearby Mission San Miguel Arcangel. Today there are more than twenty-five wineries and eighty vineyards growing premium winegrapes on rolling hills that vary from 213m to 579m (700 to 1900 ft) in elevation.

It is a very pretty spot, and if you are interested in visiting the mission, which, incidentally, is the only one in the chain that has the original wall and ceiling decorations unretouched, why not combine it with a visit to a winery.

The following establishments have winetasting rooms.
(The telephone area code is 805.)
Baron Vineyards, 1981 Penman Springs Road, ph 239 3313 - Chardonnay, Cabernet Sauvignon, Firehouse Red, Firehouse White, Sauvignon Blanc, Muscat Canelli, White Zinfandel - **open daily.**
Caparone, 2280 San Marcos Road, ph 467 3827 - Cabernet Sauvignon, Merlot, Zinfandel, Brunello, Nebbiolo - **open daily, 11am-5pm.**
Creston Manor Vineyards & Winery, cnr, Highway 101 and Vineyard Drive, Templeton, ph 434 1399 - Sauvignon Blanc, Chardonnay, Pinot Noir, Cabernet Sauvignon, White Zinfandel - **open daily 10am-5pm.**

Eberle Winery, Highway 46, 6km east of Highway 101, ph 238 9607 - Cabernet Sauvignon, Chardonnay, Muscat Canelli - **open daily 10am-6pm (summer), 10am-5pm (winter).**

Estrella River Winery at Laura's Vineyard, 5620 Highway 46 East, ph 238 6300 - Cabernet Sauvignon - **open daily 10am-5pm.**

Farview Farm Vineyard, Bethel Road, off Highway 46 West, ph 434 1133 - Chardonnay, Merlot, Zinfandel, Cabernet Sauvignon, and late harvest wines - **open daily, except Wednesday, 10am-5pm.**

Harmony Cellars, Highway 1 between Morro Bay and Cambria, ph 927 1625 - White Zinfandel, Chardonnay, Johannesberg Riesling, Pinot Noir, Cabernet Sauvignon - **open Mon-Fri 11am-5pm, Sat-Sun 10am-6pm.**

Hope Farm, cnr Highway 46 West and Arbor Road, ph 238 6979 - Cabernet Sauvignon, Zinfandel - **open Wed-Sun 11am-5pm.**

Martin Brothers, Highway 46, 1km east of Highway 101 - Aleatico, Chardonnay, Dry Chenin Blanc, Zinfandel, Cabernet Sauvignon, Nebbiolo and Grappa di Nebbiolo - **open daily 11am-5pm.**

Mastantuono Winery, 100 Oak View Road, Templeton, ph 238 0676 - Zinfandel, Chardonnay, Sauvignon Blanc, Cabernet Sauvignon, Muscat Canelli - **open daily 10.30am-6pm (summer), 10am-5pm (winter).**

Mission View Estate Vineyards & Winery, 13350 North River Road (east of San Miguel), ph 467 3104 - Cabernets, Zinfandel, Chardonnay, Sauvignon Blanc - **open daily 10am-5pm.**

Twin Hills Ranch Winery, Lake Nacimiento Drive, ph 238 9148 - Chardonnay, Zinfandel, Cabernet Sauvignon, White Zinfandel, Zinfandel Rose - **open Wed-Sun 11am-6pm (summer), 11am-5pm (winter).**

York Mountain Winery, York Mountain Road, off Highway 46 West, ph 238 3925 - Chardonnay, Cabernet Sauvignon, Merlot, Pinot Noir, Zinfandel - **open daily 10am-5pm.**

SAN SIMEON

The seaside hamlet of San Simeon is visited by over a million people each year, but few of them get to do more than drive through the village. They are all on their way to, or from, one of the greatest monuments to money in the world - **Hearst Castle**, or to give it its current name, the Hearst San Simeon State Historical Monument.

HEARST CASTLE

In 1865, George Hearst bought a 40,000 acres Mexican land grant which stretched for 64km (40 miles) along the coast. He built a comfortable ranch house, and ran herds of cattle and sheep. His only son, the newspaper magnate-to-be William Randolph, was particularly enamoured of the property and when it became his after the death of his father's widow, Phoebe Apperson Hearst, he had already commenced work on the incredible Casa Grande, on a hill which he called Cuesta Encantada (the Enchanted Hill). He had engaged well-known and respected architect Julia Morgan, apparently given her a blank cheque and kept her on a very loose rein. What an imagination that lady had! The end result almost defies description, and I strongly recommend that you join the queues to see how the other half lived.

Firstly there is the house itself, with over 100 rooms, filled with priceless art treasures, including 15th century Gothic fireplaces, 16th century Spanish and 18th century Italian ceilings, Renaissance paintings, Flemish tapestries, ancient Egyptian statues - the list goes on. There is also a private theatre used to show first-run movies. To accommodate the guests lucky enough to be invited for the weekend, there are three lavishly decorated guest houses, and two swimming pools - one outside that would have made Nero feel at home, and one inside, actually built underneath the tennis courts, that could have been built by Saladin, and accommodated

194 CALIFORNIA AT COST

him, and his harem. Unbelievable!

All the above is still there in all its splendour for everyone to see. What is not there are the beautifully landscaped gardens and pagoda, and the largest private zoo in the world. All that is left are a few deer and zebras which seem to get on quite well with the cattle, although they look quite strange all grazing together.

There are four different tours that can be taken, and each lasts 1 hour and 45 minutes, including the time spent in the bus from the visitor centre up the mountain to the estate (approx 15 minutes).

At the ticket box the information for each tour tells how many stair-steps are included, but don't let this put you off. They are not steep, and there are plenty of stops while the guides tell you about points of interest.

Tour 1 - main floor of the castle, assembly room, refectory, morning room, billiards room, theatre, one guest house, gardens and both pools. This is recommended for the first visit.

Tour 2 - upper floors of the main building, Mr Hearst's private Gothic suite, libraries, Celestial Suite, kitchen and both pools.

Tour 3 - new wing of the main building, guest bedrooms, bathrooms, sitting rooms on three levels of one wing of the castle, one guest house, gardens, and both pools.

Tour 4 - (offered April-October) overview of the Enchanted Hill, includes both levels of Hearst's Casa del Mar, extensive views of gardens and buildings, wine cellar, a 'hidden terrace' and both pools (does not visit interiors of main building).

Evening Tour - offered on selected evenings in Spring, Fall and Winter - includes highlights of the most popular daytime tours, and offers a glimpse into the 1930s lifestyle of W.R.

Hearst (according to the notice board).

Tours 2, 3, 4 require 300 stair-steps, Tour 1 has 150 stair-steps. The Evening Tour has 377 stair-steps.

Those tours which visit the theatre also show some of Mr Hearst's home movies, with some of his friends - Marion Davies (of course), Charlie Chaplin, Clark Gable, etc, in short all people you know too.

By the bye, William Randolph was Patty's grandfather.

> Be warned though, if you want to tour the castle, book well in advance, don't just turn up or you will probably be disappointed.

BIG SUR

Firstly, it must be said that Big Sur is not a town, it is a 145km (90 miles) stretch of rugged coastline that extends north from San Simeon to the Monterey Peninsula, with the ocean on one side and the San Lucia Mountains on the other.

The entire area has only 1500 residents, who have no intention of turning it into a tourist mecca. So, not only is there no town, there is nothing but natural beauty, where you can hike, have picnics, fish, or sit on the beach (the water is too cold to swim).

Having said all that, there are a couple of places you can stay, apart from camping, which is not really an option for people who have come from overseas.

Ventana Inn, on California 1, 55km (34 miles) south of Monterey, ph (408) 667 2331, is a wilderness resort on a 98ha (243 acres) oceanfront ranch, set high in the mountains. It has 59 luxurious guest rooms that are heavily booked, especially in summer, restaurant, swimming pool, and rates for doubles begin at $170 per night.

Big Sur Lodge in Pfeiffer-Big Sur State Park, about 53km (33 miles) south of Monterey on California 1, ph (408) 667 2171 has 61 cabins on over 324ha (800 acres) of towering trees, a restaurant, and heated outdoor swimming pool. Doubles start at $70 per night.

Beaches and Parks

Julia Pfeiffer Burns State Park, on California 1, about 18km (11 miles) south of Pfeiffer Big Sur State Park, has an area of 729ha (1800 acres). The centre of the park is a natural amphitheatre, and paths lead to a spot where you can see a waterfall dive dramatically into the ocean.

Pfeiffer Beach is reached by taking California 1 for 1km past the entrance to Pfeiffer Big Sur State Park, then turning right onto Sycamore Canyon Road, which travels a further 2km to the beach. It is bisected by a colourful stream, and offshore are rock formations which the sea has carved with tunnels and arches.

Pfeiffer Big Sur State Park has cottages, a restaurant and a grocery. The park is along California 1 in Big Sur and has an area of 332ha (821 acres). Attractions include the Big Sur River, with its trout and salmon, and the Pfeiffer Falls.

Andrew Molera State Park is about 5km (3 miles) north of Big Sur, and has to be a haven for hikers as there are no roads. There is plenty of wildlife, though.

Camping is allowed at these parks.

Point Lobos

Located south of Carmel, off California 1, Point Lobos is one of the best spots for whale watching on the Monterey Peninsula. The 506ha (1250 acres) Point is a living natural history museum with its teeming land and sea life, primeval cypress groves, meadows and wildflowers, great grey rocks and outcroppings and occasional white sandy beaches. It is thought that Robert Louis Stevenson used Point Lobos as a model for Spyglass Hill in *Treasure Island*.

The conglomerate pebbles of the Reserve range from thumbnail-size to several inches in diameter, and are the only record known of rocks from the Eocene Period. The Monterey

Cypress, known in the Pleistocene era, is making its last stand here.

Offshore, Bird Island is a sanctuary for large flocks of cormorants, pelicans, gulls and other waterfowl. The Reserve is in fact, the northernmost breeding ground of the California brown pelican.

When cars pull into the viewing area, dozens of squirrels and chipmunks appear as if by magic, and they look so cute that everyone starts diving into their bags to find something to feed them. The animals are quite used to this, and are so tame they almost adopt a 'hurry up' attitude. Feeding them is actually sounding their death knoll, and there are large signs that read "Do Not Feed the Animals". Because of the fickle nature of man, the area may not always be as popular as it is today, or for some unknown reason, it may in future years become off-limits to visitors, then these little creatures will starve to death because they will have forgotten how to forage for themselves. So, be strong! Don't feed them, just take their photos.

NOTES

THE MONTEREY PENINSULA

CARMEL

The village of Carmel-By-The-Sea has attracted writers and artists since the turn of the century because of its natural beauty. As usually happens, those who could afford a slice of paradise followed in their wake, and the end result is a conglomeration of houses, boutiques and galleries that literally shriek 'money'. This is a good place to window-shop, but you need a very healthy wallet to actually buy. It's all done in very good taste, of course, with illuminated retail signs banned, and even the petrol stations have an inferiority complex and try to look like something else. Trees come into their own here; any that fall are left where they lie; and those in the middle of a proposed road have definite right of way, which does help to slow down the traffic, but makes life difficult for bus drivers.

Houses do not have street numbers, so locations are pinpointed by naming the closest cross streets.

TOURIST INFORMATION

The Carmel Business Association, Vandervort Court, on San Carlos Street, between Ocean and 7th, ph (408) 624 2522, has maps and brochures. It is open Mon-Fri 9.30am-4pm.

There is a Tourist Information Center at Mission Patio, on Mission Street, between 5th and 6th, ph (408) 624 1711, which is open Mon-Fri 9am-4pm, but is mostly for arranging accommodation.

A free weekly newsletter, *Carmel Pine Cone* can be picked up at any newsstand, and has details of current events.

200 CALIFORNIA AT COST

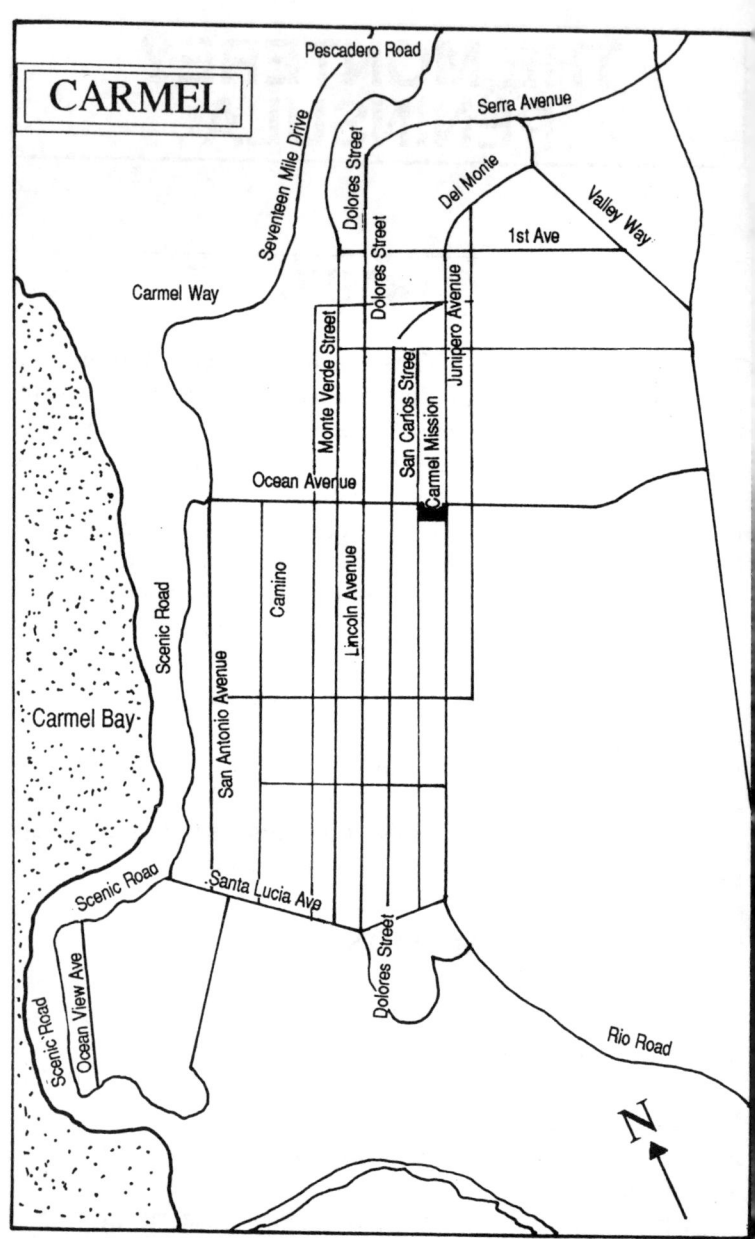

ACCOMMODATION

Personally, I think it is better to stay in Monterey and visit Carmel and its attractions for the day, but that is only my opinion. Here is a selection of lodgings in Carmel, with prices for a double room per night in US dollars, which should be used as a guide only.

The telephone area code is 408.

Highlands Inn, on Highway 1 about 6km south of Carmel, ph 624 3801 - 142 rooms, restaurant, cocktail lounge - $225-650.
Quail Lodge, 8205 Valley Greens Lodge, ph 624 1581 - 100 rooms, restaurant, cocktail lounge, swimming pools, tennis courts - $145-245.
Hofsas House, San Carlos between 3rd & 4th, ph 624 2745 - 38 rooms, swimming pool, saunas, complimentary continental breakfast- $80-150.

EATING OUT

As with the accommodation, restaurants tend to fit into the Expensive category. The creme de la creme is *The Covey* at Quail Lodge, 8205 Valley Greens Drive, ph 624 1581, which serves continental cuisine with a French emphasis. It is open every evening from 6.30pm, and accepts all major credit cards. Reservations are necessary, as are jackets for the men.

For a reasonably-priced lunch, try the *Tuck Box* on Dolores Street between Ocean & 7th Avenue, ph 624 6365. It serves home-style food and is open Wed-Sun 8am-4pm.

SHOPPING

The most attractive shopping plaza is *The Barnyard*. It is on California 1, off Carmel Valley Road, and has more than sixty shops and restaurants, housed in raw wood buildings reminiscent of old farm barns. It is all set in landscaped surroundings with a windmill and even a water tank.

One of the drawcards is the *Thunderbird Bookshop*, ph 624

1803, which includes a restaurant that serves lunch daily from 11am to 3.30pm, and dinner Tues-Sun 5.30-8pm.

Two of America's most famous photographers, Ansel Adams and Edward Weston, lived in Carmel, and two galleries which specialise in their works are the *Weston Gallery*, 6th Avenue between Dolores and Lincoln Streets, and *Photography West Gallery*, Dolores Street between Ocean and 7 Avenues, ph 625 1587.

For boutiques, the main shopping strip is along Ocean Avenue between Mission and Monte Verde Streets.

Also on Ocean Avenue, across from the park, is *Carmel Plaza* with 50 shops and restaurants.

SIGHTSEEING

Mission San Carlos Borromeo de Carmelo in Rio Road, ph 624 3600, is one of the largest and most interesting of the California missions. In fact, it was the favourite of their founder, Fr Junipero Serra, to the point that he requested to be buried here. He rests in the sanctuary, his grave marked with a stone sarcophagus.

The cemetery beside the church contains the seashell-decorated graves of 3000 Native Americans, and other things worth seeing are the old mission kitchen, the first library in the State, the high altar, the cell where Fr Serra died, and the sacred vessels he used when celebrating Mass.

17-MILE DRIVE

A leisurely trip on this world-renowned drive is a 'must'. Every turn in the road opens breath-taking views of the rock-bound coast of Carmel Bay, the high cliffs along the Pacific Ocean, and the white sands of Monterey Bay. It winds its way through dense forests, past stately mansions, and four of the world's most famous golf courses. The Lodge at Pebble Beach, which is open to the public, is a delightful place to stop for a snack.

The Drive can be entered through four gates:
Carmel Gate at San Antonio Street, north of Ocean Avenue;

THE MONTEREY PENINSULA 203

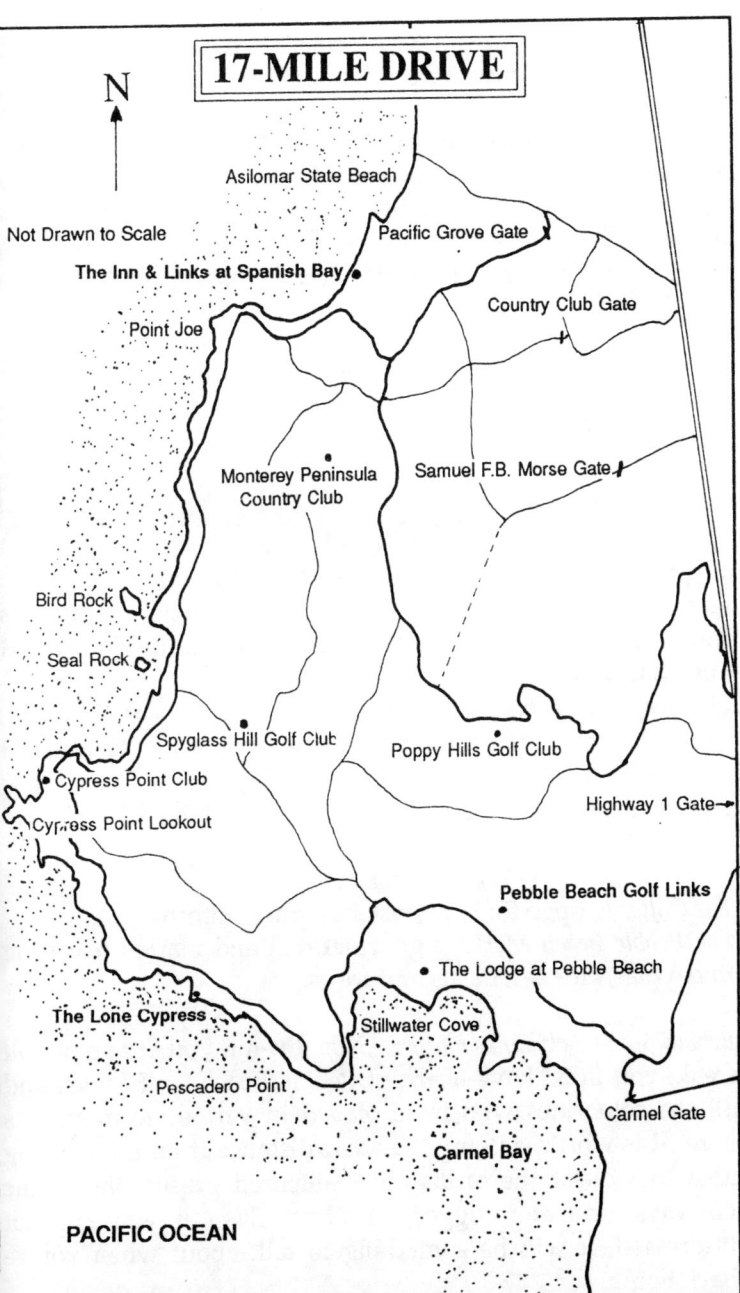

Carmel Hill Gate, just off California 1 between Monterey and Carmel; Pacific Grove Gate at Sunset Drive and 17-Mile Drive;

Country Club Gate near Country Club Center on Forest Ave.
When you pay the $6 per car admission, you are given a brochure with a map and information on 27 points of interest. Most of the points are places where you can get a good view of some of the great natural scenery, but there are a couple of man-made things that are worth mentioning.

> The prices to stay there are through the roof, but it is a good place for lunch or dinner at one of the following: *The Dunes* - casual regional cuisine; *The Bay Club* - Northern Italian cuisine, for dinner only; *The Clubhouse Bar and Grill* - informal.

The Inn and Links at Spanish Bay, ph (408) 624 3811, is the latest addition to Pebble Beach, and it has 270 rooms with lovely views, three restaurants, a spa, swimming pool, eight tennis courts and membership privileges at the nearby Beach and Tennis Club.

The Lodge at Pebble Beach, ph 624 3811, has 161 guest rooms, and pretty much the same facilities and prices as The Inn, but again you can stop at one of the following:

The Tap Room - casual pub with golf memorabilia;

Club XIX - French cuisine;

The Cypress Room - regional cuisine;

The Gallery - open for breakfast and lunch, informal;

The Pebble Beach Market - gourmet deli and market featuring fine wines, cheeses, meats and fruits.

Pebble Beach Golf Links and Pro Shop. Even if you are not a golf freak, you must have heard of Pebble Beach Golf Links, and all the celebrities who have played in various tournaments here. It is worth walking the short distance from the parking area to look at the brilliantly manicured greens, the scenic fairways, and the rugged coastline. Even if you are not impressed, it will be something to talk about when you're back home.

PACIFIC GROVE

Otherwise known as "Butterfly Town, USA" because of the thousands of orange and black monarch butterflies who migrate here every November and stay around until March, Pacific Grove is a small town in the north-west corner of the Monterey Peninsula. Originally the home of the Costanoan Indians, it became a religious settlement in the 1870s for the Methodist Retreat Association of San Francisco. Ministers would set up tents, hold services under the pine trees, and make sure that anyone venturing into the water was suitably attired. It wasn't long before people began to settle permanently and the town has many houses that date from the late 19th century. Needless to say, it was not exactly a swinging community (alcohol was banned until 1969) and locals referred to the town near Carmel-by-the-Sea as "Pacific Grove-by-God".

Pacific Grove Chamber of Commerce, cnr Forest and Central Avenues, ph (408) 373 3304, can advise on accommodation and restaurants, and local attractions.

Worth visiting are:

Point Pinos Lighthouse, on Ocean Boulevard at the north-west point of the peninsula, is the only early lighthouse on the Californian coast that has been preserved in its original condition, except for the introduction of electricity. It dates from 1856, and the beacon originally used sperm oil. Tours of the lighthouse are available on the weekends, and for information phone 372 4212.

The American Tin Cannery, 125 Ocean View Boulevard, ph 372 1442, is a discount shopping outlet with shops offering well-known brand names - Van Heusen, Royal Doulton, Maidenform, to name a few. There are also a few good restaurants in the centre, particularly the First Watch. The shops are open daily, Mon-Wed and Sat 10am-6pm, Thurs-Fri 10am-9pm, Sun 11am-5pm, the hours of the restaurants vary.

MONTEREY

The main town on the peninsula, Monterey once had a much loftier title - the capital of Northern California. That was in 1770, when the Spanish Crown established the city of Monterey.

The original inhabitants of the area were the Ohlone Indians, then Juan Rodriguez Cabrillo spied Monterey when he was sailing to Spain in 1542, and it went on Spain's list of places they needed to consolidate their position in the New World. In 1602, Sebastian Vizcaino was looking for a harbour for ships sailing from the Philippines, decided upon Monterey, and named it in honour of the Count of Monterey, Viceroy of Spain.

Mexico ruled the city from 1821 until July 7, 1846, when Commodore John Drake Sloat officially raised the United States flag.

The most famous resident of Monterey was John Steinbeck, author of *Cannery Row*, *Sweet Thursday*, *East of Eden*, *The Grapes of Wrath*, and many other equally depressing books, many of which were set in Monterey and in Salinas Valley, where he was born in 1902.

HOW TO GET THERE

By Air
Monterey Peninsula Airport is serviced by United Airlines, Wings West, West Air and Pacific Coast Airlines.

By Road
Monterey is 530km (330 miles) north of Los Angeles, and 210km (130 miles) south of San Francisco, via US 101 or California 1.

THE MONTEREY PENINSULA

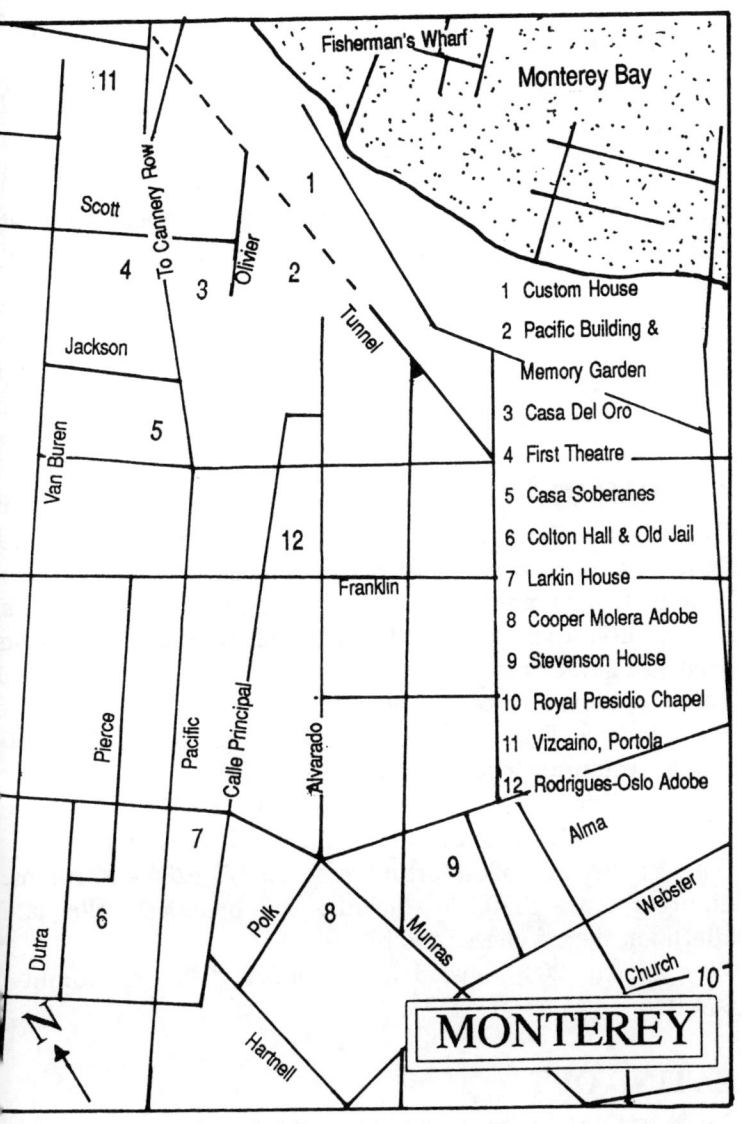

TOURIST INFORMATION

The Monterey Peninsula Chamber of Commerce, Rodrigues-Osio Adobe, 380 Alvarado Street, ph (408) 649 1770, has maps and pamphlets on the whole of the peninsula.

Monterey Visitors Center, Lake El Estero at Franklin and Camino El Estero, ph (408) 649 1770, is open Mon-Sat 9am-6pm, Sun 9am-5pm (April-Oct), Mon-Sat 9am-5pm, Sun 10am-4pm (Nov-March).

There are also several free publications - *Monterey Peninsula Review*, *This Month on the Monterey Peninsula* and *Key* - which are available at most hotels and shops.

ACCOMMODATION

Over three million people visit Monterey each year, so while there is a lot of accommodation available, it is still wise to book well in advance. Here is a selection of hotels, with prices for a double room per night in US dollars, which should be used as a guide only.

The telephone area code is 408.

The Monterey Plaza, 400 Cannery Row, ph 646 1700 - 290 rooms, restaurant, cocktail lounge - $145-195.

Monterey Bay Inn, 242 Cannery Row, ph 373 6242 - 47 rooms, health club - $120-329 (includes continental breakfast).

Old Monterey Inn, 500 Martin Street, ph 375 8284 - 10 rooms, dining room - $170-230 (includes full breakfast, plus late afternoon sherry, cheese and bikkies).

Way Station, 1200 Olmsted Road, ph 372 2945 - restaurant - $69-169.

EATING OUT

Apart from in the big-name hotels, most of the restaurants in Monterey are found on Fisherman's Wharf, or along Cannery Row. In either place, it makes choosing your meal a lot easier if you enjoy fish, for that is the main item on offer, naturally enough, I suppose. Most restaurants have good views of the harbour, and while you are waiting for your food to arrive, you can watch the otters playing in the water. In fact, some of the restaurants advertise that live entertainment is provided by the local marine life.

> Eating out in Monterey is not a cheap exercise, but each restaurant has a copy of the menu outside, so you know what you are up for before you enter.

As there's not really much difference in the standards, maybe you should let price be your guide. Most accept all major credit cards.

Probably the best-known restaurant is *The Whaling Station Inn*, 763 Wave Street, just above Cannery Row, ph 373 3778. It's been around for over twenty years, and apart from seafood, has steak and pasta, an award winning wine list, and children's menus. It comes in the Expensive category, but is value for money, and is only open for dinner.

Another old time favourite is *Old Fisherman's Grotto*, 39 Fisherman's Wharf #1, ph 375 4604, which also offers steak, pasta and chicken. It is open for lunch and dinner, and is rated moderate/expensive.

If fish is not your bag, try *Gianni's Pizza*, 725 Lighthouse Avenue, ph 649 1500. It's open Mon-Thurs 4-11pm, Fri-Sat 11.30am-midnight, and doesn't take credit cards, but it does serve good Italian fare, and has a full cocktail bar.

ENTERTAINMENT

There are five movie theatres in Monterey, and four live theatres, and your hotel can provide you with current programs and session times.

For bars with live music, try *Doc Rickett's Lab*, 95 Prescott Avenue, ph 649 4241, or *Mark Thomas Outrigger*, 700 Cannery Row, ph 372 8543. Another venue is *The Club*, 321D Alvarado Street, ph 646 9244, but the entertainment changes nightly, so it could be a band, or a rock video, or a disco.

SHOPPING

There are stores throughout the downtown area, but it is best to head for Cannery Row where there are several malls and plazas, offering all types of goods at reasonable prices. The American Tin Cannery Shopping Mall, on Ocean View Road, between Eardley and Dewey Avenues is very good for sportswear and shoes.

The shops on Fisherman's Wharf are mainly craft and souvenir stores.

SIGHTSEEING

Monterey's **Path of History** is a walking tour of the early Spanish and Californian buildings and homes, but unfortunately, some of them are now private residences, and not open to the public, so they can only be viewed from the outside.

The places listed here are those that can be visited, and each charges a small admission fee.

Custom House

Built about 1827, Custom House, 1 Custom House Plaza, is the oldest government building on the Pacific Coast, and is where Commodore John Drake Sloat raised the United States flag. When Monterey was under Mexican rule, the principal source of revenue was the custom duties collected from foreign shipping companies. When San Francisco became California's major port, the building was abandoned. It now houses displays from an 1830s cargo ship. Open daily 10am-5pm.

Pacific Building and Memory Garden

The Pacific Building, 10 Custom House Plaza, was built in 1847, and over the years has acquired just about everything from a tavern to a courtroom. It is now a museum with exhibits of California's early history (from Native Americans to the the canning industry era) in the 1930s. It is open daily 10am-5pm.

Casa del Oro

Situated behind the Pacific Building, cnr Olivier and Scott Streets, Casa del Oro was built in 1843 as quarters for American seamen left at the port under consular care. In 1849, Joseph Boston and Company leased the property and used it as a general store. The name, which means 'House of Gold' is thought to stem from miners keeping their gold in a safe on the premises during the Gold Rush days.

Today the house is owned by the state, and the Monterey History and Art Association have preserved it as a general store, and stocked it with items that would have been available in the mid-19th century. It is open Wed-Sun 10am-4.30pm.

California's First Theatre

Directly opposite the Casa del Oro is a building dating back to 1846. It was built by Jack Swan, a sailor, as a boarding house and tavern, and the first stage performance was given by the soldiers of the New York Volunteer Regiment in 1847.

The building was given to the state in 1906, and still looks the same as in its early days. The tavern still operates, and members of the Troupers of the Gold Coast still tread the boards. It is open Tues-Sun 10am-5pm.

Casa Soberanes

This mediterranean-style house at 336 Pacific Street, was built in 1830 by Don Jose Rafael Estrada, the warden of the Custom House. Now it is completely furnished, and has an extensive collection of works of local artists. It can be visited by guided tours only, Fri-Wed 10am-4pm (closed noon hour).

Colton Hall and Old Jail

Colton Hall is at 522 Pacific Street, and was named after Rev Walter Colton, US Navy Chaplain, who co-founded the state's first newspaper, empanelled the state's first jury, and built the state's first public building. Colton Hall was planned as the town hall and public school, and it was there in 1849 that California's Constitution was written, and the great seal of the state designed. Upstairs there is now a museum, and next door is the Old Monterey Jail, with remnants of prisoners' scribblings. Open daily, 10am-5pm, closed for lunch noon-1pm.

Larkin House

The two-storey adobe at 510 calle Principal, was built in 1835, and was the home of Thomas Oliver Larkin, US Consul to Mexico from 1843 to 1846, and also served as the consular office. It is now furnished with many original pieces, and is a museum of architecture. Next door is the house used by William Tecumseh Sherman, which has a museum depicting the influence of both these men on Californian history. There are guided tours daily, except Tues, 10am-noon, 1-4pm.

Cooper Molera Adobe

Captain John Cooper, the half-brother of Thomas Larkin, was a dealer in general merchandise and hides, tallow, and sea otter pelts. As business improved, he expanded his one-storey home to a two-storey, erected large barns, and enclosed the one hectare (2.5 acres) complex with a high adobe wall. It is found on the corner of Polk and Munras Streets, and is the best example of early Californian life. Open Thurs-Tues, with guided tours 10am-noon, 1-4pm.

Stevenson House

It was in the house at 530 Houston Street that Robert Louis Stevenson lived during the autumn of 1879, when he wrote *The Old Pacific Capital*, an account of life in Monterey at that time. He had come from Scotland to persuade Fanny Osbourne to marry him.

Built in the late 1830s, the house belonged to Don Rafael Gonzales, first Administrator of Customs of Alta California. In 1856, it was bought by Juan Giradin, who made some additions, and rented out rooms, which explains why Stevenson was staying here. At the time Robert Louis was poor, unknown, and ill, and not much of a bargain in the marriage stakes, but marry they did, and apparently lived happily ever after.

Several rooms of the house are filled with Stevenson memorabilia and guided tours are available Thurs-Tues 10am-noon, 1-4pm. There is some talk of a ghost sometimes being seen in one of the upstairs children's bedrooms, but it didn't show up when I was there.

Royal Presidio Chapel
The old adobe building with a towering belfry at 550 Church Street, is a mission church founded by Father Junipero Serra in 1770.

Vizcaino, Portola and Serra Landing Site

On June 3, 1770, Don Gasper de Portola and Fray Junipero Serra arrived at Vizcaino's original landing site, now south of the Monterey Presidio on Pacific Street.

Cannery Row

The name remains, but thank goodness all the canning operations have gone. The man who made the area famous in the 1940s, John Steinbeck, returned in the 1960s and had this to say: "The beaches are clean where they once festered with fish guts and flies. The canneries which once put up a sickening stench are gone, their places filled with restaurants, antique shops and the like. They fish for tourists, now, not pilchards, and that species they are not likely to wipe out."

It is indeed Steinbeck Country now, and at every turn you are reminded of some aspect from his books. A bronze bust of him, on the corner of Cannery Row and Prescott Avenue, shows how much the locals appreciate the fact that he made Monterey so familiar to people all over the world.

The Spirit of Monterey Wax Museum is in The Monterey Cannery at no 700, and it has life-size reproductions of all the characters of Steinbeck's novels. Open daily, 9am-9pm, **admission is $6 adults, $4 children.**
For fans of Steinbeck, it must be revealed that some of the

businesses on the Row have taken names from Steinbeck's books, and are not at the original locations. To help sort the sheep from the wolves, here is a list of authentic places.

Cannery Row Antique Warehouse, is on the 700 block of the Row. Built in 1929, it was Dora Flood's bordello in *Cannery Row*, which was taken over by her sister Flora in *Sweet Thursday*.

Pacific Biological Laboratories, 800 Cannery Row, is now a private club. In the late 1930s, when Edward F. (Doc) Ricketts owned this marine laboratory, John Steinbeck bought a part interest in it, and worked with 'Doc' as a marine biologist off and on. Doc's Lab plays an important part in *Cannery Row*, *Sweet Thursday*, *Travels with Charley*, *Sea of Cortez* and *Log of Cortez*. It is also the setting for the short story, *The Snake*.

Wing Chong's Market, 835 Cannery Row, was originally owned by Wing Chong, but in *Cannery Row*, Steinbeck called it Lee Chong's Heavenly Flower Grocery. In *Sweet Thursday* it was bought by the dapper Mexican Joseph Rivas and his wife Mary. It is now The Cannery Row Shell Co.

Kalisa's "Between Pacific Tides", 851 Cannery Row, was La Ida's Cafe, owned by Wide Ida in *Sweet Thursday*.

Hopkins Marine Station, China Point, was the location of Chin Kee's Squid Yard in *Sweet Thursday*. The point was originally a Chinese settlement. Steinbeck attended a class in General Zoology in 1923 at Hopkins Marine Station.

Monterey Bay Aquarium

Situated at 886 Cannery Row, ph 648 4888, Monterey Bay Aquarium is open daily 10am-6pm, and **admission is $9.75 adults, $7.25 students 13-18, $4.50 children 3-12.**
Monterey Bay is part of the Monterey submarine canyon, an undersea chasm that covers hundreds of square kilometres,

and reaches depths greater than 3050m (10,000 ft). Scientists and engineers from the Aquarium Research Institute use the bay as a vast laboratory, and video technology beams their research work live to the auditorium in the Aquarium on Mondays and Tuesdays from noon to 3pm. The show is called *Live from Monterey Canyon*, and it is not unusual for the scientists to discover some animal that has never been seen before. If you are not lucky enough to be there on those days, don't despair, there is still plenty to see - tide pools, coastal streams, touching pools, rocky shores, and kelp forests, with all the appropriate animals swimming around. They even have the 'sandy shore', which is actually an aviary. Feeding times, which are subject to change so it is best to check, are:

Sea Otters - 11am, 2pm, 4.30pm;
Kelp Forest - 11.30am, 4pm.

If you want to see absolutely everything, allow two to three hours for a visit. You can't take your own food inside, but there is a cafe and a cafeteria, and, of course, a gift and bookstore.

Fisherman's Wharf

Not to be compared with San Francisco's Fisherman's Wharf, this one is lined with craft shops, boating and fishing operations, seafood restaurants and fish markets. It is crowded day and night, and it is surprising that, although there is so much competition, the prices in the restaurants are still quite high. I guess it is because there are so many tourists that every eatery get's its fair share of customers.

If you are tired of just looking at the water, and want to get out on it, the Wharf is a good place to pick up a boat or a cruise. Make sure that you have warm clothing, though, as it can get very cold out on the bay.

Princess Monterey Cruises at the end of the Wharf, ph 372 2628, have 45-minute cruises departing on the hour from noon to 6pm daily in summer - **$6 adults, $3 children.**

In winter, they have 2-hour whale-watching cruises,

departing on the hour from 10am to 4pm. Reservations must be made, and sometimes trips have to be cancelled because of sea and weather conditions. These trips can get a bit rough, so if you are not a good sailor, forget them. The **cost is about $18 per person.**

Monterey Sport Fishing at no 90, ph 372 2203, offers deep-sea fishing trips, and you can rent all equipment. Reservations are necessary, and the **costs range from $25 to $50**, depending on times and how much you need to hire.

Chris' Fishing Trips, at no 48, ph 375 5951, have cod trips and salmon trips all year, and albacore trips in autumn. You can rent all the gear, buy a fishing licence, and organise a box lunch from the shop. Reservations are necessary, and **prices range from $25 to $70.**

SPORT AND RECREATION

The following covers golf courses and tennis courts that are open to the public in the whole of the Monterey Peninsula.

Golf

Laguna Seca Golf Club, York Road, off Monterey-Salinas Highway 68, ph 373 3701 - 18-hole, par 71, 5587m (6110 yds).
Green fees: $35 every day; $17 twilight rate (after 2pm PST, and 3pm PDT); power carts $21.
Del Monte Golf Course, 1300 Sylvan Road, Monterey, ph 373 2436 - 18-hole, par 72.
Green fees: $45 every day; twilight $15 every day; golf carts $12/rider; hand-pull rental $5.
Pacific Grove City Golf Course, 77 Asilomar Avenue, Pacific Grove, ph 375 3456 - 18-hole, par 70, 5030m (5500 yds).
Green fees: $8 for 9 holes weekdays, $9 weekends; $12 for 18 holes weekdays, $14 weekends; power carts $17, push carts available.
Pebble Beach Golf Links, ph 624 3811; Golf shop, ph 624 6611 - 18-hole, par 72, 6217m (6799 yds).

Green fees: $200, $75 twilight; golf cart included; caddie $30/bag.

The Links at Spanish Bay, 17-Mile Drive and Congress Road, Pebble Beach, ph 647 7500; Reservations, ph 624 6611 - 18-hole par 72, 6236m (6820 yds).
Green fees: $125, $55 twilight; golf cart included; caddie $30/bag.

Poppy Hills Golf Course, 3200 Lopez Road, 17-Mile Drive Pebble Beach, ph 625 2035 - 18-hole, par 72, 6264m (6850 yds).
Green fees: $70; golf carts $20. Carts are mandatory for all group play.

Rancho Canada Golf Club, Carmel Valley Road, 1.6km from Highway 1, ph 624 0111 - two 18-hole championship courses West Course par 72, 6047m (6613 yds); East Course, par 71 5883m (6434 yds).
Green fees: $44 every day, $22 twilight; power carts $21.

Spyglass Hill Golf Course, Stevenson Drive and Spyglass Hill Road, Pebble Beach, ph 624 3811; Golf shop, ph 624 6611 - 18-hole, par 72, 6227m (6810 yds).
Green fees: $145; golf cart included; caddie $30/bag.

USNPS Golf Course, south end of Garden Road, behind Monterey County Fairgrounds, ph 646 2167 - 18-hole, par 79 5186m (5672 yds). **Green fees:** $8 weekdays, $10 weekends golf carts $10.

Tennis

Beach and Tennis Club, 17-Mile Drive, Pebble Beach - 14 courts $15 per 1.5 hours, if courts are available.

Carmel Valley Inn, Carmel Valley Road and Los Laureles Grade (CV), ph 659 3131 - 6 courts, reservations necessary.

Carmel Valley Racquet Club, Rancho San Carlos Road, Carmel Valley, ph 624 2737 - 18 courts - if available.

Doubletree Hotel of Monterey, Fisherman's Wharf, ph 649 4511 3 courts.

Hyatt Racquet Club, 1 Old Golf Course Road, Monterey, ph 372 1234 ext 56 - 6 courts, 2 lit for night play.

Meadowbrook Swim & Tennis Club, 1553 Kimball Avenue

Seaside, ph 394 6629 - 9 courts, 2 light for night play.

Mission Tennis Ranch, 26260 Dolores Street, Carmel, ph 624 4335 - 6 double courts, 2 single courts. Reservations necessary.

Monterey Tennis Center, Jack's Park, 401 Pearl Street, Monterey, ph 372 0172 - 4 lighted courts, 9am-9pm weekdays, 9am-6pm weekends. Reservations necessary.

Pacific Grove High School, 615 Sunset Drive, Pacific Grove - 5 courts - available to the public when school classes are not in session.

Pacific Grove Community Center Courts, 515 Junipero Street, Pacific Grove - 5 courts.

Tularcitos School, Via Contenta and Pilot Road, Carmel Valley - 2 courts - open to the public.

Via Paraiso Park, Via Paraiso & Marin Street, Monterey - 2 courts - open to the public.

NOTES

SAN FRANCISCO

The City by the Bay, San Francisco is probably one of the best-known cities in the United States. Its attributes have been lauded in movies and songs, and it is indeed a place where you can 'leave your heart'. The city has an area of 122 sq km (47 sq miles), on the tip of a peninsula bounded by the Pacific Ocean and San Francisco Bay. It is a busy, cosmopolitan city that sprawls over a series of hills that have been the setting for so many car chase sequences in the movies.

San Francisco is a city of many symbols - the beautiful Golden Gate Bridge, mist-shrouded Alcatraz Island, frenetic Fisherman's Wharf, sophisticated Nob Hill, bell-clanging Trolley Cars - and those hills.

HOW TO GET THERE
Getting to San Francisco is covered in the Travel Information chapter.

TOURIST INFORMATION
The Visitor Information Center is in the Benjaman Swig Pavilion, in the lower level of Hallidie Plaza at the corner of Market and Powell Streets, ph (415) 391 2000.
It is open Mon-Fri 9am-5.30pm, Sat 9am-3pm, Sun 10am-2pm, and always seems to be very busy.

The Center has a 24-hour recorded listing of daily events and activities on 391 2001.

ACCOMMODATION
Although San Francisco has over 45,000 hotel rooms, it is still wise to book in advance because around 3 million people visit

the city each year. Accommodation ranges from the super deluxe hotels to budget motels.

> There is a company you might consider contacting called Discount Hotel Rates. Their address is 3 Sumner Street, San Francisco, California, 94103, ph (415) 252 1107, fax (from overseas) 1-415-252 1483. They advertise that they can obtain discounts of 10% to 60% on listed prices at quality hotels, from $45 European-style pensiones, to $275 rooms at five-star resorts. Some of the hotels on their brochure are: The Pan-Pacific, The Mark Hopkins, The Hyatt Regency, The Nikko, The Cathedral Hill, The Orchard, The King George, The Californian, The Richelieu, The Lombard, The Quality, The Parc Fifty-Five, The Savoy and The Hotel Union Square. They can also arrange accommodation in Sonoma and Napa Wine Country. I have not personally used this service, but have had some good reports, and no bad ones.

Anyway, here is a selection of hotels with prices for a double room per night, which should be used as a guide only.
The telephone area code is 415.

Super Deluxe
Mark Hopkins Inter-Continental, 1 Nob Hill, ph 392 3434 - 392 rooms, restaurant, cocktail bar - $220-305.

Four Seasons Clift Hotel, Geary and Taylor Streets, ph 775 4700 - 329 rooms, restaurants, cocktail lounges - $205-345.

Fairmont Hotel, cnr Mason and California Streets, ph 772 5000 - 596 rooms, restaurants, cocktail lounges - $175-295.

Westin St Francis, 335 Powell Street, ph 397 7000 - 1200 rooms, restaurants, cocktail lounges - $180-260.

San Francisco Hilton, 333 O'Farrell Street, ph 771 1400 - 1914 rooms, restaurants, cocktail lounges - $190-250.

Huntingdon Hotel, 1075 California Street, ph 474 5400 - 140 rooms, restaurant, cocktail lounge - $185-235.

Deluxe
Holiday Inn Union Square, 480 Sutter Street, ph 398 8900 - 400 rooms, restaurant, cocktail lounge - $170-245.

Prescott Hotel, 545 Post Street, ph 563 0303 - 167 rooms, restaurant, cocktail lounge - $160-180.

222 CALIFORNIA AT COST

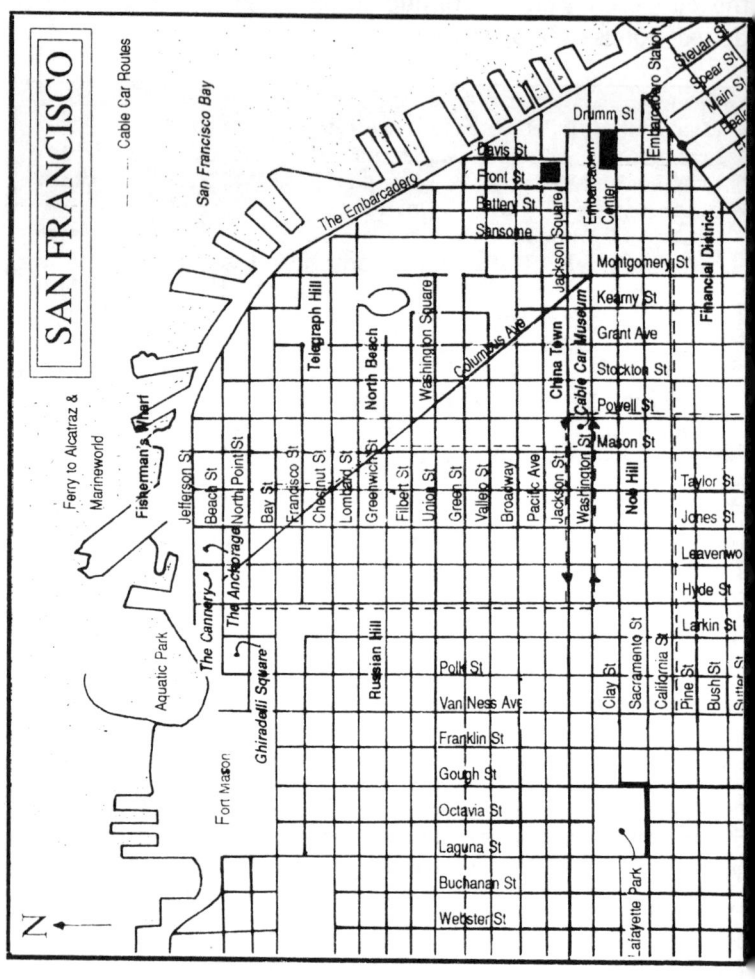

SAN FRANCISCO 223

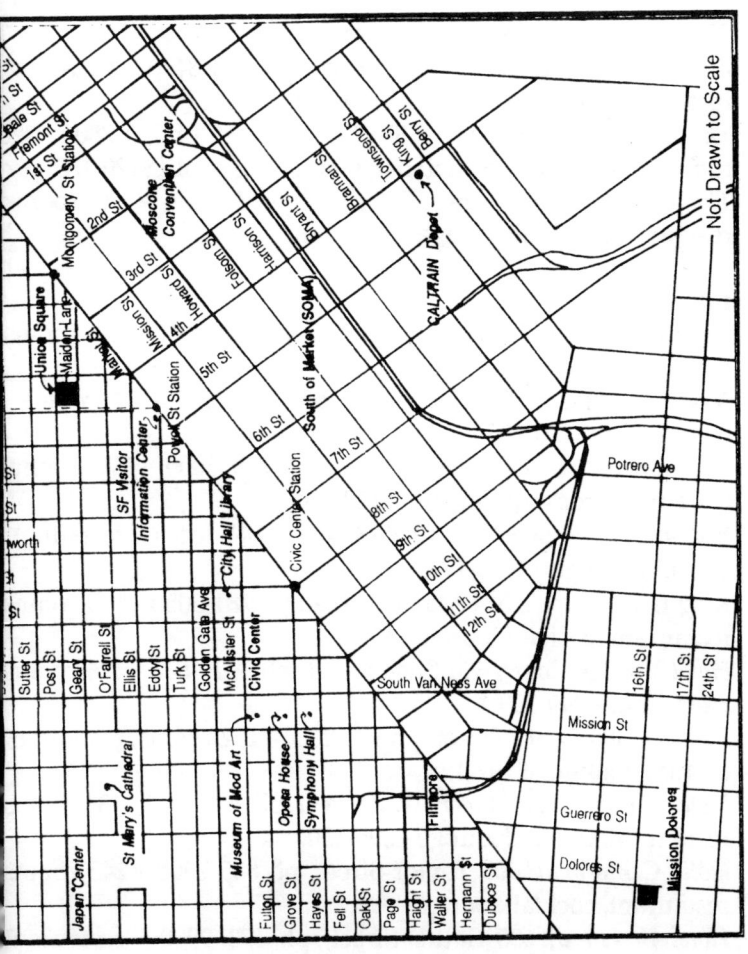

Sheraton at Fisherman's Wharf, 2500 Mason Street, ph 362 5500 - 525 rooms, restaurant, cocktail lounge - $149-169.

Inn at the Opera, 333 Fulton Street, ph 863 8400 - 48 rooms, restaurant, cocktail lounge - $120-215.

The Handlery Union Square, 351 Geary Street, ph 781 7800 - 375 rooms, restaurant, cocktail bar, swimming pool - $120-155.

The Orchard, 562 Sutter Street, ph 433 4434 - 96 rooms, restaurant, cocktail lounge - $110-140.

First Class

Galleria Park Hotel, 191 Sutter Street, ph 781 3060 - 177 rooms, restaurants, cocktail lounge - $130-145.

Monticello Inn, 127 Ellis Street, ph 392 8800 - 91 rooms - restaurant - $120-135.

Shannon Court, 550 Geary Street, ph 775 5000 - 173 rooms, restaurant, cocktail lounge - $120-130.

Bedford, 761 Post Street, ph 673 6040 - 144 rooms, restaurant, cocktail lounge - $110-175.

King George Hotel, 334 Mason Street, ph 781 5050 - 143 rooms, restaurant, cocktail lounge - $112.

Hotel Vintage Court, 650 Bush Street, ph 392 4666 - 106 rooms, restaurant - $99-129.

Raphael, 386 Geary Street, ph 986 2000 - 152 rooms, restaurant, cocktail lounge - $107-128.

Hotel Union Square, 114 Powell Street, ph 397 3000 - 131 rooms, restaurant, cocktail lounge - $95-130.

Hotel Californian, 405 Taylor Street, ph 885 2500 - 243 rooms, restaurant, cocktail lounge - $94.

Hotel Beresford, 635 Sutter Street, ph 673 9900 - restaurant, cocktail bar - $85-94.

Andrews Hotel, 624 Post Street, ph 563 6877 - 48 rooms, restaurant next door - $82-119.

Lombard Hotel, 1015 Geary Street, ph 673 5232 - 100 rooms, restaurant (breakfast and lunch daily, dinner Thurs-Sat) - $69-93.

Cornell Hotel, 715 Bush Street, ph 421 3154 - 45 rooms (all non-smoking), restaurant - $65-95.

Budget

Pacific Bay Inn, 520 Jones Street, ph 673 0234 - $65-75.

Adelaide Inn, 5 Isadora Duncan, ph 441 2261 - 18 rooms (shared facilities) - $42-48.

Sheehan Hotel, 620 Sutter Street, ph 775 6500 (old YWCA) - doubles with private facilities $55.

AYH-Hostel At Union Square, 312 Mason, ph 788 5604 - 218 beds, 30 with private bath - AYH Membership required - from $14 per person.

LOCAL TRANSPORT

From the Airport

SFO is 24km (15 miles) south of downtown San Francisco, a 20 to 30 minute trip by car.

The following companies operate services from the airport.

Airport Express, 865 Post Street, ph 775 5121, have a service every 20 minutes from 5.30am and 10.30pm between SFO and Union Square hotels. Other areas by reservation. **Fare is $9 adults, $7 children 5-11.**

Yellow Airport Shuttle, 80 Charter Oak, ph 282 7433, have a twenty-four hour service from SFO. **Reservations are required, and fares are $9 adults, $5 children 6-12.**

SFO Airporter, 923 Folsom Street, ph 495 8404, has a non-stop motor coach service between SFO and Downtown, Union Square. No reservations are need, and there are departures to and from the airport every twenty minutes, 5am-11pm. **Fare is $8 one-way, $14 round trip.**

Marin Airporter, ph 461 4222, services the greater North Bay. Departures every half hour, 6am-midnight. No reservations needed. **One way fares $9-13 adults, half-fare for children 5-12.**

Public Transport

San Francisco Municipal Railway (MUNI), 949 Presidio Avenue, ph 673 6864, is responsible for the operation of buses, trolley cars, metro street cars and the historic cable cars.

There are seventy-five public transit lines, including express lines during peak hours and a service to Candlestick Park for sporting events. Wheelchair access varies per route, but all Metro stations are fully accessible.

The standard fare is $1 ($2 for cable cars), and exact change is required. There are monthly, 1-day and 3-day passes available. Transfers are free with fare, and are valid for two changes of vehicle in any direction for a limited time of around 90 minutes. A full colour street and transit map can be bought at **local bookstores for $2.**

Cable Cars

The cable cars operate daily 6am-1am, **the fare is $2,** and exact change is not required. Tickets can be purchased on board, or beforehand at self-service ticket machines. A conductor will collect the fare or ticket after you board.

MUNI operates thirty-seven cars on three lines, Powell-Mason Line, Powell-Hyde Line, and the California Line. The route names appear on the front and back of each car, and along the roof in different colours.

Although the cable cars are often crowded with tourists taking a ride for the fun of it, they are a legitimate form of transport, and the best way to get from, say, Fisherman's Wharf to Union Square, and to the San Francisco Shopping Centre at Market and 5th Streets, a must for any dedicated shopper.

There are a few things to remember about riding the cable cars:

* Board at designated stops - look for the maroon and white cable car stop signs, or the yellow band painted between the rails. It is not necessary to wait in line and board at the beginning of a route. In fact, if you walk to the next stop you

will not have so long to wait, as some people only go on or two stops so they can say they rode on a cable car.
* Watch for signs indicating *Do Not Board in This Area*.
* Wait on the footpath and wave to the gripman to stop.
* Board on either side when the car has stopped.
* Keep clear of the space between the gripman and the lever when you wish to alight, and wait for the car to stop.
* If you miss your stop, wait for the next. The cars stop at almost every corner on their routes, so it won't be a long walk back.

The History of the Cable Car

Since they are so much a part of the city, it is only fair to know something of their history. The cable car was introduced to San Francisco on August 2, 1873, by Scottish wire cable manufacturer Andrew Hallidie, after he witnessed an accident in which a horse-drawn carriage faltered and rolled backward downhill, dragging the horses behind it.

The first cable car travelled down Clay Street on Nob Hill, and was an immediate success. It not only created a vital link in the public transportation system, Hallidie's invention also opened the door for building on steep hills, which until that time was thought to be impossible.

Throughout the late 1800s, there were 600 cars operated by eight transit companies, covering twenty-one routes and a total of 52.8 miles. Then came the earthquake of 1906, which, with the fires that followed, destroyed almost the entire system. When the city was rebuilt, only a few lines were restored, the other routes being serviced by electric trollies. The number of cable cars dwindled. Referendums in 1947 and 1954 allowed the cable cars to continue operating, although the service was cut back to the current three lines.

In 1982, the system was shut down again and an enormous two-year restoration was undertaken, including cars, track and cables. The trackway and the Washington & Mason house rebuilding cost the city $63.5 million. State and ral funds, plus $10 million in private donations, paid for the work. An additional $4 million was spent on renovating the cable cars.

BART

Bay Area Rapid Transport, 800 Madison Street, Oakland, ph 788-BART, has rail lines linking San Francisco with East Bay and Daly City. In San Francisco, trains run underground along Market Street, stopping at Embarcadero, Montgomery & Powell Streets and the Civic Center.

Trains run:
6am-midnight Mon-Sat,
9am-midnight Sun, and fares vary according to distance travelled.
All trains and stations are wheelchair accessible, and for information regarding schedules, fares, and special services, phone the number above.

Streetcars

These are gradually being replaced by the MUNI Metro, a subway that will run alongside and under BART in the downtown area. Presently there are five lines, with the letters J, K, L, M and N, and they all travel up and down Market Street past the Civic Center, then proceed in different directions.

AC Transit

Buses connect San Francisco with East Bay cities in Alameda and West Contra Costa counties, including Oakland and Berkeley.

In San Francisco, AC transit buses depart daily from the Transbay Terminal at 1st and Mission Streets. During peak hours, buses run eight to thirty minutes apart, and in off-peak at fifteen to sixty minute intervals. Complete timetable information can be obtained from drivers, or by phoning 83 2882. *Fares* vary according to distance travelled, and m buses accommodate wheelchair passengers.

Caltrain

There is a *daily rail service* between San Francisco and San Jose, 5am-10pm, with a *midnight service* from SF to San Jose on Fri and Sat.
Mid day and weekend trains run one to two hours apart, but there are extra services during peak hours.

Connections can be made at the San Francisco station to Golden Gate transit buses for points in Marin County.
 At the San Jose station, the Santa Cruz/Caltrain Connector shuttlebus provides service to Santa Cruz.
Fares vary with distance travelled. Call 557 8661 for detailed information.

Samtrans

Buses service San Mateo County and provide transportation to and from downtown San Francisco. Exact fare is required, and varies with distance travelled. Contact SamTrans, ph 761 7000, for exact routes and fares. Most buses provide wheelchair service.

Golden Gate Transit Bus Service

This company runs a daily service between San Francisco and North Bay communities, including Sausalito, Mill Valley, Tiburon, San Rafael and points as far north as Santa Rosa.
 In the city, buses stop along Lombard and Van Ness Streets, Geary Boulevard, and in the Financial District.
 Contact Golden Gate Transit, ph 332 6600, for exact timetables. Fares vary according to distance, and many buses are wheelchair accessible.

Amtrak

Trains depart from Oakland and San Jose daily.
There is a shuttle service to and from SF, departing from TransBay Terminal and CalTrain Station.

Ferry Services

Golden Gate Transit Ferry Service, ph 332 6600, operates daily between the San Francisco Ferry Building at the Embarcadero, and terminals in Larkspur and Sausalito.

The first ferry from SF to Sausalito leaves at 7.50am Mon-Fri, 11.30am Sat-Sun, *and the last ferry* leaves Sausalito at 7.20pm Mon-Fri, 6.10pm on Sat-Sun.

The first ferry from SF to Larkspur leaves at 7am Mon-Fri, 10.45am Sat-Sun, *and the last ferry* leaves Larkspur at 7.35pm Mon-Fri, 5.45pm Sat-Sun.

Red & White Fleet, ph 546 2700, has ferries departing daily from Pier 43 1/2 at Fisherman's Wharf for destinations including Sausalito, Angel Island, Alcatraz.
The service to Marine World Africa USA in Vallejo departs from Pier 41. Phone for times, timetables and advance purchase information.

Blue & Gold Fleet, ph 705 5555, sail under the Golden Gate and Bay Bridges and around Alcatraz Island on a 95-minute tour of the San Francisco Bay. Tours depart from Pier 39 daily.

Taxis

As with any city in the world, this is the most expensive way to travel, but if you need one, there's no problem in picking one up, and it doesn't cost any more to phone for one.
Here are a few phone numbers:
Allied Taxi, ph 826 9494;
City Cabs, ph 468 7200;
De Soto Cabs, ph 673 1414;
Luxor Cabs, ph 282 4141;
Pacific, ph 986 7220;
Veteran's Cabs, ph 552 1300;
Yellow Cabs, ph 626 2345.

Car

Driving in San Francisco is a whole new ball game.

Firstly, one-way streets abound, but these are clearly marked on most street maps, so it is best to plan your journey before starting out.

Secondly, cable cars have absolute right-of-way, which is only fair as they can hardly jump off their tracks to avoid a collision. Also, during rainy days the tracks tend to be slippery, so it is best to avoid them. Lastly, there are those hills.

Always use low gear when driving down them, and when parking on a hill there are a few laws to observe. **Yes, laws!**
You must engage the hand brake;
put the car into gear;
if facing downhill, the wheels must be turned towards the kerb;
if facing uphill, the wheels must be turned away from the kerb.

Failure to observe these laws will result, at best, in a parking ticket, at worst, the car will not be there when you return, and who knows how much damage it will have done on its merry way down the hill.

In fact, you may not have to worry about the parking laws at all, because finding a spot on the street is not that easy. There are metered zones, five-minute parking zones, disabled zones, commercial zones, and no parking zones, which are all clearly marked.

Don't ignore the restrictions because the local police are very efficient at towing away illegally parked cars, and it costs a fortune to get them out of hock.
There are plenty of parking stations in the congested areas, but they are not cheap. **Also many of the hotels do not provide parking for guests.** In short, a car can be a nuisance

in the city, and with the good public transport system, you don't really need one.

But it is, of course, a bonus if you want to travel further afield, and here is a list of car rental companies.

Avis, 675 Post Street, ph 885 5011 (toll free 800-331-1212); at SFO, ph 877 6780; at Oakland Airport, ph 562 9000.

Budget, 321 Mason Street, ph 875 6850 (toll free 800-527-0700); at SFO, ph 875 6850; at Oakland Airport, ph 568 2552.

Hertz, 433 Mason Street, ph 771 2200 (toll free 800-654-3131); at SFO, ph 877 1600; at Oakland Airport, ph 568 1177.

EATING OUT

San Francisco has around 3,300 restaurants, so obviously if you ate out every night, it would take almost ten years to try them all. It would also reduce your bank balance considerably.

Following is a selection rated on the price of a main course:
Expensive - $20+;
Moderate - $10-20;
Reasonable - under $10.

DOWNTOWN

Donatello Ristorante in the Donatello Hotel, 501 Post Street, ph 441 7182 - northern Italian cuisine - open Mon-Fri 11.30am-2pm, daily 6-11pm - **Expensive.**

Marrakech Moroccan, 419 O'Farrell Street, ph 776 6717 - premier Moroccan restaurant for 22 years - open nightly 6-10pm - **Moderate.**

Trader Vic's, 20 Cosmos Place, ph 776 2232 - Polynesian cuisine - open Mon-Fri 11.30am-2.30pm, nightly 5-11pm, supper Mon-Sat till 12.30am - **Expensive.**

Salmagundi, 442 Geary Street, ph 441 0894 - gourmet souperie, plus quiches and salads - open daily 11am-midnight - **Reasonable.**

Lehr's Greenhouse, 74 Sutter Street, ph 474 6478 - the city's finest Angus steaks and seafood in a garden setting - open daily 6.30am-10pm - **Moderate**.

NOB HILL

Bella Voce Ristorante & Bar, Fairmont Hotel, cnr Mason & California Streets, ph 772 5199 - Italian - open daily 6.30am-3pm, 5.30-11pm - **Expensive**.
Big Four, Huntington Hotel, 1075 California Street, ph 771 1140 - American - open for breakfast, lunch and dinner - **Expensive**.

UNION SQUARE

John's Grill, 63 Ellis Street (between Stockton and Powell), ph 986 3274 - SF landmark, used for the movie *The Maltese Falcon* - large menu - open Mon-Sat 11am-10pm, Sun 5-10pm - **Moderate**.
"Lefty" O'Doul's, 333 Geary Street, ph 982 8900 - cafeteria-style American food in a room studded with sports photos and memorabilia - **Reasonable**.
Iron Horse Restaurant, 19 Maiden Lane, ph 362 8133 - a landmark restaurant serving elegant northern Italian food - open Mon-Sat 11.30am-10.30pm, Sun 4.30-10.30pm - **Moderate**.

FISHERMAN'S WHARF

Alcatraz Bar & Grill, Pier 39, ph 434 1818 - California cuisine, pizza and fish - **Reasonable**.
Gaylord's, Ghirardelli Square, ph 771 8822 - Indian cuisine - open daily 11.45am-2pm, 5-11pm - **Moderate**.
Chowders, Pier 39, Space A-3, ph 397 4737 - light meals including chowder in a sour-dough bowl, grilled crab sandwiches - open daily 10.30am-8.30pm (until 10.30pm Fri-Sun) - **Reasonable**.
Neptune's Palace, Pier 39, ph 434 4424 - Seafood - open for lunch and dinner daily aa.30am-9pm - **Expensive**.

For light lunches, there are a couple of places along Beach Street, that have good sandwiches, without the crowds on the main Jefferson Street.

CHINATOWN

Imperial Palace, 919 Grant Avenue, ph 982 8889 - open Sun-Thurs 11.30am-1am, Fri-Sat 11.30am-2am - **Expensive**.
Hang Ah Tea Room, 1 Hang Ah Street off Sacramento Street, ph 982 5686 - open daily 10am-9pm - **Reasonable**.
Cathay House, 718 California Street, ph 982 3388 - landmark restaurant since 1938 - open daily for lunch and dinner until 9.30pm - **Moderate**.

COW HOLLOW/UNION STREET

Prego, 2000 Union Street, ph 563 3305 - Italian cuisine - open daily 11.30am-midnight - **Moderate**.
L'Entrecote de Paris, 2032 Union Street, ph 931 5006 - traditional French cuisine - open Mon-Thurs 11.30am-11pm, Fri-Sat until midnight, Sun until 10pm - **Expensive**.
Sushi Chardonnay, 1785 Union Street, ph 346 5070 - Japanese buffet - open Tues-Sun 11.30am-2pm, Tues-Thurs 5.30-10pm, Fri Sat 5.30-11pm, Sun 5-10pm - **Moderate**.
Perry's, 1944 Union Street, ph 922 9022 - open daily 9am-2am - **Reasonable**.

ENTERTAINMENT

The Bay City has more than its fair share of bars, discos, and performing arts venues, so here is only the tip of the iceberg.
San Francisco's version of Half-Tix is STBS, on Stockton Street at Union Square. Payment for half-price tickets is in cash only. Full price advance tickets may be purchased with Mastercard or Visa. Open Tues-Sat noon-7.30pm.

For full information on cultural performances and nightlife, get hold of the pink section of the Sunday *San Francisco Examiner and Chronicle*, or a copy of *Key* from your hotel or a newsstand. Or, you could ring the theatres listed below.

Theatres

Cable Car Theatre, 430 Mason Street, ph 861 6895.
Mason Street Theater, 340 Mason Street, ph 981-SHOW.
Marines Memorial Theatre, 609 Sutter Street, ph 771 6900.
Theatre on the Square, 450 Post Street, ph 433 9500.
Zephyr Theatre, 25 Van Ness Street, ph 861 6895.

Cinemas

There are over thirty cinema complexes in San Francisco, and their programs and show times are listed in the publications mentioned above.

Cabaret

The *Club Fugazi*, 678 Green Street, ph 421 4222, has become an institution with its show "Beach Blanket Babylon" that has been running since 1974. Show times are Wed-Thurs 8pm, Fri-Sat 7pm & 10pm, Sun 3pm & 7pm (under-21s admitted to the 3pm show only).
New Orleans Room at the Fairmont Hotel, 950 Mason Street, ph 772 5259. Top quality live shows are offered nightly 8pm-midnight, with no cover change.
Johnny Loves, 1500 Broadway at Polk, ph 931 8021 - supper club atmosphere complemented by live jazz and bistro-style menu - bar open daily 5pm-2am, dinner nightly 6-10pm.

Headline Concerts

Greek Theatre, UC Berkeley, ph 762 2277
Oakland Coliseum, ph 762-BASS
Shoreline Amphitheatre, Mountain View, ph 762-BASS
Slims, 333 Eleventh Street, ph 621 3330
The Warfield, 982 Market Street, ph 775 7722.

Jazz

Bajones, 1062 Valencia Street, ph 282 2522
Jazz At Pearl's, 256 Columbus Street, ph 291 8255
Kimball's, 300 Grove Street, ph 861 5555
Lascaux, 248 Sutter Street, ph 391 1555
Pasand Lounge, 1875 Union Street, ph 922 4498
Tropical Haight, 582 Haight Street, ph 558 8019.

Blues - R & B

Lou's Pier 47, 300 Jefferson Street, ph 771 0377
Last Day Saloon, 406 Clement Street, ph 387 6343
Rockin Robins, 1840 Haight Street, ph 221 1960.

Dance Clubs - SoMa (South of Market Street)

Club DV 8, 540 Howard Street, ph 777 2217
DNA Lounge, 375 11th Street, ph 626 1409
Holy Cow, 1535 Folsom Street, ph 861 6906
Paradise Lounge, 1501 Folsom Street, ph 861 6906
Townsend, 177 Townsend Street, ph 974 6020.

Comedy

Cobb's Club, 2801 Leavenworth Street, ph 928 4320
Holy City Zoo, 408 Clement Street, ph 386 4242
Improv, 401 Mason Street, ph 441 7787
Punch Line, 444 Battery Street, ph 397PLSF.

Bars

Buena Vista Cafe, 2765 Hyde Street
The Fillmore Grill, 2301 Fillmore Street
Golden Gate Bar & Grill, 3200 Fillmore Street
Hard Rock Cafe, 1699 Van Ness
Margaritaville, 1787 Union Street

Pierce St Annex, 3138 Fillmore Street
Rockin Robins, 1840 Haight Street
SF Brewing Co, 155 Columbus Avenue
Southside, 1190 Folsom Street.

Pubs

Ginberg's Pub, 400 Bay Street
Harrington's Pub, 460 Larkin Street
Penny Farthing Pub, 900 Bush Street
Tarr and Feathers, 2140 Union Street
Clancy's Saloon, 734 Irving Street,
S. Holmes Esq Public House & Drinking Salon, 480 Sutter St.

SHOPPING

Union Square

The grass and treed area of *Union Square* is bordered by Powell, Geary, Stockton and Post Streets, and surrounded by department stores:
I Magnin, Macy's, Neiman-Marcus, FAO Schwarz, Gucci and Hermes are found on **Stockton Street;**
a block to the east, **Grant Avenue** has a variety of stores, including Tiffany & Co;
north on **Post Street** are Brooks Brothers, Cartier, Gump's and Sak's Fifth Avenue, as well as upmarket boutiques and jewellery stores;
the Chanel boutique and the Morris building are in **Maiden Lane,** which runs between Stockton and Kearny Streets.

Two blocks south, at 865 Market Street, near 5th Street, is the *San Francisco Shopping Centre*, a nine level mall, with the top four levels occupied by Nordstrom department store. The other levels have over ninety specialist stores and restaurants.

Embarcadero Centre

Situated on Sacramento Street, near the foot of Market Street, the Centre consists of the lower three levels of four adjoining skyscrapers, and covers eight city blocks. There are over 140 stores and restaurants, and some of the best shopping in San Francisco.

Fisherman's Wharf

Pier 39
The pier was once used by cargo ships, but now it has over 100 specialty shops and restaurants, a 2-level carousel, a video game arcade, and is always crowded with tourists. There is a light-hearted carnival atmosphere, with free entertainment, and it's worth a visit, even if you don't intend to shop.

The Anchorage
Situated on Jefferson Street, between Leavenworth and Jones Streets, has some good restaurants and entertainment, but I wasn't too impressed with the shops.

The Cannery
In the next block, heading east, the building was originally the Del Monte peach canning plant. It now has over fifty specialty shops and restaurants, covering three floors. I think it has more to offer than The Anchorage.

Ghirardelli Square
On the corner of North Point and Larkin Streets, Ghirardelli Square is named after Domingo Ghirardelli, an Italian chocolate manufacturer who arrived in San Francisco in 1849. He built the complex of red brick buildings between 1900 and 1916. The chocolate company decided to sell the building and relocate in the early 1960s, so Mrs William P. Roth and her son, William Matson Roth, bought the property to save it from demolition. Extensive renovation work was carried out over

the next six years, and Ghirardelli Square now has fourteen buildings and eight levels containing shops, theatres, restaurants, cafes, and a chocolate shop. There's an information booth in the middle of the central plaza where you can pick up a copy of a free booklet that sets out a walking tour of the Square.

SIGHTSEEING

If you have hired a car, there is a **49-Mile Scenic Drive** that you can take which covers all the major sights, and also allows for some terrific views of the bay and ocean.

Maps can be obtained from the Visitor Information Center at Powell & Market Streets, and you are advised to follow the map to the letter, as it uses many one-way streets. Some people have tried to do the trip in the reverse direction, only to end up in a complete muddle.

For those who are going to rely on Shanks's pony and public transport, the following section is divided into the various districts of San Francisco.

FISHERMAN'S WHARF

This area has to be the biggest tourist spot in the city, and one the locals rarely visit.

It is located along Jefferson Street, between Hyde Street and the Embarcadero, on the northern waterfront.

It is easily reached from the Downtown area by cable car, and the trip allows great views of the Bay, Alcatraz, Lombard Street, and the Victorian houses on Russian Hill.

Strange as it may seem to the visitor, the Wharf is still the centre of the city's fishing industry, with over 200 boats per day bringing in their catches.

Day and night, the area is always teeming with people, and there are always plenty of buskers vying for your attention, and your money. On Beach Street, from the cable car turntable at the end of Hyde Street to the Maritime Museum, there are dozens of stalls offering hand-made and home-made goods.

Maritime Museum, ph 556 3002, looks a bit like a ship, and was built in 1939, as a bathing house. Now it contains whaling, fishing and sailing exhibits, and a large collection of model ships, including one of the *Preussen*, the largest wind-powered ship ever built. All in all, it is a very interesting place to visit, *and is open daily (in summer) 10am-6pm, Wed-Sun (winter) 10am-5pm.*

Aquatic Park is directly in front of the Museum, and from its eastern end the **Hyde Street Pier** stretches out into the water. Moored at the pier are five historic ships - *Balclutha, Eureka, C.A. Thayer, Eppleton Hall* and *Alma* - and all are open to the public. In fact, seven of San Francisco's historic ships are National Historic landmarks, and two more are in this area - the submarine *Pampanito* is berthed at Pier 45, and *Jeremiah O'Brien* is docked at Pier 3, Fort Mason.

Also on the Hyde Street Pier is the Small Boat shop where museum boat-builders conserve original small craft and construct replicas.

Walk back to Jefferson Street, turn left and continue walking along past the fish restaurants on one side, and the Cannery and Anchorage Shopping Centres on the other. Then you come to Pier 45, where the submarine museum is housed, and which is, incidentally, the real Fisherman's Wharf; then Pier 43 1/2, from where the Red & White Fleet ferries leave; then Pier 43, where you buy tickets for trips on the Red & White ferries; then Pier 41, from where the Blue & Gold ferries leave; then Pier 39. (For those who are wondering, as I did, what happened to all the even numbered piers, they are south of the Bay Bridge, though for some reason they seem to start with 24.)

Pier 39 has already been mentioned in the Shopping section, but it really deserves more than that. It is at this pier that you get your tickets for trips on the *Blue & Gold ferries*, and also where you can take a *Cable Car Fun Tour* around the city. I hasten to add that, although they look like the cable cars, they are actually buses impersonating cable cars, and can therefore travel to many more places than the real thing.

There are also young boys on cycle-rickshaws, hollering for you to hire them to take you on short trips.

For those interested in looking for Victorian houses, the *Victorian Shop* at Pier 39 has maps, and can arrange tours of those that are open to the public.
For more information, ph 781 4470.

Another of the Pier's attractions is *The San Francisco Experience*, on the 2nd level, near the entrance. It is a 220-seat theatre with seven screens, thirty-two speakers, three projectors, surroundsound and fog simulator, which combine to allow viewers to feel the earth shake during the 1906 earthquake, and watch the city erupt into flames. Other aspects of the city's history are also featured, and the show lasts about half an hour. It runs more or less continuously in summer. To check for times and ticket prices, ph 982 7394.

Other attractions at Fisherman's Wharf include: **The Wax Museum**, 145 Jefferson Street, ph 885 4975, open Sun-Thurs 9am-11pm, Fri 9am-midnight in summer, with shorter hours in winter; **Ripley's Believe It or Not! Museum**, 175 Jefferson Street, ph 771 6188, open daily 9am-midnight in summer; **Guinness Museum of World Records**, 235 Jefferson Street, ph 771 9890, open daily 10am-11pm in summer.

Now let's take a few ferry trips from Fisherman's Wharf.
Alcatraz Island
In 1775, Spanish explorer Juan Manuel de Ayala charted San Francisco Bay, and named the island "La Isla de los Alcatraces" - the Island of the Pelicans - its only inhabitants.

Sitting in the middle of the Bay, the island was an ideal defensive location, and in 1853 the Army began to build fortifications, some of which are still in situ. During the Spanish-American War, the island became a confinement facility for prisoners-of-war. In 1933, control passed to the newly formed Federal Bureau of Prisons, and it was redesigned as a maximum security facility to house 'incorrigible' civilian inmates from other Federal institutions. So it became 'The Rock', made even more famous by Hollywood in movies about such inmates as Al 'Scarface' Capone and Robert Stroud, known as 'The Birdman of Alcatraz', who actually did not have a window in his cell in this prison so did not have any feathered visitors, but did keep birds in other places where he was detained.

During its time as a Federal prison, thirty-six men tried to escape, in fourteen separate attempts, and three men actually made it off the island. However, it is presumed that they perished in the cold, swift waters of the Bay, as none of them were ever seen again.

The Prison closed on March 21, 1963, due to the expense of its upkeep. Then in 1969, a group of Native American Indians cited an 1868 treaty, and claimed and occupied the island. They wanted to establish the island as a cultural, spiritual and educational centre, and although they didn't achieve this, they did draw attention to the problems of the American Indians.

In 1972, Alcatraz was made part of the Golden Gate National Recreation Area, administered by the National Park Service, and it now has over 750,000 visitors every year.

The Red & White Fleet run tours to the island, and tickets can be purchased at Pier 41.

An excellent 35-minute audio tour of the cellblocks is available, and can be purchased with your ferry ticket for a **total cost of $8.75 adult, $4.25 child 5-11.**

> Don't expect to be able to buy a ticket for the same day, though, you have to book at least one day in advance, sometimes more. The ferries have snack bars on board for those people who can't go a couple of hours without food, but more importantly, especially if you have children with you, they have toilets. The only *toilets* on the Rock are at the dock, and they are those portable-type affairs that really should only be used in an emergency. Plans are afoot to build restrooms, but work is progressing slowly.

Upon arrival at the island you are provided with a map of a self-guiding walk, and a ranger gives a short talk on the facilities, or lack thereof, and the pitfalls of wandering off the beaten track, then you can watch a 12-minute audio-visual presentation of the history of the island. You are then free to continue the walk up to the cellblocks, pick up your audio gear, and experience life in prison.

A visit to Alcatraz is a very interesting way to spend a few hours, and although the brochures advise a certain degree of fitness is required, I did not find the uphill walk daunting in the least, and I am not exactly a fitness freak.

One thing to bear in mind, though, is that you should allow at least ten minutes to walk from the cellhouse down to the dock, and the last ferry leaves at 4.15pm. I would suggest that you don't miss it.

Sausalito

A picturesque seaside village, 13km (8 miles) from Downtown, Sausalito can best be reached by ferry, and there is a choice of two companies.
The Red & White Fleet leaves from Pier 43 1/2 Fisherman's Wharf and **the return trip costs $9;**
Golden Gate Ferry leaves from the San Francisco Ferry Building, at the end of Market Street, and **the return fare is $8.** You can also travel to Sausalito by Gold- en Gate bus for $1.95 one-way, but it is a very ordinary way to get there.

> **Comment**
> Last time I visited, I went from Pier 43 1/2, but mistakenly returned by the other ferry, and can guarantee that it is a very long walk along The Embarcadero back to Fisherman's Wharf, where I was staying. Of course, I could have hired one of the cycle-rickshaws that were lying in wait for people who don't look at a ferry before they climb aboard, but it didn't look very far on my map. *C'est la vie*.

Sausalito is a town where people go to walk, shop, eat and drink, although I must say that some people take bicycles over on the ferry for healthier visits. But, getting back to the majority of people, the town's main street, Bridgeway, and two of the side streets, Princess and Caledonia, are shop after shop, after bar after shop. Some are supposed to be factory outlet shops, but I couldn't see that there was much difference in their wares or prices than could be found at Fisherman's Wharf.

The Village Fair, at 777 Bridgeway, is a complex of 30 shops and restaurants, and is one of the main attractions.

Angel Island
The Red and White Fleet sails to this 295ha (730 acres) state park from Pier 43 1/2, and the round trip fare, which includes admission to the park, is $8 adults, $5 children 5-11.

The park is open from 8am to sunset, and is very popular for hiking, cycling, fishing and picnicking. The ferries land at Ayala Cove where there are picnic facilities, barbecues and restrooms. These are also available at West Garrison. The 19km (12 miles) of hiking trails circle the island, and also lead to the top of Mount Caroline Livermore, 237m (776 ft) above the Bay.

Angel Island is rumoured to have been a pirate stronghold, and many think that there is a strong possibility of buried treasure on its shores. Dig away if you feel like it, but I don't think anyone has actually found anything of value.

Another way to get to the island is by ferry from Tiburon.

TELEGRAPH HILL

The Hill was named after the Morse Code Signal Station of 1853, and has stepped streets, garden lanes, cottages. It was home to numerous artists and writers.

Coit Tower, ph 274 0203, at the top of Filbert Street, honours Lillie Hitchcock Coit who bequeathed $125,000 for the beautification of San Francisco. A 360 degree view of the city can be obtained from the top of the tower, and inside are a history museum and Art Deco murals. The eccentric Ms Coit apparently chased fire engines, becoming a fire company mascot during the 1850s. The shape of the tower is said to represent a fire hose nozzle.

The tower is open daily 9am-4.30pm (10am-5.30pm March-Sept), and admission is $3 adults, $1 children.

The **Filbert Street Steps** begin at the east end of the Coit Tower parking lot, and the picturesque walk leads past clapboard houses with plenty of greenery, to the Embarcadero.

NORTH BEACH

This area is situated between Chinatown and Fisherman's Wharf and its colourful Barbary Coast past is still present in the neon-lit Broadway, with its strip joints, transsexual revues, and X-rated (and even lower) theatres.

It is a predominantly Italian district, with lots of Italian restaurants and bocci ball courts, and a piazza, **Washington Square Park**, which is dominated by the Church of St Peter and St Paul.

North Beach was the scene for the beginning of the Beat movement, and **Upper Grant Avenue** still has some remains of that Bohemian culture. Bars that were favourites of the Beat generation, such as Specs, Vesuvio's and Tosca, are worth visiting for their displays of memorabilia from the period. Across from the Tosca Cafe is **City Lights**, 261 Columbus Avenue, ph 362 8193, the first paperback bookstore in the country. It was the centre of the Bohemian movement in the 1950s, and still has an excellent range.

RUSSIAN HILL

The hill is mostly residential, but it has some lovely green parks and gardened cul-de-sacs, and offers great views of the Bay. Its most popular feature, though, is **Lombard Street**, 'the crookedest street in the world'. It is actually only one block, between Hyde and Leavenworth Streets, that is crooked but it is worth walking, or driving down it as it is so unique. It is also very pretty with plenty of flowers and greenery. I should emphasise the 'down' in that last sentence, as it would not be nearly so attractive walking or driving up. The nearby block, from Hyde to Leavenworth, is the steepest in the city.

CHINATOWN

Bordered by Kearny and Powell Streets on the east and west, and by Vallejo and Bush Streets on the north and south, Chinatown is a replica of all the Chinatowns all over the world (outside China). The Pagoda Gates are on Grant Avenue, and the centre of the district is **Portsmouth Square**, where the first Chinese immigrants settled in the 1850s. More than 100,000 Chinese San Franciscans live within a 20-block radius. This is the most densely populated area in the city.

Attractions in the district include the usual array of restaurants, shops, herb pharmacies and markets; Old St Mary's Church, California's first cathedral, built in 1854 by Chinese labourers; and Kong Chow Temple, the oldest family association in the United States.

NOB HILL

Originally settled by railroad and mining magnates Charles Croker, Leland Stanford, Mark Hopkins and Collis Huntingdon, Nob Hill can be reached by any of the three cable car lines. The mansions were all destroyed in the earthquake of 1906, the sole survivors on the hill being the Fairmont Hotel, 950 Mason Street, which had been built just prior to the earthquake, and the Pacific Union Club, 1000 California Street, a brownstone built in 1886 for silver king James Flood. In reality, only the shell of the Fairmont survived, the interior was refurbished and the hotel opened on the first anniversary of the earthquake.

The Neo-Gothic Episcopalian **Grace Cathedral**, the largest Gothic structure in the West, was built in 1928, and is found at 1051 Taylor Street. It is worth a visit for the doors at the top of the Cathedral steps. They are a copy of Lorenzo Ghiberti's *Doors of Paradise*, cast in bronze from the artist's original work.

FINANCIAL DISTRICT

Beginning at Montgomery Street and extending east towards the Embarcadero, this district is the 'Wall Street of the West', and its streets were among the first in San Francisco. They housed banks during the days of the Gold Rush, and after the discovery of the Nevada silver mines, San Francisco became firmly established as the financial centre of the West.

A.P. Giannini Plaza, between Pine and California Streets, is a combination mall and office building that commemorates the Italian banking magnate who, in 1904, opened the Bank of Italy which later became the Bank of America, one of the world's largest financial institutions.

The Wells Fargo Museum, 420 Montgomery Street, has artifacts, gold specimens, and photos of the Old West, including wanted posters. It also has a reconditioned nine-passenger stagecoach.

Transamerica Building, between Clay and Washington Streets, is the most striking feature on the City's skyline. Known locally as the 'Pyramid', albeit a rather convoluted one in shape, it is a 48-storey building, rising 260m (853 ft) from the street. There is a small lookout window on the 27th floor, which is open to the public.

Jackson Park Historical District, on the 700 block of Montgomery Street, is a small park surrounded by lanes and Victorian architecture. The original area's bordellos and criminals have been replaced by law offices, the best known being that of Melvin Belli, lawyer to the rich and famous.

SOMA (South of Market)

Situated between the Mission district and the industrial waterfront, SoMa is rapidly becoming the nightlife centre of the City. It was once called 'south of the slot' because of the cable car tracks on Market Street, and only contained old warehouses and industrial land. Now it is comparable to the SoHo district of New York City, but on a smaller scale.

MISSION

Mission Dolores, the sixth Franciscan mission on El Camino Real, was originally an Indian village that was settled by the Spanish in 1776. The Mission was named for the nearby lagoon, the Laguna de Nuestra Senora de los Dolores, and it and the Officers Club in the Presidio are the oldest buildings in San Francisco.

During the 1800s, the Mission district underwent a complete change of character, and was home to dance halls, saloons, gambling houses and race tracks. Then Germans and Scandinavians took up residence and the Spanish influence was completely eradicated.

After the earthquake, palm trees were planted, and the new buildings were topped with red tile roofs, reviving the Spanish look, and the mission was refurbished. In the wake of World War II many Hispanics returned to the area, and now the majority of the city's Mexican, Colombian, Nicaraguan, Guatemalan and Salvadoran population reside in the district.

The original Levi Strauss factory is located in Valencia Street.

The heart of the district is **24th Street**, which has a collection of shops and an outdoor market.

The **Mission San Francisco de Asis**, or Mission Dolores, is on the corner of Dolores and 15th Streets, ph 621 8203, and is open daily 9am-4.30pm, with a small admission charge. It has a mini-museum behind the chapel and a 20th century basilica next door, but the piece de resistance is the cemetery which has several famous and infamous residents.

Dolores Street is a very pretty street with stately palm trees along its centre, and it leads to **Dolores Park**, a peaceful spot with pepper and magnolia trees.

CASTRO

The Castro is around the junction of Market and Castro Streets, and is a hang-out for the gay population. The big times of the year for the locals are Halloween and the Gay Freedom Day Parade in June.

TWIN PEAKS

The original Spanish settlers named these hills 'Los Pechos de la Chola', which means 'The Breasts of the Indian Maiden'. Whatever you wish to call them, they offer the best views of central San Francisco, and are reached by following Market Street, which becomes Portola Drive. Don't be confused by the modern name, they are not the Twin Peaks of TV fame. Those particular peaks are in the State of Oregan.

HAIGHT-ASHBURY

The capital of the 'hippies' in the 1960s, with their free-love, anti-war, psychedelic drug culture, Haight-Ashbury became world famous. It now seems that while many people from other countries remember that time, the district itself has forgotten it. It is now, as it was before the hippie 'invasion', an upper-middle class neighbourhood, with some of the best Victorian houses in the City. Situated between two parks, the Golden Gate and Buena Vista, it is becoming a popular gathering place for the 'arty'.

GOLDEN GATE PARK

Golden Gate Park stretches from the Haight-Ashbury district to the ocean, and is one of the biggest metropolitan parks in the country, measuring approximately 5.6km (3.5 miles) long and 0.8km (0.5 miles) wide.

Originally sand dunes, it was landscaped in the early 1900s by John McLaren, and is now a very green area with lakes, a

250 CALIFORNIA AT COST

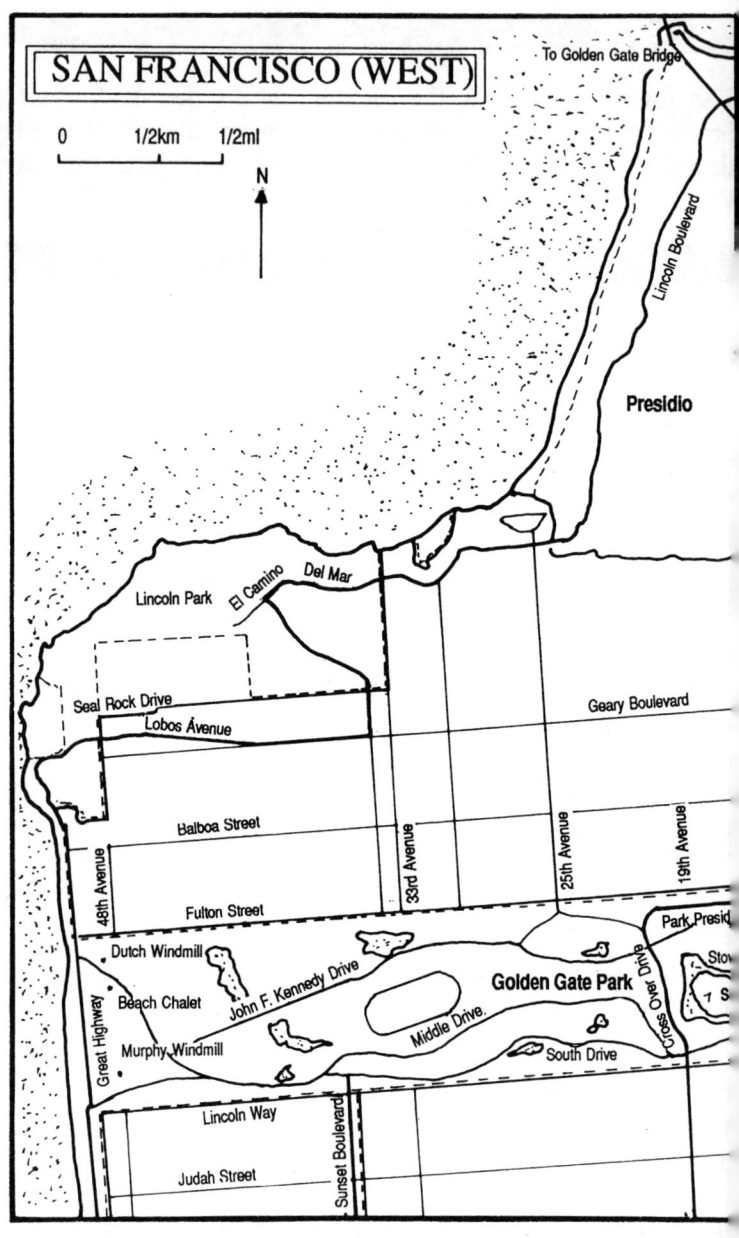

SAN FRANCISCO 251

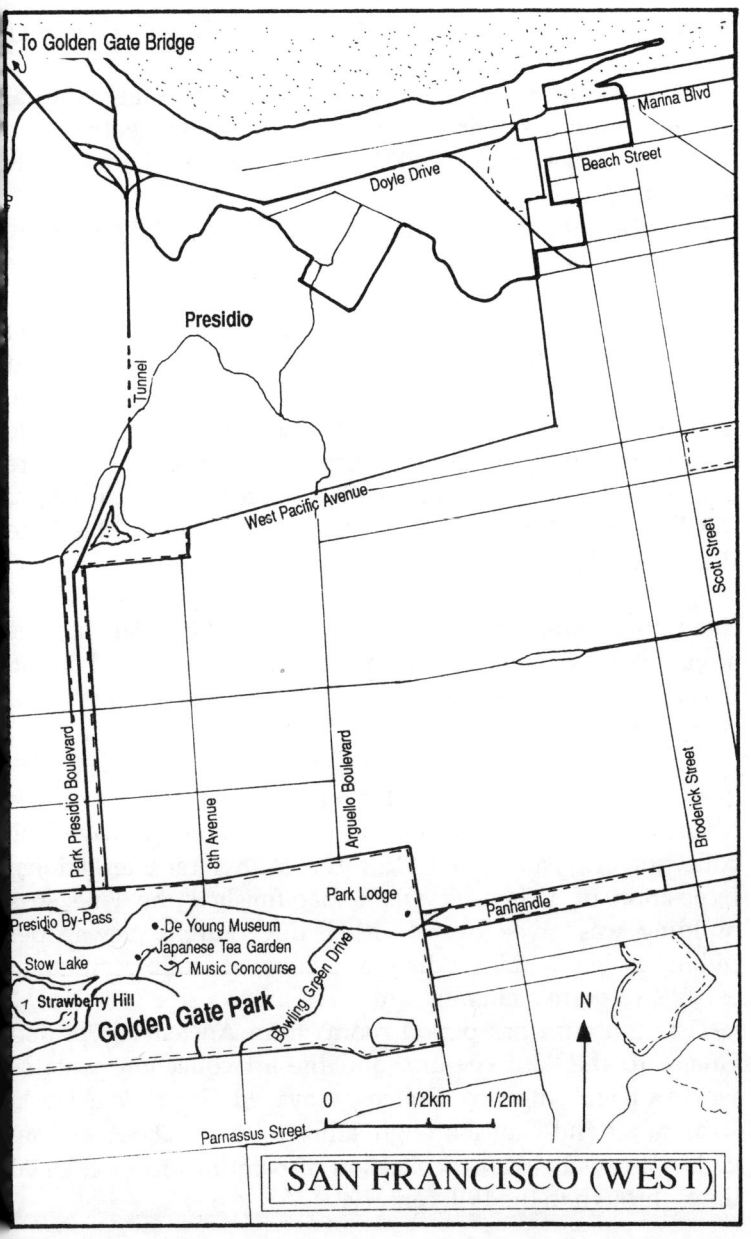

golf course, a polo field, a flycasting pool, tennis courts, a bowling green, a ball field, a riding academy, and a children's playground.

Apart from these, there are some very interesting cultural places within the park, and the information centre is in McLaren Lodge, ph 666 7200, just inside the park on John F. Kennedy Drive.

On weekends the Lodge is closed, but maps of the park are available at the kiosk near the carousel.

The *Golden Gate Park Culture Pass* is worth considering if you intend visiting the various museums, etc. It costs $10 and allows one single admission to the Asian Art Museum, California Academy of Sciences, Conservatory of Flowers, de Young Museum and the Japanese Tea Garden. Passes are available at the Visitor Information Center in Hallidie Plaza; TIX Bay Area, Union Square; McLaren Lodge in Golden Gate Park; and all participating attractions.

The **Conservatory**, ph 666 7017, is to the right of the entrance along John F. Kennedy Drive, and is modelled after a London garden house. It was built in 1879, and contains a myriad of plants and flowers.

The de Young Memorial Museum, ph 863 3330, is on the Music Concourse, which runs off John F. Kennedy Drive. The collection originated at the California Midwinter International Exposition of 1894, and when that finished the Fine Arts building was given over to M.H. de Young, a newspaper publisher who had been director-general of the Exposition, to establish a permanent museum.

The museum has period rooms from Ancient Egypt and Greece to the 20th century, and the art collection contains works of Fra Angelico, Rubens, Goya, El Greco, van Dyck, Rembrandt and Gainsborough, among others. The American gallery presents a good collection of paintings from colonial times through to the 19th century.

Opening hours are Wed-Sun 10am-5pm (to 8.45pm first Wed of the month). **Admission is $5 adults, $2 children 12-17, under 12 free.**
There is a cafe in the museum, open 10am-4pm, and a garden for al fresco dining.

The **Asian Art Museum**, ph 668 8921, is an annex of the de Young Museum, and features one of the most comprehensive Oriental art collections in the world, including the world-famous Avery Brundage Collection. There are conducted tours daily.

The **Japanese Tea Garden**, ph 666 7101, was crafted by a group of Osaka craftsman for the 1894 Midwinter International Exposition, and is a great place to take a break from the museums. There are pagodas, shrines, buddhas, and a Japanese tea room complete with kimono-clad waitresses.

> *Comment*
> It has always intrigued me how Japanese ladies shuffle along in those kimonos, and I have often wondered how they get on when they are in a hurry. Well, when at these gardens I found out. An errant, extremely small mouse wandered into the tea room, causing much disturbance, and all the waitresses except the lady in charge, hitched up their kimonos and ran in all directions. The aforementioned lady kept her cool, picked up a piece of wood, and despatched the mouse with a minimum of fuss. The little drama was worth the entry fee of $1 to the gardens.

The **California Academy of Sciences**, ph 221 5100, on the other side of the Music Concourse, is a three-in-one museum exhibiting natural history, astronomy and marine life displays.

The *Steinhart Aquarium* is home to more than 14,500 specimens of fish, as well as aquatic mammals, invertebrates, reptiles and amphibians. It is one of those aquariums where you walk through the middle of the tank, rather like walking on the ocean floor. There is also a hands-on area where little kids (and not so little kids) can pick up sea urchins and starfish. If you are finishing your tour of California in San Francisco it is quite possible you are a bit jaded in the aquarium department, but I am still wondering how many starfish per year are lost, or at least extremely disadvantaged, because of these hands-on exhibits.

The *Morrison Planetarium* has seven different shows a year, and explores black holes, quasars, pulsars, UFOs, neutron stars and other mysteries of the universe. The *Earth and Space Hall* has exhibits on many inexplicable things.

The *Wattis Hall of Man* has exhibits on human societies and their adaption to the environment. Exhibits cover arctic, tropical, temperate and desert regions. There are also displays of birds, insects, gems and mammals from different regions, and stones from the stomachs of dinosaurs.

The Academy of Sciences is open daily 10am-5pm (to 7pm in summer) and **admission is $6 adults, $3 children 12-17, $1 children 6-11. The Planetarium shows are $2.50 adults, $1.25 children 17 and under.**

The **Strybing Arboretum and Botanical Gardens** cover an area of 28ha (40 acres) and contain the *Garden of Fragrance*, the *Moon-Viewing Garden* and the *New World Cloud Forest*.

Other attractions in the park include **Stow Lake** which is open to rowing and paddle boats, and the **Dutch Windmill** along the beach front. A large stretch of John F. Kennedy Drive is closed to cars on Sundays from dawn till dusk to allow cyclists, roller skaters and strollers a free go.

PRESIDIO

The military base of San Francisco for over 200 years, the Presidio was founded by Colonel Juan Bautista de Anza and the Spanish settlers in 1776. The Mexicans took over the post in 1822, and the United States made it a possession of the government in 1846.

The Presidio was an active military establishment during the Civil War and was used for training Union soldiers. During World War II it was the home base for the Fourth Army, and now it is home to the Sixth Army.

With an area of around 646ha (16 acres), there are hiking trails through the property, but first stop should be the **Presidio Army Museum**, on Funston Avenue, near Lincoln Boulevard, ph 561 4115.

It has historical displays related to old San Francisco, and a collection of military uniforms and weapons. The nearby **Officers' Club**, on Moraga Avenue, includes part of the original Presidio, one of the first buildings constructed in the City.

GOLDEN GATE NATIONAL RECREATION AREA

The Golden Gate National Recreation Area is a 12,524ha (31,000 acres) metropolitan park that stretches north from San Francisco throughout the Bay Area. In the city area it forms a narrow band along the ocean front, then along the shoreline of the Bay from the Golden Gate Bridge to Aquatic Park.

Fort Point, ph 556 1693, is situated underneath the Golden Gate Bridge and is a three-tiered brick building built in 1853 to fortify the Bay during the Civil War, but it was never used for active defence. Situated at the end of Marine Drive, it is the only brick fort west of the Mississippi. It has a collection of cannons, a small museum, and a gift store. Free guided *tours are offered Wed-Sun*. The fort is closed on Mon and Tues.

From the Fort there is a footpath leading up to the observation area astride the Golden Gate Bridge, or if you are driving, take Lincoln Boulevard.

The **Golden Gate Bridge** is one of the longest suspension bridges in the world, with a main span of 1280m (4200 ft). For those who love statistics, the following information should suffice:

Length of one Cable - 2331.7m (7650 ft)

Diameter of Cable - 92.4cm (36.4 ins)

Wires in each Cable - 27,572

Total Wire used - 128,744km (80,000 miles)

Weight of Cable (suspenders & accessories) - 24,892 tonnes (24,500 tons)

Cable Contractor - John A. Roebling's Sons Company, Trenton and Roebling, New Jersey.

If you are game enough, you can walk across the bridge, along a daunting side path - not for the faint-hearted.

The Bridge has become the emblem of San Francisco, and indeed it seems to beckon you from most parts of the waterfront. The Oakland Bay Bridge, which many first-time visitors mistake for the Golden Gate, is in two sections, seeming to be propped up in the middle by Treasure Island. The Bay Bridge has two levels of traffic, the Golden Gate only one. Both bridges have a toll charge, the Bay Bridge for westbound traffic, the Golden Gate for southbound traffic.

Golden Gate Promenade is a 6km (3.5 miles) shoreline path that begins at Fort Point and continues to Aquatic Park, near Fisherman's Wharf. It allows access to the Presidio (see above), then the next detour should be to the Palace of Fine Arts.

Palace of Fine Arts

Situated at 3601 Lyon Street, at Marine Boulevard, the rococo Palace of Fine Arts is the only surviving building from the 1915 Panama-Pacific International Exposition, which celebrated the opening of the Panama Canal. It was almost demolished to make way for a real estate development, but in the mid-1960s it was saved by Walter Johnson and several millions from his private bank account.

The Palace is home to **The Exploratorium**, voted by *Scientific American* as "the best science museum in the world".

It is a 'hands-on' spectacle to the nth degree and you should plan to spend at least an hour, more if possible, adding a new dimension to your sensory organs.

The Exploratorium is open Tues-Sun 10am-5pm, Wed until 9.30pm, ph 561 0362.

Admission is $8 adults, $4 children 6-17. Near the Palace of Fine Arts is a lake that teems with ducks and swans, and is a great place for a picnic.

Next stop along the shoreline is the **Marina**, where some of the City's best-looking, best-equipped and top-priced yachts are docked, then nearby is **Marina Green**, a park that parallels the bay and is popular with cyclists, joggers, sunbathers and kite-fliers.

Fort Mason Center, Marina Boulevard and Buchanan Street, ph 441 5706, is a cluster of old army barracks and warehouses that were once a major military embarkation point. Now it is home to a variety of non-profit organisations, cultural groups, and environmental organisations, including Greenpeace. There is also a 5-star vegetarian restaurant and a selection of community art schools.

Permanently docked at the Fort is the **SS Jeremiah O'Brien**, a World War II Liberty Ship, and the only one of the original 2751 in original condition. Visitors are welcome to explore the ships (Mon-Fri 9am-3pm, Sat-Sun 9am-4pm), and an admission fee is charged, ph 441 3101.

Then it's a downhill walk to the Municipal Pier and Aquatic Park, where we began our tour.

NOTES

SPORT AND RECREATION
Golf
Golden Gate Park Course, 47th Avenue & Fulton, ph 751 8987 - 9 holes, over 1240m (1357 yds) - par 27.

Lincoln Park, 34th Avenue and Clement Street, ph 221 9911 - 18 holes, over 4646m (5081 yds) - par 68.

Harding Park, Skyline and Harding Park, ph 664 4690. Two courses: Harding Park - 18 holes, over 6069m (6637 yds) - par 72; Fleming Course - 9 holes, over 2118m (2316 yds) - par 32. Both courses have driving ranges and electric or pull carts.

Tennis
Most of the neighbourhood parks have tennis courts, phone the San Francisco Recreation & Park Department, 558 3643, for details.

Golden Gate Park Tennis Complex, ph 753 7032 (reservations ph 753 7101).

San Francisco Tennis Club, 645 Fifth Street, ph 777 9000.

Golden Gateway Tennis Club, 370 Drumm Street, ph 433 2936.

Bicycles
Start To Finish, 599 Second Street at Brannan, ph 243 8812; and 1619 Fourth Street, San Rafael, ph 459 3990. Rent mountain bikes, helmets, locks and everything you need.

Horse Riding
Golden Gate Park Stables, John F. Kennedy Drive, next to polo field, ph 668 7360.

Windsurfing
SF School of Windsurfing, Lake Merced, ph 750 0412 - lessons and rentals available.

Boating
Bay & Delta Yacht Charters, 3020 Bridgeway, Sausalito, ph 381 9503.

Swimming
North Beach Pool, Lombard & Mason Streets, North Beach, ph 274 0200.
Rossi Pool, Arguello & Anza Streets, Richmond, ph 666 7014.
Sava Pool, 19th Avenue and Wawona Street, Sunset, ph 753 7000.
Sheehan Hotel Pool and Fitness Centre, 620 Sutter and Mason Streets, ph 775 6500.

Health & Fitness Clubs
Bay Club Marathon Plaza, 303 Second Street, ph 543 9100.

Spectator Sports
Oakland Athletic Baseball, Oakland/Alameda County Coliseum, Hegenberger Road off 1-880. Accessible by BART. Tickets,
ph 638 6000.
San Francisco Giants Baseball, Candlestick Park, Exit of Highway 101.
San Francisco 49ers Football, Candlestick Park.
Golden State Warriors Basketball, Candlestick Park.

Horse Racing
Thoroughbred racing season August-January. Quarter horse racing February-April - Bay Meadows, intersection of Hillsdale Boulevard at Bayshore Freeway/US 101 (San Mateo), ph 574 7223.

TOURS
Walking Tours
City Guides, ph 557 4266, are sponsored by Friends of the San Francisco Public Library. Schedules can be obtained from any public library, the Visitor Information Centre, or the Holiday Plaza.
SF Heritage Walk, ph 441 3004. Based at the Haas-Lilienthal House, this group offers guided architectural tours to Victorian houses, as well as others along similar lines.

Friends of Recreation and Parks, McLaren Lodge, Golden Gate Park, ph 221 1311, have guided tours of the park, focusing on its history and flora.

The Strolling Nosh, ph 441 4221, is a tour focusing mainly on Fisherman's Wharf.

Sightseeing Tours
If you would rather see things on your own at your own pace, sightseeing maps are available at the Convention and Visitors Bureau at Halladie Plaza, or at the SF Municipal Railway at 949 Presidio Avenue,
Room 222.

If you prefer to join a group and have a local expert point out attractions, contact one of the following:
Cable Car Charters, Pier 41, ph 922 2425.
Gray Line Tours, ph 558 9400.
Carriage Charter, Pier 33, ph 398 0857.
Great Pacific Tour Co, 518 Octavia Street, ph 626 4499.

Gray Line Tours leave from the Transbay Terminal at 1st and Mission Streets (day tours) and from Union Square (evening tours). They have a free shuttle bus service between centrally located hotels and these departure locations. For hotel pick-up times, ph 558 9400.

Following is a sample of their tours.
Tour 1 - Deluxe City Tour - **$25 adult, $12.50 child** - 3.5 hours. Views San Francisco from Treasure Island (weather permitting), passes the Civic Center, Opera House, Davies Symphony Hall, then visits Old Mission Dolores. A stop is made at Twin Peaks, then a drive through Golden Gate Park with a visit to the Japanese Tea Gardens. Next stop Cliff House to see Seal Rock, then drive through the Presidio Army Base and across the Golden Gate Bridge with a stop at Vista Point North. The Tour concludes at Fisherman's Wharf.

Tour 12 - Muir Woods & Sausalito - **$28 adult, $14 child** - 3.5

hours. Drive across the Golden Gate and along Highway 1 to stroll through Muir Woods and admire the fabled Redwood, then on to Sausalito for a wander through the boutiques and galleries.

These tours can be **combined for a cost of $41.50 adult, $20.75 child.**

Tour 3 - San Francisco by Night, including Chinatown - **$25 adult, $12.50 child** - 3 hours. A 4 hour version of this tour can also be taken with dinner included.

Tour 6 - California Wine Country - **$42 adult, $21 child** - 9 hours.

Gray Line also have Heart of San Francisco package tours of up to 8 days/7 nights duration, ph 800 633 3000 (outside USA ph 818 988 7844).

NOTES

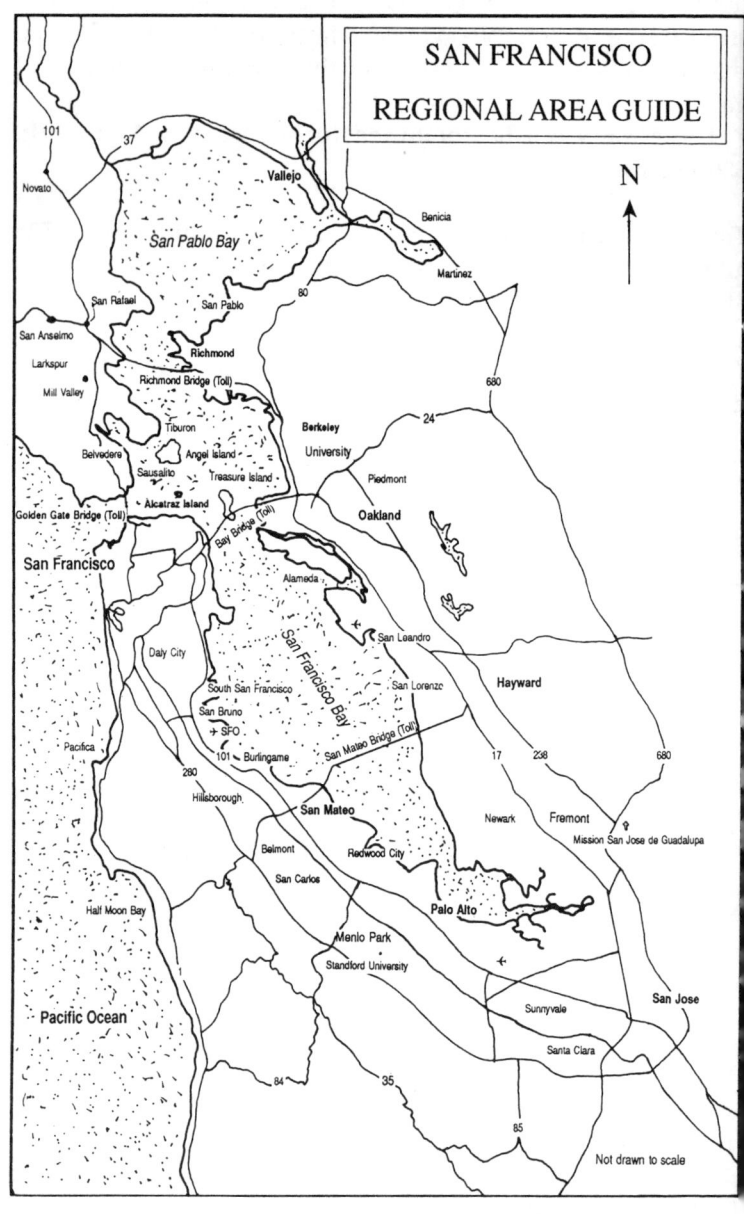

SAN FRANCISCO BAY AREA

San Francisco Bay, according to geologists, is a drowned river valley caused by glaciers melting around 10,000 years ago. This raised the sea level and caused the ocean to fill a canyon previously formed by the Sacramento and San Joaquin Rivers. Whatever the cause, the result is an extremely scenic and photographic Bay with a few interesting places to visit on day trips from San Francisco.

OAKLAND

The largest of the East Bay cities, Oakland was settled in the mid-19th century, but received a boost in population after the 1906 Earthquake with people wanting to get out of the city. They were able to live in Oakland, but they had to work in San Francisco, and by the 1930s there were thousands of people commuting every day. Their lives were made easier by the building of the Bay Bridge, an engineering feat which spans 7.2km (4.5 miles) of water. The building of the bridge also enabled more people to move to Oakland, and today the population of this industrial port is around 340,000.

HOW TO GET THERE
If travelling by car, drive over the Oakland Bay Bridge. A direct bus travels from the Transbay Terminal, Mission and 1st Streets.
BART connects Powell Street to Oakland City Center.

SIGHTSEEING

In the heart of the city is **Lake Merritt**. It has an area of 67ha (155 acres) and is the world's biggest saltwater tidal lake located within a city. Set in the middle of Lakeside Park, off Grand Avenue, the lake is the favourite spot with the locals. Part of it is a refuge for wild ducks and waterfowl, and the winter bird count can go as high as 5000. On the western side of the lake there are canoes, rowboats and sailboats for hire.

Lakeside Park
Lakeside Park is home to **Children's Fairyland**, ph (510) 832 3609, which you enter through the home of the *Old Woman Who Lived in a Shoe*, to visit over sixty nursery-rhyme locales.

This is a great place for the kids, and also puts the mums and dads up a notch when the kids realise that the oldies know more nursery rhymes then they do. There are also clowns, dancers, musicians, storytellers, and magic shows, and puppet shows are held at 11am, 2pm and 4pm. The hours change according to the season so it is best to phone in advance.

Oakland Museum
A few blocks from the lake is **Oakland Museum**, 1000 Oak Street, ph (510) 238 3401, which opened in 1969. An internationally acclaimed museum, it has Babylonian hanging gardens, lily ponds and courtyards, but the theme of the exhibits is pure California.

The museum is open Wed-Sat 10am-5pm, Sun noon-7pm, and though there is no **general admission charge,** there could be fees for special exhibitions. There is a snack bar and a book and gift shop.

The famous writer Jack London, author of such classics as *Call of the Wild* and *White Fang,* grew up in Oakland, and this favourite son is remembered by **Jack London Square** at the foot of Broadway. A bust of London overlooks the square, probably gazing at the **First and Last Chance Saloon**, 56 Jack London Square, ph 839 6761, where he did some of his writing, and most of his drinking. The corner table in the saloon, where he habitually sat, has been kept the same as it was seventy years ago, and there are many photos and other memorabilia. Next door is the Jack London Cabin which, when London lived in it during the Klondike gold rush, was situated on the north fork of Henderson Creek in the Yukon.

Oakland Zoo

Oakland Zoo is in Knowland State Park, and is an open-rage zoo with a train that takes visitors around. There is also a 380m (1250 ft) Jungle Lift that goes up over the African Veldt area. The zoo is open daily 10am-4.30pm, and **admission is $5.50 per car.**

For more detailed information on Oakland, and maps, etc, call into the **Oakland Visitors Bureau**, 1000 Broadway, Suite 200, ph 839 9000, open Mon-Fri 9am-noon, 1-5pm.

BERKELEY

Home to one of the nation's finest educational institutions, Berkeley is a real college town, and life seems to revolve around the University of California-Berkeley and its 32,000 students.

HOW TO GET THERE

By car, drive over the Oakland Bay Bridge, keep left, then turn off onto Ashby Avenue. A bus service runs from the Transbay Terminal, Mission and 1st Streets.

BART travels from the city to Berkeley.

SIGHTSEEING

The University was founded in 1868, and covers over 485ha

(1200 acres). It is easily toured with a map obtainable from the Student Union information desk on the 2nd floor at the corner of Telegraph Avenue and Bancroft Way, ph 642 4636. Free guided tours are available Mon-Fri at 1pm and take about 1.5 hours. Near the Student Union building are stalls selling everything from falafels to tarot cards to craft items. This is the hub of the student activities.

The **Berkeley Marina Yacht Harbor** is probably the only non-university related attraction in the town. It is a $2 million complex on the shores of San Francisco Bay, where hundreds of private boats and yachts are moored. Apart from oohing and aahing over the boats, there are sandy beaches, play areas for the children, picnic spots, trails and lookout points, and a 90m (300 ft) fishing pier. A great place to spend a few hours.

MARINE WORLD AFRICA USA

In a State where theme parks abound, this 65ha (160 acres) complex is well worth a visit. It is not only devoted to animals from the sea, there are also lions, tigers, elephants, birds, butterflies, etc, etc.

HOW TO GET THERE

Marine World Africa USA, ph (707) 643-ORCA (recorded message) is in Marine World Parkway, Vallejo, just off Interstate Highway 80, so if travelling by car from San Francisco, cross over the Bay Bridge and stay on Highway 80.

The *Red and White Fleet* have a catamaran service from Pier 41 that takes 55 minutes, including a short bus ride.

SIGHTSEEING

Firstly, it should be pointed out that there is a full schedule of shows at the park, so it is best to get there early, pick up your map, note the entertainment times, plan an itinerary, and stick to it. Otherwise you will find yourself running around in circles, missing out on star attractions, and generally feeling disappointed, especially if you do not have time to make another visit.

Aquatic shows include:
the *Killer Whale/Dolphin Show*, the *Sea Lion Show*, and the *Water Ski and Boat Show*, which is held on a 22ha (55 acres) lake that was once a golf course.

Land animal shows include:
the *Elephant and Chimpanzee Show*, the *Parrot and Predatory Bird Show*, and the *Tiger and Lion Show*.

In the Africa part of the complex there is:
Butterfly World, which has to be seen to be believed;
the *Wildlife Show* at the Ecology Theater explains the delicate balance of nature;
Tiger Island, a must; and the *Small Animal Petting Corral* where, for the price of a bag of food, you can make some new friends.

There is also a great children's playground, called the *Gentle Jungle*, that combines adventure and education.

As would be expected, a wide variety of fast food is available, or you can try the restaurant for something a bit more up-market. Or, at the other end of the scale, you can take your own food. Barbecue facilities are provided.

Marine World Africa USA is open daily 9.30am-6.30pm from Memorial Day through Labor Day, Wed-Sun 9.30am-5.30pm throughout the rest of the year.
Admission is $21.95 adults, $15.95 children, which covers all the shows, but not the camel and elephant rides, which are around $5.

MUIR WOODS

Muir Woods, a 222ha (550 acres) redwood forest, is home to *Sequoia sempervirens*, the coast redwood, which can live for thousands of years. The trees can reach heights of around 110m (360 ft), but around here they average about 73m (240 ft). One of the incredible things about them, though, is that their roots go no deeper than 2m (6 ft).

HOW TO GET THERE
From San Francisco, take US Highway 101 north. There are plenty of signs to tell you when to turn left onto State Highway 1.

> The secondary road leading to the Woods has a lot of S bends, with few places to pull over. Before you start out, check your tyres and brakes, and make sure you have plenty of petrol.

SIGHTSEEING
At the entrance to the Woods, a cross section of a fallen tree shows growth rings that prove that it was alive before England was conquered by the Normans (1066)! This puts you in the mood to appreciate these monsters, and to wander along the needle-carpeted trails. The best time to visit is during the week, when the serene nature of the Woods can also be appreciated. During the weekends, the place is packed and becomes more like a theme-park.

As with most natural attractions, the Woods had to be saved from civilisation at one stage. In the early 1900s, a company wanted to dam Redwood Creek, from which the trees receive their water supply, but a nearby landowner, William Kent, lobbied the president, Theodore Roosevelt, to proclaim the area a national monument. Fortunately he was successful, and the area was named after the great Scottish-American naturalist, John Muir.

There are *several hiking trails*, but make sure you follow the signs to **Cathedral Grove**, a group of redwoods that resemble the walls of a chapel, and **Family Circle**. The latter shows how the redwood reproduce, and you can see younger trees formed in a circle around the stamp of a parent tree.

If you are feeling energetic, you can follow a trail up the slopes of **Mount Tamalpais**, a 784m (2570 ft) peak that is locally known as Mt Tam, and is one of the Bay Area's most prominent landmarks.

There is a visitor centre, gift shop and snack bar, but there are picnic areas along the hiking trails and that is really the best way to go. The park is open daily 8am-sunset, and there is no admission fee.

TIBURON

Inhabited by the Miwok Indians as far back as 100BC, the town of Tiburon was 'settled' by railroad workers when the first wood-burning locomotives began chugging into Point Tiburon in 1884. Today the residents are mostly 'yuppies' who commute into San Francisco each day.

HOW TO GET THERE
The quickest way to go is by *Red and White Fleet ferry* which leaves from Pier 41 at Fisherman's Wharf. Golden Gate Transit has a bus service to Tiburon from downtown San Francisco.

If you are travelling by car, cross over the Golden Gate Bridge and stay on US Highway 101 until the Tiburon Boulevard exit, then stay on California 131. The one-way trip is around 29km (18 miles).

SIGHTSEEING
Main Street is a succession of shops and restaurants with marvellous water views, but don't expect to pick up a bargain, this is an expensive village. If you are just a little tired of

shopping, take the self-guided tour through the **Richardson Bay Wildlife Sanctuary**, 376 Greenwood Beach Road.

The half a kilometre walk takes you back to nature, and several hundred species of birds live in the reserve. During winter sea lions and harbour seals can be seen along the shoreline. A magnificent Victorian home, **Lyford House** is also on the property.

Connected to Tiburon by a causeway is the island of **Belvedere**, which is only 2km long and less than 1 km wide, but has some of the most expensive homes in the Marin County. It is also the site of the historic San Francisco Yacht Club.

NOTES

WINE COUNTRY

NAPA VALLEY

The valley stretches from the San Pablo Bay in the south to the base of Mt St Helena in the north, a distance of 48km (30 miles). Its width varies from 1.6km to 8km, and it is protected on both sides by low mountains. It is a very scenic valley that would probably attract visitors even if it didn't produce some of the world's best wines.

A History

Napa Valley has for many years been the best-known of California's wine growing districts, and most people mistakenly think that it was probably the first. Prior to 1823, the valley was inhabited solely by the Wappo Indians. In 1823, Father Jose Altimira visited the area looking for a suitable site to build a mission, but he decided in favour of Sonoma.

The next years saw many explorers visit the valley, but the first person who thought of settling there was George Yount. He was given a grant of land by General Mariano Vallejo, and built the first structure in the County in 1836. He also planted the first grapes, the coarse Mission variety, in order to have wine for his own table.

In 1858, Charles Krug, a German, decided to put Napa wine onto a business footing for the first time, although he was still using the Mission grapes. He was followed, in 1860, by George Belden Crane, who decided that German grapes were better than the native Missions. The wines of the era from 1870 through to the beginning of the 20th century all had a predominately German flavour, and the names of Jacob and Frederick Beringer and Jacob Schram are among those still

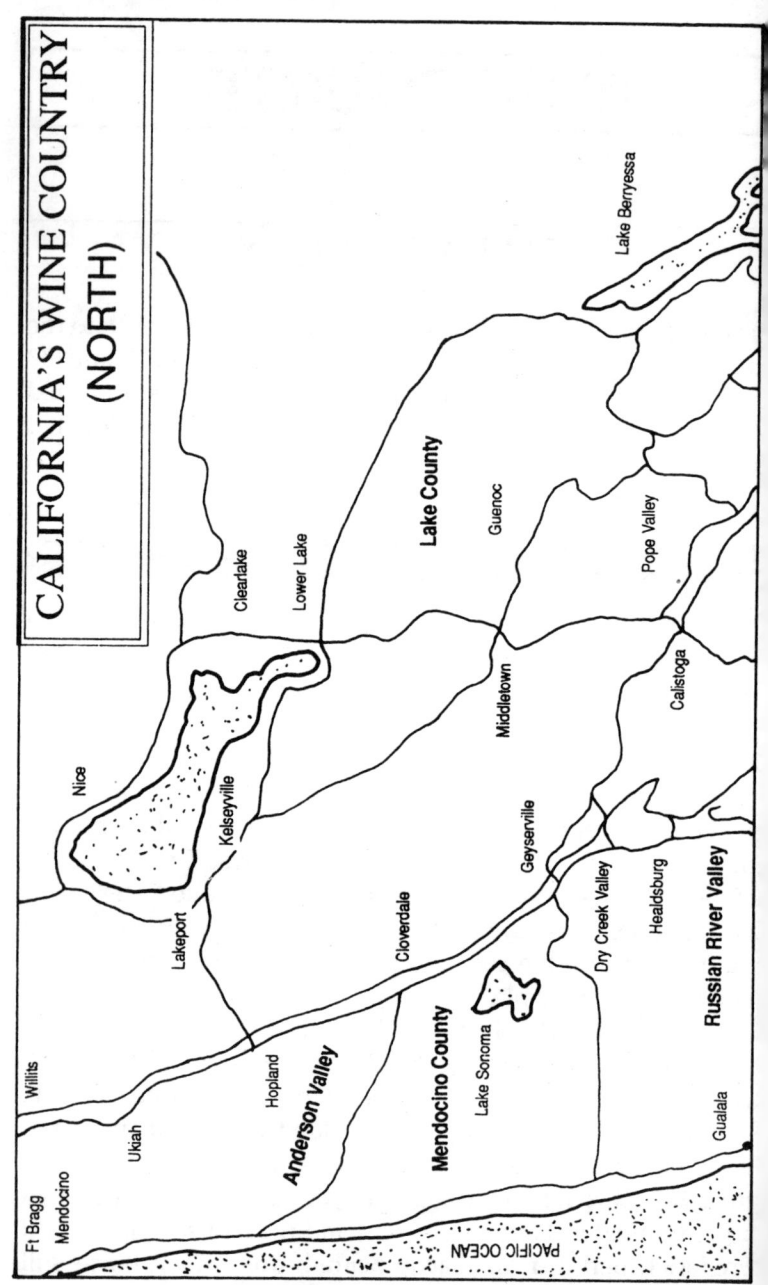

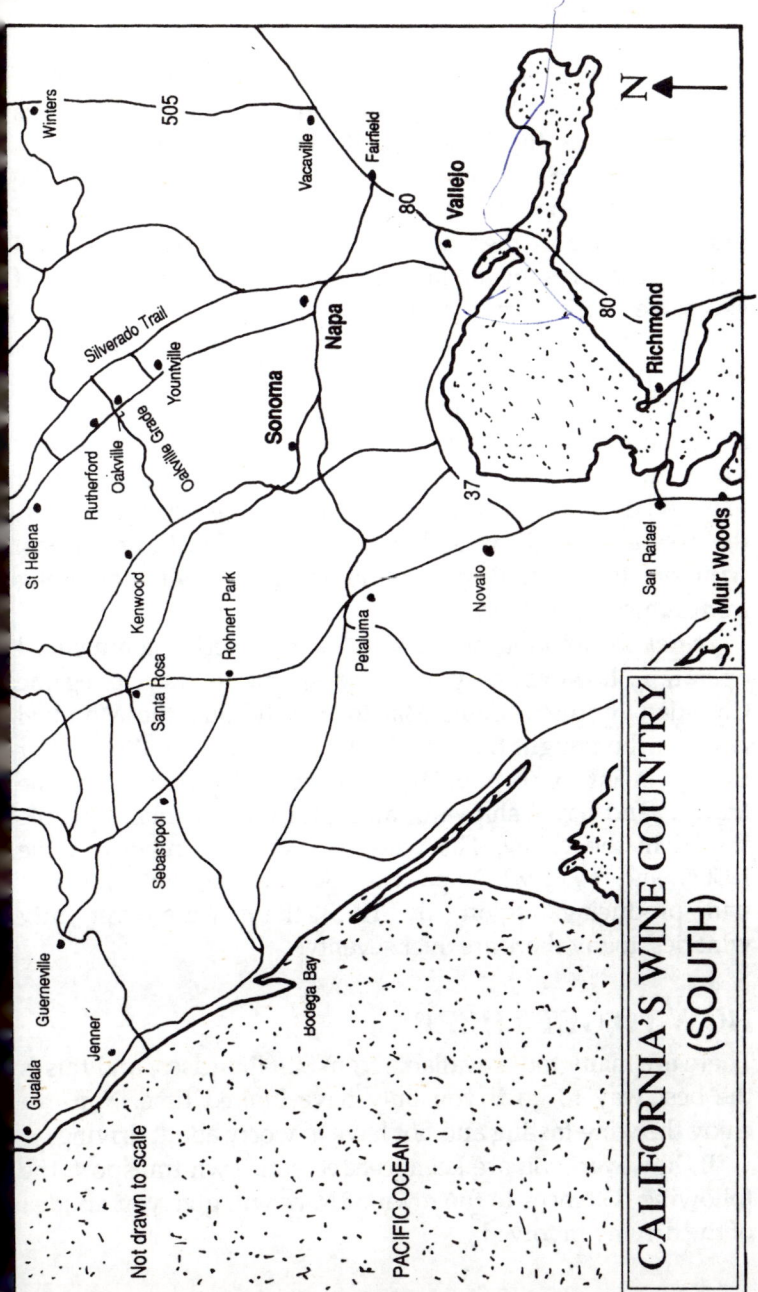

heard today.

In the late 19th century, mining became an important industry, and the Silverado, immortalised by Robert Louis Stevenson, was the largest producing silver mine in Napa County. In 1860, quicksilver was discovered in the Mayacamas Range, north-west of Calistoga. Quicksilver was much in demand then as it was used to recover gold and silver from ores by amalgamation; in the manufacture of explosives; and in drugs and paints.

From 1864 to 1903, Napa County was one of California's leading producers of quicksilver.

Then in the 1880s and 90s, interest was revived in wines from the region, and many of the cellars that can be visited today are from that period. The wine's reputation continued to grow, then along came Prohibition and the Depression, but the area apparently was able to ride out both those storms, with the Beringer, Beaulieu and Inglenook wineries going from success to success.

After Prohibition about sixty new wineries commenced operation, however only a few were able to survive, eg the Christian Brothers, Louis Martini family, and the Mondavi family, who bought the old Charles Krug winery. World War II saw an influx of population in the valley because of the Mare Island naval shipyard, and after the war many people stayed in the valley. The wine industry was reborn in the 1950s, and by 1963 Napa was once again **the** American wine-producing region. By 1975, there were over fifty wineries, today there are over seventy.

HOW TO GET THERE

There are many tours available from San Francisco, and this is the best way to go if you only have limited time. You can enjoy the wine-tasting and not have to worry about driving.

If, however, you are keen to have your own transport, the following distances to the town of *Napa* will give you an idea of the driving involved.

To Napa	
From Calistoga -	45km (28 miles)
Oakland -	80km (50 miles)
Sacramento -	95km (59 miles)
San Francisco -	82km (51 miles)
San Jose -	138km (86 miles)
San Rafael -	68km (42 miles)
Santa Rosa -	66km (41 miles)
Sonoma -	24km (15 miles)
St Helena -	29km (18 miles)

Two main roads run the length of the valley, from Napa to Calistoga - **Highway 29,** the more popular as it passes through a string of small villages giving access to a greater number of wineries; and the **Silverado Trail**, which runs parallel to 29, but on the eastern edge of the valley, away from the wineries.

Greyhound Bus Lines have frequent services from San Francisco to the Napa and Sonoma Valleys.

TOURIST INFORMATION

The Napa Valley Conference and Visitors Bureau, 1310 Napa Town Center, ph (707) 226 7459, is open Mon-Fri 9am-5pm, Sat-Sun 11am-3pm, and can provide maps and information.

There is also the Tourist Tower, 4076 Byway East, Napa, ph (707) 253 2929. They have guide books and winery tour maps, and can arrange balloon Rides, accommodation, and even sell you a T-shirt.

A free publication that is put out weekly is the *Wine Country Review*, and it has information on all the wineries, and current events and opening times. You can pick it up at most establishments in Napa and Sonoma.

ACCOMMODATION

The following is a sample of accommodation available in the valley, with prices for a double room per night in US dollars, which should be used as a guide only.

The telephone area code is 707.

Auberge du Soleil Resort, 180 Rutherford Hill Road, Rutherford, ph 963 1211 - 48 rooms, restaurant, cocktail lounge, swimming pool, tennis courts - $350-725.

Meadowood Resort, 900 Meadowood Lane, St Helena, ph 963 3646 - 70 rooms, restaurant, cocktail lounge, swimming pool, golf course, tennis courts - $235-500.

The Vintage Inn, 6541 Washington Street, Yountville, ph 944 1112 - 80 rooms, restaurant, cocktail lounge, swimming pools, tennis courts - $144-204.

Silverado Country Club & Resort, 1600 Atlas Peak Road, Napa, ph 257 0200 - 280 rooms, restaurants, cocktail bar, swimming pools, tennis courts, golf course - $130-235.

John Muir Inn, Highway 29 at Trower, Napa, ph 257 7220 - 60 rooms, swimming pool, continental breakfast - $70-150.

Roman Spa - Hot Springs Resort, 1300 Washington Street, Calistoga, ph 942 4441 - 60 rooms, swimming pool, hot mineral pools - $64-120.

Golden Haven Spa and Resort, 1713 Lake Street, Calistoga, ph 942 6793 - 28 rooms, swimming pool, mineral pool - $49-115.

EATING OUT

The Napa Valley has a good selection of restaurants, some at the wineries, some in the townships.

Following is a selection, which has been rated by the cost of a main course:

Expensive - $20+;

Moderate - $10-20;

Reasonable - under $10.

The Diner, 6476 Washington Street, Yountville, ph 944 2626 - Mexican and American, popular with locals - open Tues-Sun 8am-3pm, 5.30-9pm - **Reasonable.**

Compadres, 6539 Washington Street, Yountville, ph 944 2406 - Mexican - open Mon-Fri 11am-10pm, Sat-Sun 10am-10pm - **Moderate.**

The French Laundry, 6640 Washington Street, Yountville, ph 944 2380 - family-owned, country French cuisine - open

Wed-Sun for dinner, reservations are essential - **Expensive.**
Mustards Grill, 7399 St Helena Highway, Yountville, ph 944 2424 - wood-burning oven and grill - open daily 11.30am-10pm - **Moderate.**
Tra Vigne, 1050 Charter Oak Avenue, St Helena, ph 963 4444 - Italian/American cuisine - open Sun-Thurs noon-9pm, Fri-Sat noon-10pm, reservations suggested - **Moderate.**
Or, for something a bit different, try Saturday Dinner or Sunday Brunch on board the Sternwheeler *City of Napa*. Reservations are required - contact the Napa River Boat Co, 1400 Duhig Road, Napa, ph 226 2628.

Trips, without meals, are available from $12 per person.

SIGHTSEEING
Although the main reason for visiting the Napa Valley is the wineries, there are interesting things the area has to offer.

The Napa Valley Wine Train, 1275 McKinstry Street, Napa, is a great way to explore the valley. Over 50 km (around 32 miles) of track between the town of Napa and the vineyard north of St Helena are covered during luncheon and dinner trips. The trains have restored Pullman lounges and the Dining Car is a thing of beauty where gourmet food and local wines are served. For prices, schedules and reservations, ph 253 2111.

Vintage 1870 - Yountville, ph 944 2451, is an 110-year-old winery which has been restored and converted into restaurants and shops.

Silverado Museum, 1490 Library Lane, St Helena, ph 963 3757, is dedicated to the life and works of Robert Louis Stevenson, who spent his honeymoon in the Napa Valley in 1880. It has over 7000 items pertaining to his life, including manuscripts, letters, photographs and first editions, as well as personal effects. The museum is open Tues-Sun noon-4pm and there is **no admission charge.**

Hurd Beeswax Candle Factory, 3020 St Helena Highway (California Highway 29), ph 963 7211, is an old-fashioned country store that also has a demonstration beehive and an open workshop where you can watch the handcrafting of beeswax candles. It is part of the Freemark Abbey complex.

Bale Grist Mill, 5km north of St Helena on Highway 29, is a State park featuring a water-powered grain mill built in 1846 by Dr Edward Turner Bale. There are hiking trails in the grounds and a small museum, which is open daily and charges a small entrance fee.

Bothe-Napa Valley State Park is set between St Helena and Calistoga on Highway 29. A very scenic 727ha (1800 acres) park, it is open daily and has hiking, picnic and camping facilities, and a swimming pool. For information and reservations, ph 942 4575.

Sharpsteen Museum, 1311 Washington Street, Calistoga, ph 942 5911, is an unusual museum developed by former Disney producer Ben Sharpsteen. Exhibits include dioramas of the town of Calistoga as it was in 1865.
The museum is open daily
10am-4pm (summer)
noon-4pm (winter) and there is **no admission charge.**

Old Faithful Geyser of California, 1299 Tubbs Lane, Calistoga, ph 942 6463, is the oldest and most famous of the Calistoga geysers. One of the few geysers in the world (in fact, I think there are only three) that erupts on a regular basis, Old Faithful only seems to deviate from its regular 40-minute performance when there are earthquakes within a 500 mile radius. There are picnic areas in the park, and a gift shop, and it is *open daily*
9am-6pm (summer),
9am-5pm (winter). **Admission is $4.50 adults, $2 children over 6.**

The Petrified Forest, 4100 Petrified Forest Road, Calistoga, ph 942 6667, can be a little disappointing if you expect to see thousands of trees that have been turned into stone, as the name suggests. Still it is interesting to see what the volcanic ash from Mount St Helena's eruptions have done to some of the redwoods that were covered. Even more interesting to some is proof that the area was under water before the redwood forest developed.

There is a picnic area, and a gift shop, and *the forest is open to visitors daily* 10am-6pm (summer), 10am-5pm (winter). **Admission is $3 adults, $1 children under 12.**

The town of *Calistoga* has other attractions apart from Old Faithful, the Petrified Forest and the vineyards, and they are **mud baths**. The area's geothermal springs were first put to use by Sam Brannan, who became the State's first millionaire as a result of building a hotel and spa in the town. He even dreamed up the name 'Calistoga', a combination of 'California' and 'Saratoga', the popular East Coast resort.

The mud is made from imported peat, local volcanic ash, and the boiling mineral springs, and the resulting thick sludge has a temperature around 32 to 38C. The idea is that you lower your naked body into a stone tub full of mud for about ten minutes, then you have a warm shower, then a whirlpool bath, then go into the steamroom, then wrap yourself into a blanket so as to cool down slowly. To complete the experience you then are supposed to have a massage.

The whole event takes about one and a half hours, and you feel completely rejuvenated.

Mud baths are not recommended for people with high blood pressure, or for pregnant women.

Venues offering the baths are:
Lincoln Avenue Spa, 1339 Lincoln Avenue, ph 942 5296;
Golden Haven Hot Springs Spa, 1713 Lake Street, ph 942 6793;
Calistoga Spa Hot Springs, 1006 Washington Street, ph 942 6269;
and *Dr Wilkinson's Hot Springs*, 1507 Lincoln Ave, ph 942 4102.
Appointments are necessary at all the above, and should be made about a week in advance.

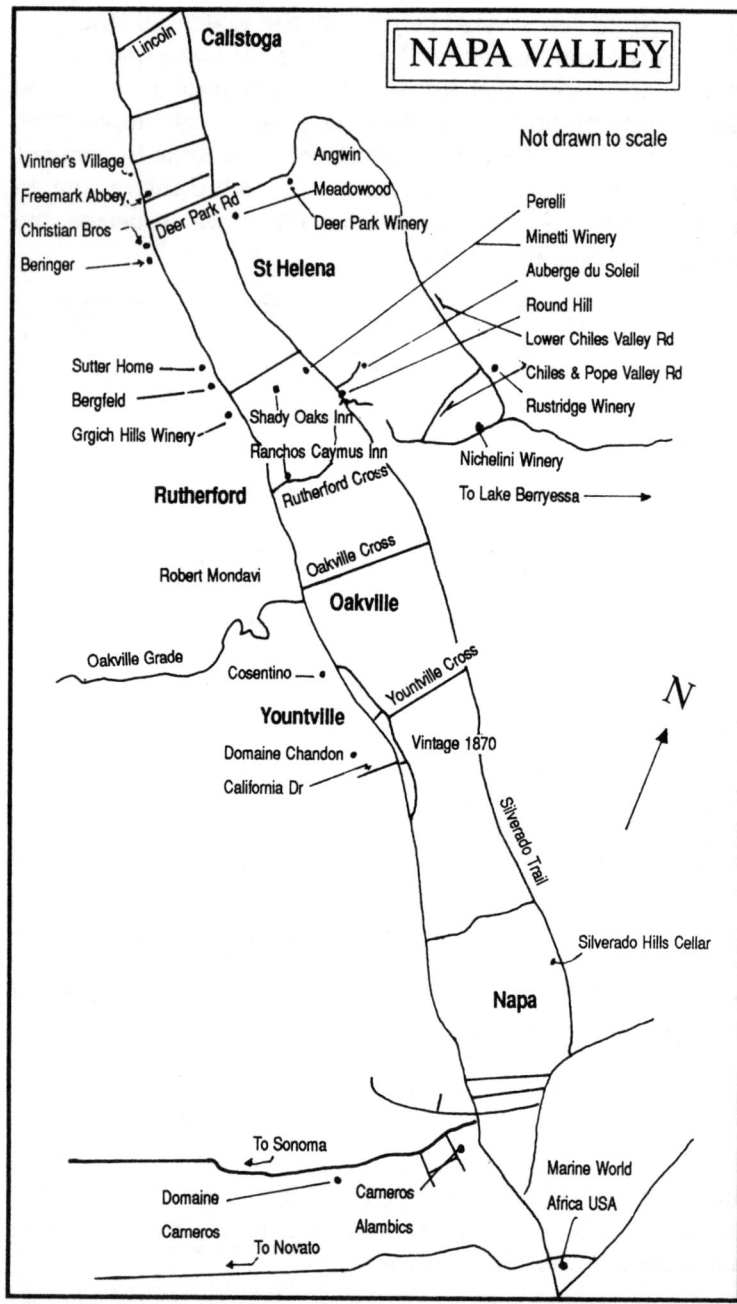

Robert Louis Stevenson Park is 8km (5 miles) north of Calistoga on California 29, and is an undeveloped 1616ha (4000 acres) park with hiking trails and little else. It is open daily and has no admission fee.

WINERIES

Following is a list of wineries in the Napa Valley that are open for tours, tasting and sales. It is suggested that you phone ahead for opening hours.

Napa

Carneros Creek, 1285 Dealy Street, Napa, ph 253 9463.
Clos Du Val Wine Co Ltd, 5330 Silverado Trail, Napa, ph 252 6711.
Domaine Carneros, 1240 Duhig Road, Napa, ph 257 0101.
Hakusan Sake Gardens, cnr Hwys 29 & 12, Napa, ph 258 6160.
The Hess Collection, 4411 Redwood Road, Napa, ph 255 1144.
Lakespring Winery, 2055 Hoffman Lane, Napa, ph 944 2475.
Merlion Winery, 880 Vallejo street, Napa, ph 226 5568.
Monticello Cellars, 4242 Big Ranch Road, Napa, ph 253 2802.
Mont St John Winery, 5400 Old Sonoma Rd, Napa, ph 2558864.
RMS Vineyards, 1250 Cuttings Wharf Rd, Napa, ph 2539055.
Stag's Leap Wine Cellars, 5766 Silverado Trail, Napa, ph 944 2020.
Trefethen Vineyards, 1160 Oak Knoll Ave, Napa, ph 255 7700.

Yountville

Cosentino Winery, 7415 St Helena Hwy, Yountville, ph 9441220.
Domaine Chandon, California Drive, Yountville, ph 944 2280.
Sinskey, Robert Vineyards, 6320 Silverado Trail, Yountville, ph 944 9090.

St Helena

Beaulieu Vineyard, 1960 Highway 29, St Helena, ph 963 2411.

Bergfeld 1885 Wine Cellars, 401 St Helena Highway, St Helena, ph 963 7293.

Beringer Vineyard, 2000 Main Street, St Helena, ph 963 7114.

Cain Cellars, 3800 Langtry Road, St Helena, ph 963 1616.

Chateau Boswell, 3468 Silverado Trail, St Helena, ph 963 5472.

Chateau Napa-Beaucanon, 1695 St Helena Highway, St Helena, ph 963 1886.

Christian Bros, 2555 Main Street, St Helena, ph 963 0765.

Conn Creek Winery, 8711 Silverado Trail, St Helena, ph 963 9100.

Domaine Napa Winery, 1155 Mee Lane, St Helena, ph 963 1666.

Ehlers Lane Wine Co, 3222 Ehlers Lane, St Helena, ph 963 0144.

Folie A Deux Winery, 3070 St Helena Highway, St Helena, ph 963 1160.

Freemark Abbey Winery, 3022 St Helena Highway, St Helena, ph 963 9694.

Heitz Cellars, 436 Highway 29, St Helena, ph 963 3542.

Hanns Kornell Champagne, 1091 Larkmead Lane, St Helena, ph 963 2334.

Charles Krug Winery, 2800 Main Street, Highway 29, St Helena, ph 963 5057.

Markham Winery, 2812 St Helena Highway, St Helena, ph 963 5292.

Louis M. Martini, 254 St Helena Highway, St Helena, ph 963 2736.

Milat Vineyards, 1091 St Helena Highway, St Helena, ph 963 0758.

Napa Creek Winery, 1001 Silverado Trail, St Helena, ph 963 9456.

Nichelini Vineyards, 2950 Sage Canyon Road, St Helena, ph 963 3357.

Prager Winery & Port Works, 1281 Lewelling Street, St Helena, ph 963 3720.

Raymond Vineyard & Cellars, 849 Zinfandel Lane, St Helena, ph 963 3141.

V. Sattui Winery, cnr Highway 29 & White Lane, St Helena, ph 963 7774.

Charles Shaw, 1010 Big Tree Road, St Helena, ph 963 5459.

Spring Mountain, 2805 Spring Mountain Road, St Helena, ph 963 5233.
Sunny St Helena Winery, 1000 Main St, St Helena, ph 963 7777.
Sutter Home Winery, 277 St Helena Highway, St Helena, ph 963 3104.
Vintners Village, 3111 N St Helena Hwy, St Helena, ph 963 4082.
Whitehall Lane Winery, 1563 St Helena Hwy, St Helena, ph 963 9454.

Calistoga

Chateau Montelena, 1429 Tubbs Lane, Calistoga, ph 942 5105
Clos Pegase, 1060 Dunaweal Lane, Calistoga, ph 942 4981.
Cuvaison Winery, 4500 Silverado Trail, Calistoga, ph 942 6266.
Sterling Vineyard, 1111 Dunaweal Lane, Calistoga, ph 942 3300.
Stonegate Winery, 1183 Dunaweal Lane, Calistoga, ph 942 6500.
Wermuth Winery, 3942 Silverado Trail, Calistoga, ph 942 5924.

Oakville

Chateau Potelle, 3875 Mt Veeder Road, Oakville, ph 255 9440.
De Moor Winery, 7481 St Helena Hwy, Oakville, ph 944 2565.
Robert Mondavi Winery, 7801 St Helena Highway, Oakville, ph 226 1395.
Silver Oak Cellars, 915 Oakville Crossroad, Oakville, ph 944 8808.
Villa Mt Eden, 620 Oakville Crossroad, Oakville, ph 944 2414.

Rutherford

Cassayre-Forni, 1271 Manley Lane, Rutherford, ph 944 2165.
Caymus Vineyards, 8700 Conn Creek Road, Rutherford, ph 963 4204.
Franciscan Vineyards, 1178 Galleron Road, Rutherford, ph 963 7111.
Grgich Hills Cellar, 1829 St Helena Highway, Rutherford, ph 963 2784.

Inglenook Napa Valley, 1991 St Helena Highway, Rutherford, ph 967 3359.
Peju Province, 8466 St Helena Highway, Rutherford, ph 963 3600.
Rutherford Hill, 200 Rutherford Hill Road, Rutherford, ph 963 7194.
Rutherford Vintners, 1673 St Helena Highway, Rutherford, ph 963 4117.
Sequoia Grove, 8338 St Helena Highway, Rutherford, ph 944 2945.
St Supery Vineyards & Winery, 8440 St Helena Highway, Rutherford, ph 963 4507.

TOURS
The following are not your run-of-the-mill tours, but they are very popular in this neck of the woods.

Ballooning
I am not going to pretend that I have first-hand knowledge of this type of adventure, but I have been reliably informed that it is an unforgettable experience (I didn't argue with that one); and that once you have tried it, you can't wait for the next opportunity to take another flight!

There are several companies in Napa that specialise in hot air balloon rides, which usually include coffee before the flight, and a champagne brunch afterwards.

So, if you are game, contact one of the following:
   Napa Valley Balloons, Inc, ph (800) 253 2224;
   Napa Valley Balloon Safari, ph (800) 255 0125;
   Bonaventura Balloons, ph (707) 944 2822;
   Napa's Great Balloon Escape, ph (707) 253 0860;
   American Balloon Adventures, ph (800) 333 4359.

If you have ever wondered, as I did, why balloon flights are always at such an uncivilized hour, wonder no more. It is because as the earth heats up, the air above becomes more turbulent, and makes the flights too bumpy.

Gliding

While we are on the subject of aerial tours:
Calistoga Gliders of Napa Valley, 1546 Lincoln Avenue, Calistoga, ph 942 5000 - **1 person ride $79, 2 person ride $110.**

SPORT

Golf

The following are the public courses in the Valley.
Chardonnay, 2555 Jamieson Canyon Road, Napa, ph 257 8950.
Chimney Rock, 5320 Silverado Trail, Napa, ph 255 3363.
Mt St Helena, Napa City Fairgrounds, Calistoga, ph 942 9966.
Napa Municipal, 2295 Streblow Street, Napa, ph 255 4333.
Vineyard Knolls, 1129 Dealy Lane, Napa, ph 255 7388.
Meadowood Resort, 900 Meadowood Lane, St Helena, ph 963 3646, and *Silverado Resort*, 1600 Atlas Peak Road, Napa, ph 257 0200, are hotel courses. Call the above numbers for tee times and availability of play.

Cycling

The Napa Chamber of Commerce can provide suggestions for touring the Valley by bicycle, and can provide you with a list of bike routes. The following companies can provide the bikes.
   Napa Valley Bike Tours, 4080 Byway East, Napa, ph 255 3377.
   Jules Culver Bicycles, 1227 F Lincoln Avenue, Calistoga, ph 942 0421.

Horse Riding

There are over 1200ha (3000 acres) of trails at *Wild Horse Valley Ranch*, 8km (5 miles) east of Napa, ph 224 0727.

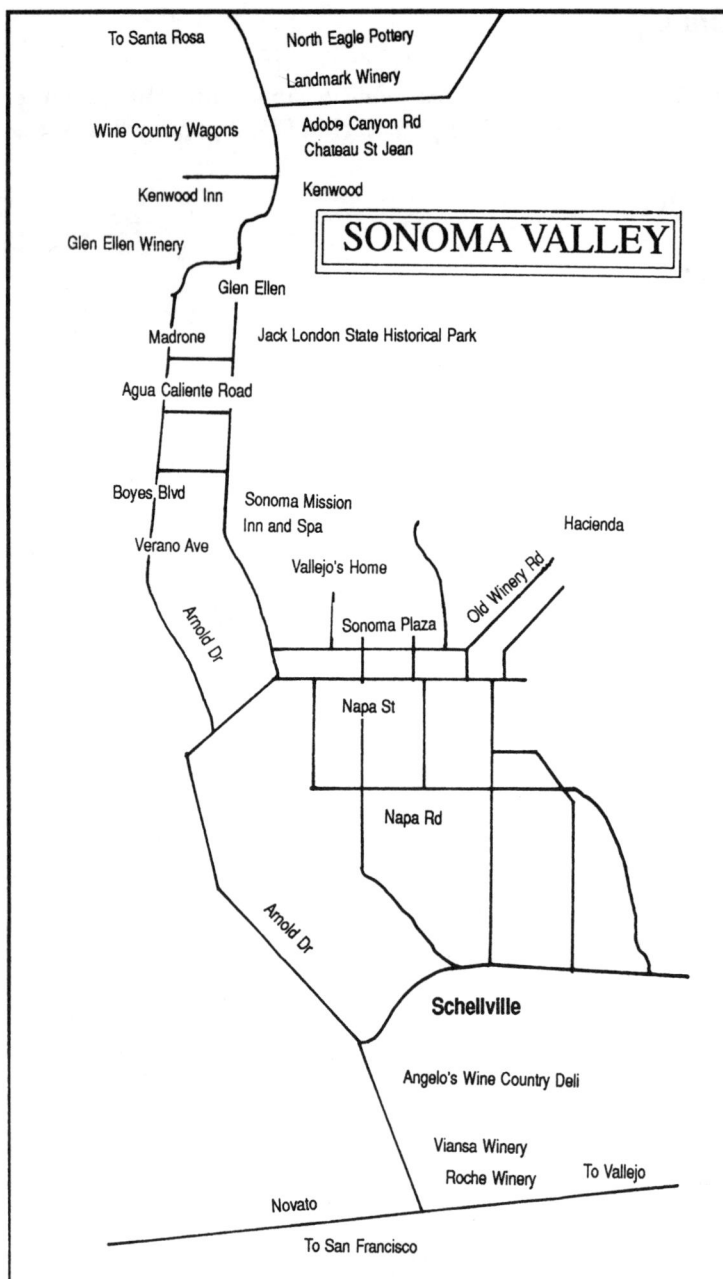

SONOMA VALLEY

Also known as the *Valley of the Moon*, Sonoma is 63km (39 miles) north of the Golden Gate Bridge, and 27km (17 miles) from Napa.

A History

The original inhabitants of Sonoma County were the Miwok, Wappo and Pomo Indians, who thrived in the peaceful valley living off the land and the sea. During the early 1800s, Russian explorers travelled down the Pacific Coast of California to find a suitable spot to raise produce for their settlement in Sitka, Alaska. They established a settlement at Ross, built a fort, a chapel and a stockade, and started work. They traded with the Indians, the Mexicans living in the area and Yankee traders, and explored the Russian River and Mt St Helena. They also grew grapes, indicating the potential of the northern part of the state for viticulture. However, the locals were not impressed with the Russian presence, and there was a huge sigh of relief when they sold out to John Sutter in 1841.

In 1823, Father Jose Altimira, accompanied by General Mariano Vallejo, established the last of the California missions, Mission San Francisco Solano de Sonoma. Vineyards were planted along with other crops, and all was going along nicely until orders for secularization arrived from Mexico in 1834. General Vallejo was given orders to establish a pueblo, and the town of Sonoma was designed around a plaza with a church, and residential and commercial buildings. Many of these early buildings have been restored and can be visited.

Although Vallejo tried to encourage settlers to the area, he did not rate well in the popularity stakes and was more likely to upset the people already there than to attract newcomers. Also, the Mexican government prohibited Americans from owning land, and at one stage actually expelled all 'foreigners' from the area, but told them to leave their weapons behind. This was probably the straw that broke the camel's back, and a series of skirmishes led to the Bear Flag Revolt on June 14, 1846, when the rebels surrounded Vallejo's house and seized him and his family.

The home-made flag with the grizzly bear motif flew over the Sonoma plaza for nearly a month, then when the war between Mexico and the United States broke out in July, 1846, it was replaced by the Stars and Stripes.

The discovery of gold in the Sierra Foothills hastened the development of Northern California, with French, Italian, German, Spanish and English settlers moving into the Sonoma area. Unsuccessful in their search for gold, they turned their attention to agriculture, and more importantly, viticulture.

HOW TO GET THERE
From San Francisco, drive north on Highway 101, turn right onto Highway 37, left onto Highway 121, then left again onto Highway 12 which travels into the town of Sonoma.

TOURIST INFORMATION
The Sonoma Valley Visitors Bureau is at 453 1st Street East, Sonoma, ph (707) 996 1090, and is *open daily*, 9am-5pm Mon-Fri, 9am-4pm Sat, 9am-3pm Sun.
They have information on all the local attractions, including the wineries, but if you want to know about places further afield, visit the Sonoma County Convention and Visitors Bureau, 5000 Roberts Lake Road, Rohnert Park, ph (707) 575 1191.

ACCOMMODATION
Following is a selection of accommodation available, with prices for a double room per night in US dollars, which should be used as a guide only.
The telephone area code is 707.

Sonoma Mission Inn & Spa, 18140 Sonoma Highway 12 (3km north of Sonoma Plaza), ph 938 9000 - 170 rooms, restaurants

cocktail bars, tennis courts, swimming pools - $145-325.
El Dorado Hotel, 405 First Street West, Sonoma, ph 996 3030 - 27 rooms, restaurant, cocktail lounge, swimming pool - $80-140 (including continental breakfast).
Sonoma Chalet Bed & Breakfast, 18935 Fifth Street West, Sonoma, ph 938 3129 - 7 rooms, spa, bicycles - $75-125 (including continental breakfast).
Vineyard Valley Inn, 178 Dry Creek Road, Healdsburg, ph 433 0101 - 24 rooms - $45-65 (including continental breakfast).

EATING OUT

The best place to dine in Sonoma is Regina's at the *Sonoma Hotel*, 110 West Spain Street, ph 938 0254.
It is open daily for lunch and dinner, and has an extensive menu, leaning towards southern American cuisine. As you would expect, it has a good wine list, but if you decide to take a bottle of something special you have picked up at a winery, this is permitted but the corkage fee is a bit over the top.

For ***Italian cuisine***, there are two eateries near the Plaza, *La Casa* and *Zino's*.
La Casa, 121 East Spain Street (opposite the Mission), ph 996 3406, is open daily 11.30am-9pm and a main meal will set you back about $10-14.
Zino's, 420 East 1st Street, ph 996 4466, is open daily 11am-10pm, and the prices are comparable to *La Casa*.

If you are in the mood for a ***picnic***, stop in at *The Sonoma Cheese Factory*, 2 West Spain Street, ph 996 1931, and choose something from their great range of gourmet sandwiches, cheeses and wines.

To combine a ***spot of history*** with a meal try the *Swiss Hotel*, 18 West Spain Street, ph 938 2884. This adobe building was originally built as another home for General Vallejo, and later was used as a hotel and restaurant. Incidentally, the menu on the wall is from 1936, and is definitely not the current price list.

SIGHTSEEING

The historical landmarks in Sonoma are all part of the Sonoma State Historic Park, whose office is at 20 East Spain Street, ph 938 1519. Tickets can be purchased at any site for any of the other sites on the same day, and all are open daily 10am-5pm.

The **Sonoma Mission**, or Mission San Francisco Solano, is at the corner of East 1st and East Spain Streets. It was the last of the twenty-one missions founded by Father Junipero Serra, and the only one founded under Mexican rule. Nothing remains of the original wooden structure built in 1823, but to the east of the chapel there is an adobe building which was added later as living quarters and is the oldest building in Sonoma. The chapel that stands today was built in 1840 by General Vallejo as a parish church, but when the mission was abandoned it saw service as a barn, winery and a blacksmith's shop. What was left of the mission property was purchased as a California Landmark in 1910, and was restored. It houses a collection of mission artifacts, and some interesting watercolours by Virgil Jorgensen.

The **Sonoma Barracks**, across the street from the Mission, were built to house General Vallejo's troops in the 1830s. When the Mexicans were ousted, the barracks continued for some time as a US Army post, then were used as a winery, a store, a law office and finally as a private home, until purchased by the State in 1958. It has a small museum on Californian history.

Toscano Hotel, next door to the Barracks, was built in 1852 and is furnished in that period. In fact, it looks as if the staff and visitors left in a hurry, as a game of cards seems to be in progress in the downstairs parlour. Free guided tours are available on weekends from 11am-4pm, and they also visit the old-style kitchen.

La Casa Grande, on East Spain Street between East 1st Street and West 1st Street, was the first home of General Vallejo, but the main wing of the building was destroyed by fire in 1867. What remains today was the servants' wing. The house was built in 1836, and it was the centre of social and diplomatic life in the area. It was also the place were eleven of the General's children were born, and where he was arrested in 1846.

Lachryma Montis, at the end of 3rd Street West and about 1km from the town square, was another home of General Vallejo, this one built in 1852. Like the Toscano Hotel, it seems that time has been suspended here. The old pendulum clock swings away and the dinner table is set, awaiting the General's arrival.

Train Town, 20264 Broadway, ph 938 3912, is located about 2km south of Sonoma Plaza, and is the best-developed scale-model railroad in the country. The 4ha (10 acres) park has over 2km of track winding through a mad-made landscape of hills and valleys and around a lake. The round trip takes about twenty minutes and half-way a stop is made at a miniature Old West town called Lakeview. Here you can peer through the windows of the one-quarter scale depot, Wells Fargo express office, houses, stores, fire station and newspaper office. Trains depart daily every 20 minutes from 11am-5pm in summer, and on weekends and holidays during winter. **Fares are $3.50 adults, $2.50 children.**

North-east of the town of Sonoma is the **Buena Vista Winery** (1800 Old Winery Road, ph 938 1266). This was originally owned by Hungarian, Colonel Agoston Haraszthy, the father of California Wines. A colourful character, Col Haraszthy first planted grapes here in the 1850s; and in 1861, he was asked by California Governor John Downey to visit Europe and bring back to California cuttings of the best European varieties.

Although not the first to import grapes, he was instrumental in cultivating certain varieties, such as Riesling, Zinfandel, Emperor and the Flame Tokay. He used his expertise to influence other growers in the area to adopt scientific methods of selective planting and good growing practices.

Much of the Colonel's work was wiped out by diseases that destroyed the imported grape vines, but by 1875, it was found that European vines could be successfully grafted onto disease-resistant Mission grape stumps. The original winery is now the tasting centre, and the venue for private parties, as well as Shakespearean productions in the summer.

Jack London State Park, 2400 London Ranch Road, Glen Ellen, ph 938 5216, is situated about 11km (7 miles) north-west of Sonoma along California Highway 12. Jack London and his wife, Charmian, bought a 566ha (1400 acres) ranch and began construction of their dream home **Wolf House**. A few weeks before they were due to move in, on August 22, 1913, the house mysteriously burned to the ground. Three years later, after becoming America's first millionaire author, Jack London committed suicide at the age of 40.

Visitors can wander around the estate, and the house of **Happy Walls** where Charmian lived after London's death, has a museum containing first editions and original manuscripts. A first floor room has been set up as London's office was, with his desk, typewriter, and artwork for his stories.

> The cottage where London lived and wrote from 1911 is still standing, and his grave is close by, marked simply by a stone boulder.
> *The park is open daily* 8am-sundown and the museum 10am-5pm, and there is a $4 per car admission fee.

WINERIES

Following are the Sonoma Valley wineries, which have tasting rooms. It is recommended that you enquire at the Visitors Bureau about opening hours.

Sebastiani Vineyards, 389 East 4th Street, Sonoma, ph 938 5532.

Buena Vista, 18000 Old Winery Road, Sonoma, ph 938 1266.
Chateau De Baun, 5007 Fulton Road, Fulton, ph 571 7500.
Glen Ellen Winery, 1883 London Ranch Road, Glen Ellen, ph 935 3000.
Valley of the Moon Winery, 777 Madrone Road, Glen Ellen.
Grand Cu, Dunbar Road, Glen Ellen.
Chateau St Jean Winery, 8555 Sonoma Highway, Kenwood, ph 833 4134.
Kenwood Vineyards, 9592 Sonoma Hwy, Kenwood, ph833 5891.
Clos du Bois Wines, 5 Fitch Street, Healdsburg, ph 433 5576.
Davis Bynum Winery, 8075 Westside Road, Healdsburg, ph 433 5852.
Landmark Vineyards, 101 Adobe Canyon Road at Highway 12, Kenwood, ph 833 0053.
Eagle Ridge Winery, 111 Goodwine Avenue, Penngrove, ph 664 9463.
Viansa Winery, 25200 Arnold Drive, Schellville, ph 935 4700.

TOURS

Hot air balloon flights are available from *Sonoma Thunder*, ph 538 7359, or you can try a flight in a bi-plane if you contact *Aero-Schellville*, ph 938 2444.

Wine Country Wagons offer tours of the wineries in the Kenwood area in Northern Sonoma Valley. The wagons are pulled by Belgian draught horses, and the 3-4 hour tour includes a gourmet lunch, all for the sum of around $50. For enquiries and bookings, ph 833 2724.

NOTES

SIERRA NEVADA

Sierra Nevada, the largest single mountain range in the country, is 690km (430 miles) long and 130km (80 miles) wide. It rose from the earth's surface a few million years ago, during the Pleistocene period, spreading glaciers carved river valleys and canyons, and created domes, cliffs and stone towers. The landscape now is dominated by peaks while there are hundreds of lakes, and canyons whose walls rise over a kilometre and a half.

The most popular spot in the Sierra is *Lake Tahoe,* a year-round resort that boasts 300 days of sunshine a year and 6m of snow in the winter. The Lake itself is thought by many to be the most beautiful in the world, and it is famous for its 99.7% clear water. Divers claim visibility at 60m, and it is a fact that something placed on a ledge at 30m can be clearly seen from the surface.

Next in the popularity stakes would probably be *Yosemite National Park* and *Yosemite Valley,* an area of incredibly spectacular scenery.

LAKE TAHOE

Completely surrounded by towering mountains, Lake Tahoe is 1897m (6225 ft) above sea level. It measures 35km (22 miles) long, with a circumference of 116km (72 miles) and an average depth of 300m (984 ft), which makes it the third deepest lake in the world. The California/Nevada border runs through the lake, with California getting the lion's share of it.

A History

The Washoe Indians lived on the shores of the lake for centuries before it was 'discovered' by Captain John Fremont and Kit Carson in 1844. The name 'Tahoe' means 'water in high place'. By the 1870s, with the help of the railway, Tahoe had become a popular resort area. It still retains that year-round popularity, with crowds flocking in summer for the swimming, boating and fishing, and in the winter for the snow and all it has to offer, and all year round for the casinos on the Nevada side. *Gambling is, of course, illegal in California.*

HOW TO GET THERE

By Air
South Lake Tahoe Airport is serviced by *American Airlines* out of LA and San Francisco. Shuttle services are available to Heavenly Valley ski fields. Cannon International Airport in Reno is serviced by *United Airlines, American, USAir, Continental, America West, Delta and Northwest.* Squaw Valley has a free shuttle service between this airport and the resort.

By Train
Amtrak runs excursions to Lake Tahoe. The 'Zephyr' runs from Oakland to Truckee in the Tahoe area.

By Bus
Greyhound has daily San Francisco-Reno services that stop at Truckee.

By Car
South Lake Tahoe can be reached via Interstate Highway 80 and US Highway 50, from San Francisco - 336km (209 miles). Truckee is situated on Interstate 80, and is 16km (10 miles) north of the lake.

TOURIST INFORMATION

The Lake Tahoe Visitor Center, Highway 89, South Lake Tahoe, ph (916) 573 2600.

The South Lake Tahoe Chamber of Commerce, 3066 US Highway 50, South Lake Tahoe, ph (916) 541 5255.

The Tahoe Chamber of Commerce, Suite 3, 950 North Lake Boulevard, Tahoe City, ph (916) 583 2371.

The US Forest Service, PO Box 731002, South Lake Tahoe, CA 95731, ph (916) 573 2600.

ACCOMMODATION

Accommodation prices around Lake Tahoe vary considerably. In South Lake Tahoe, the closer the establishment is to the casinos of Nevada, the more you have to pay. In winter, to stay at the ski-fields of Squaw Valley or Heavenly is an expensive operation. In the latter case, it might be much cheaper to arrange your accommodation before you leave home through a travel agent versed in arranging ski packages.

Here is a selection of accommodation around the lake, with prices for a double room per night in US dollars, which should be used as a guide only.

The telephone area code is 916.

North

Truckee Hotel, Bridge Street & Commerical Row, Truckee, ph 587 4444 - four-storey, Old West charm - $50-80.

Tahoe Vista Inn & Marina, 7220 North Lake Boulevard, Tahoe Vista, ph 546 4819 - 7 suites, great views, restaurant - $200+.

Sunnyside Restaurant & Lodge, 1850 West Lake Boulevard, Tahoe City, ph 583 7200 - 23 rooms, restaurant, bar - $150.

Squaw Valley

Squaw Valley Lodge, at base station of aerial tram - studio suites from $870/week; one bedroom condomin. from $1018/week.

Squaw Valley Inn - deluxe rooms from $994 per week; 2-bedroom kitchen units from $1047 per week.
Mogul Ski World, resort complete at foot of mountain - 405 rooms, swimming pools, tennis courts, restaurants - from $790 per week.

> For full information on accommodations in Squaw Valley contact Squaw Valley USA, PO Box 2007, Olympic Valley, CA 96146, ph 583 6985.

South

Inn by the Lake, 3300 Lake Tahoe Boulevard, South Lake Tahoe, ph 542 0330 - 100 rooms, swimming pool - $95-145.
Camp Richardson Resort, California Highway 89, South Lake Tahoe, ph 541 1801 - multi-purpose facility with motel rooms, cabins and campsites. Restaurant, bar and full-service marina on site - motel rooms costs $50-85.
Across the state line (also known as Stateline) are several large, luxurious 5-star hotels complete with casinos and Las Vegas-style entertainment.

The prices reflect the standards at each hotel.
For full information on these, and indeed all accommodation in the area, contact the Lake Tahoe Visitors Authority, PO Box 16299, South Lake Tahoe, CA 95706, ph toll free 800/288 2463.
Telephone lines are open
Mon-Fri 8am-6pm (Pacific Time), Sat-Sun 9am-5pm.

Heavenly Valley

Lakeland Village, on the shores of the lake - self-contained units and one to four-bedroom apartments - from $496 per week.
Holiday Lodge, one block from casinos near the shuttle - 150 rooms and suites with kitchens - outdoor/indoor swimming pools - from $263 for double room.

EATING OUT

Following is a selection of restaurants around the lake rated

Reasonable (under $10 for a main course),
Moderate ($10-20),
Expensive ($20+).

China Chef Restaurant, 10115 Commercial Row, Truckee, ph 587 1831 - Szechuan cuisine - **Reasonable.**

Col Clair's, 6873 North Lake Boulevard, Tahoe Vista, ph 546 7358 - Cajun and Creole cuisine - **Moderate.**

Captain Jon's, 7220 North Lake Boulevard, Tahoe Vista, ph 546 4819 - seafood, extensive wine list - **Expensive.**

Le Petit Pier, 7252 North Lake Boulevard, Tahoe Vista, ph 546 4464 - French, formal atmosphere - **Expensive.**

Tahoe House, California 89, Tahoe City, ph 583 1377 - continental cuisine - open for dinner only - **Moderate.**

Rosie's Cafe, 571 North Lake Boulevard, Tahoe City, ph 583 8504 - open breakfast, lunch and dinner - **Reasonable.**

Christy Hill, 115 Grove Street, Tahoe City, ph 583 8551 - California cuisine, local favourite - **Moderate.**

Top of the Tram, Heavenly Valley, ph 544 6263 - steak and seafood, open for lunch and dinner - **Expensive** (although includes cable car fare).

The Greenhouse, 4140 Cedar Avenue, South Lake Tahoe, ph 541 5800 - continental cuisine - open for dinner only - **Expensive.**

The Dory's Oar, 1041 Fremont Avenue, South Lake Tahoe, ph 541 6603 - seafood/steak - **Expensive.**

Tahoe Queen, ph 541 3364, is an authentic Mississippi sternwheeler which offers cocktails, luncheon bar and sunset dinner dance cruises with live entertainment.

SIGHTSEEING

Donner Memorial State Park, 3km west of Truckee, has an interesting museum commemorating a group of pioneers who perished during the winter of 1846-47. They were trying to cross the mountains but were stopped by snow drifts so decided to camp for the winter, with disastrous results. Some went insane, many died from exposure and hunger, and others resorted to cannibalism. The Emigrant Trail Museum is off California Highway 80, ph 587 3841, and charges a small admission fee. A monument to the Emigrants has a base that is 6.7m (22 ft) high, which was the depth of the snow they experienced. The park has campgrounds, hiking trails, and plenty of beaver, deer and porcupines.

The north shore of Lake Tahoe has several small towns with resort facilities, restaurants and some attractions, but the main focus of activity is on the south shore, around **South Lake Tahoe**, the region's biggest town.

To really appreciate the lake, you should travel completely around it, through dense forests and past granite outcroppings. The road also passes some magnificent private homes, such as **Vikingsholm**, ph 525 7232, a 38-room granite castle a few kilometres west of South Lake Tahoe. The house was designed to resemble a 9th century Norse fortress, and is open to the public during the summer for a small admission fee. Offshore there is a small island, **Fanette Island**, with a stone tea house.

Vikingsholm is situated on **Emerald Bay**, a 5km (3 miles) inlet bordered by tall pine trees. Many people think that this bay is the most scenic spot on the whole lake, and a great view of it can be obtained from a lookout on California 89. Not far from here is a hiking trail that leads to **Eagle Falls**.

Because this is a guide to California, I am not going to dwell on attractions over the Nevada border. I have mentioned the casinos, but I'm not going to list all the facilities found in them - anyway, by and large all casinos offer much the same the world over. But, there is one attraction I think you might enjoy on the north shore of Lake Tahoe, near the town of Incline Village - **Ponderosa Ranch**, the home of the Cartwright family of *Bonanza* TV fame.

Ponderosa Ranch
Tours are available of the ranch house, where you learn how the television series was filmed. Then you can explore an entire Old West town, which includes a saloon, general store,

country church and photo emporium. There are movie sets and props, gun fights, pony rides, a Mystery Mine, and fun for young and old.The Ranch is *open daily* 9.30am-5pm from mid-April through October, ph (702) 831 0691.

SKI FIELDS

Squaw Valley

Squaw Valley first achieved international recognition with the Winter Olympics of 1960, but it has undergone major infrastructure developments since then. The resort has added a complex at Squaw Creek at the base of the mountain, plus the Bath and Tennis Club at upper elevations.

The valley spans more than 1616ha (4000 acres) overlooking Lake Tahoe, and features wide-open bowls and six separate mountain peaks. More than 1143cm (450 ins) of snow falls annually.

Facilities

Cable car, six-passenger gondola, 16 double chairlifts, seven triple chairs, four surface lifts, three quad express chairs.

Uphill capacity: 47,370 skiers an hour.

Terrain

Base elevation 1890m (6200 ft), summit elevation 2758m (9049 ft), vertical drop 829m (2720 ft).

Average snowfall 1143cm (450 ins). Terrain covers 1616ha (4000 acres) - 25% beginner, 45% intermediate, 30% advanced.

Activities

Sleds, snow mobiles, ice skating, cross-country, boat rides, ballooning.

Heavenly Valley

Heavenly Valley, on the south shore of Lake Tahoe, straddles the states of California and Nevada, and is one of the largest US resorts, offering 35 sq km (13.5 sq miles) of skiable terrain. It offers descents of up to 10km (6 miles), and features the

largest vertical rise in the Tahoe basin.
Facilities
Total of 24 lifts, with a capacity of 31,000 skiers per hour, plus 50-passenger aerial tram. Six day lodges located throughout the terrain. There are three full-service bases, mid-mountain lodge.
Terrain
Elevation of 3078m (10,100 ft), vertical rise 1920m (6300 ft), runs up to 12km (7 miles), 762 to 1270cm (300 to 500 ins) of snow per season - 25% beginner, 50% intermediate, 25% expert. 60% of slopes covered by snow-making facilities.
Activities
Lil Angels Children's Ski School; sailing/cruising Lake Tahoe.

BEACHES

Kings Beach State Recreation Area is one of the few public beaches near Nevada on the North Shore. It is located on Route 28, near the intersection of Route 267, and about 20km (12 miles) north-east of Tahoe City. There is a small sandy beach, plus a few amenities, ph 546 7248.

Lake Forest Beach and Campground, ph 583 5544, on Lake Forest Road about 3km east of Tahoe City, has an inland campground with about 20 sites, and a tree-bordered stretch of sand.

Sugar Pine Point State Park, ph 525 7232, is on Route 89, about 16km (10 miles) south of Tahoe City. It extends along nearly 3.5km (2 miles) of sandy beaches, and almost 6.5km (4 miles) inland. The park also has several historic buildings, including an old mansion that is now a museum. Camping is permitted.

D.L. Bliss State Park, ph 525 7277, and **Emerald Bay State Park**, ph 541 3030, are adjoining forested parks that extend along 10km (6 miles) of shoreline. D.L. Bliss is 27km (17 miles) and Emerald Bay is 35km (22 miles) south of Tahoe City.

West of South Lake Tahoe, on Route 89, are several scenic beaches - **Baldwin Beach, Kiva Beach** and **Pope Beach**.

YOSEMITE NATIONAL PARK

The state of California has many man-made attractions that beckon visitors from all over the world, but they pale into insignificance when compared with the breathtaking majesty and beauty of Nature's creation - **Yosemite**.

Yosemite National Park has an area of 3109 sq km (1200 sq miles) which traverses the Sierra Nevada from an elevation of 610m (2000 ft) to 3962m (13,000 ft). The lower elevations have meadows with herds of grazing deer, and higher elevations are sheer granite cliffs and valleys carved by glaciers.

The glaciers moved through a canyon carved by the Merced River, with the ice working through the weak sections of granite and bypassing the solid portions, thereby widening the canyon. When the glaciers melted, the debris that had been carried with them formed a dam across the river creating Lake Yosemite. Over a period of time sediment filled in the lake, which explains the flat floor of Yosemite Valley.

The Ahwahneechee Indians, and other tribes, had been living in the valley for thousands of years before European discovery in the mid 19th century. When word got around about the incredible scenic beauty, tourists began flocking to Yosemite, causing President Lincoln, in 1864, to give public park status to Yosemite Valley and the Mariposa Grove of Giant Sequoias. It was not much later that naturalist John Muir began campaigning to have Yosemite declared a national park, and he was successful in 1890. In all, about 90% of the park has been given wilderness status.

HOW TO GET THERE

By Air

American Eagle has flights from San Francisco and Los Angeles to Merced, about 132km (82 miles) to the west of the park. From the Greyhound terminal in Merced, Yosemite VIA Bus

Lines, ph (209) 383 1563, has a service to Yosemite Valley.

By Bus
Greyhound has services from Los Angeles, Fresno, San Francisco and Sacramento to Merced, and two services daily to/from Yosemite. It should be noted that the Ameripass is not accepted for transportation between Merced and Yosemite.

By Train
Amtrak's "San Joaquin" travels from Oakland and Los Angeles to Merced. From there a direct connection to Yosemite is available from California Yosemite Tours, ph (209) 383 1563.

By Car
From San Francisco, Interstate 580, then Interstate 5 to the off-ramp for Gustine, then California 140. The latter is recommended because it is less mountainous and therefore tends to have less snowfall. If you are travelling in winter, always have chains in your car.

There are four entrances to the park - California 120 on the north-west, California 140 towards the west, California 41 on the south, and California 120 on the north-east (the latter open in summer only).

The entrance fee to the park is $5 per car.

TOURIST INFORMATION
The Visitor Center is in the Village Mall, ph (209) 372 0264, and *is open daily*
9am-6pm (April-May); 8am-7pm (summer);
8am-6pm (September-October) 9am-5pm (winter).
You can pick up a copy of a free weekly newsletter called the *Yosemite Guide* which tells of the week's happenings and also has a map for the free shuttle bus. The Center is also a mine of information on guided walks, demonstrations and hiking.

They can also fill you in on the do's and don'ts in the park - regulations that have been made to protect the environment and the visitors.

For road and weather information, phone (209) 372 4605.

ACCOMMODATION

Accommodation in Yosemite Valley includes:
The Ahwahnee, Yosemite Lodge, Curry Village, Wawona Hotel.
Available seasonally are:
Curry housekeeping units,
White Wolf Lodge and *Tuolumne Meadows Lodge.*
All accommodations are operated by the Yosemite Park & Curry Co, CA 95389, ph (209) 252 4848.

SIGHTSEEING

Yosemite Valley

It only takes up 18 sq km (7 sq miles) of the park, but the valley is a hub of activity with accommodation facilities, camping grounds, shops, restaurants and the Visitor Center. It also has some important scenic features which can be reached by a free shuttle-bus service which travels continuously through the eastern portion of the valley.

Clouds Rest, the highest mountain visible from the valley, climbs to 3025m (9926 ft), and in front of it stands *Half Dome*, a gigantic rock that seems to have been cut in half by a higher power, leaving a sheer wall that measures 610m (2000 ft).

Mirror Lake is named for the mountains that are reflected in its water; and *Royal Arches,* are granite arcs formed by glaciers.

Sentinel Rock is a large block of granite that resembles a watchtower; and *Leaning Tower* is definitely on the incline.

Cathedral Spires are granite spears rising about 610m (2000 ft) from the ground; and *Three Brothers* are named for the sons of Yosemite's greatest Indian chief.

Yosemite Falls are among the longest waterfalls in the world, cascading 740m (2425 ft) in two stages; and *El Capitan*, one of the largest monoliths in the world, rises 914m (3000 ft) from the floor of the valley.

Next to the Visitor Centre in Yosemite Village is the *Indian Cultural Museum*, with a mock village and exhibits of the culture of the Paiute and Miwok Indians who were early inhabitants.

South-West Area of the Park

Taking California 41 from the valley provides an interesting trip to the south-western area of the park, passing firstly *Bridalveil Falls*, then just before the tunnel, the lookout *Tunnel View*, which offers great views of Yosemite Valley.
Further along a side road leads to *Glacier Point* (2200m-7214 ft), and 180 degree views of the High Sierras, and views over Nevada and Vernal Falls, the Merced River, and the snowclad peaks of Yosemite's back country.

The main road then continues to the settlement of **Wawona**, where an old covered bridge leads to the *Pioneer Yosemite History Center* which has log cabins and houses dating to the 19th century, old horse-drawn vehicles, and displays of man's history in the park.

Near the park's south entrance is **Mariposa Grove**, the largest of Yosemite's three giant sequoia groves. Here there are over 200 trees that measure over 3m in diameter, but the oldest and biggest is *Grizzly Giant*, which is said to be over 2700-years-old.

You can drive to the entrance of the grove, which is 56km (35 miles) south of the valley, then you can hike through the grove, or take the free shuttle bus.

High Sierras

The High Country has over 579km (360 miles) of roads that are suitable for car travel, and 1287km (800 miles) of trails that can be followed by horse, mule, or on foot. Many guided bus tours are available, and the Visitor Center has all the necessary details. One way to set out is to follow California 120 (Tioga Road) to the top of the mountain range. The road is not open when it is snowing, but in warmer weather it crosses some splendid alpine scenery.

After passing through a stand of red fir the road continues to **White Wolf** where there is a lodge, camping ground, restaurant and a stable. Next stop is **Olmstead Point** from where a short track leads to a lookout that offers great views down towards **Half Dome** and up to **Tenaya Lake**. The lake, at 2484m (8149 ft), is a long, narrow body of water surrounded by bald rock-faces. Continuing along the road, Mt Conness (3837m-12,590 ft) comes into view, then the next stop, **Tuolumne Meadows**, gateway to the High Country.

Set at an elevation of 2621m (8600 ft), this is the largest alpine meadow in the High Sierras, and is 88km (55 miles) from the valley. It is closed in winter, but in summer offers a large camping ground, information centre, lodge, store and restaurant. In summer, the surrounding hillsides are covered in brilliantly coloured wildflowers.

The road then continues into **Tioga Pass**, the highest vehicular pass in California.

SPORT AND RECREATION

Horse Riding

There are stables near Curry Village, Wawona, White Wolf and Tuolumne Meadows, and they all offer tours of differing lengths through out the park. For full information contact Yosemite Park & Curry Co, CA 95389, ph (209) 252 4848.

Swimming

There are lots of streams, rivers and waterfalls that beckon a hot hiker, but remember that the water is very cold, and the rocks nearby are very slippery.

Cycling
Bikes can be rented from stands at Yosemite Lodge and Curry Village.

Mountain Climbing
The Yosemite Mountaineering School at Curry Village offers classes for beginners, intermediate and advanced climbers, and the Visitor Center has full details.

Skiing
Badger Pass is the oldest ski resort in California, having opened in 1935. Facilities include one triple-chair lift, three double-chair lifts, one T-bar, a rope-tow for beginners, a child-care centre, and a fast-food area. The runs are rated 50% intermediate, 35% beginner, 15% expert. Instruction is available, as is rental equipment.

For cross-country enthusiasts, there are 145km (90 miles) of marked trails, and 35km (22 miles) of machine-groomed track from Badger Pass to Glacier Point are set several times a week. Overnight accommodation is available at Glacier Point Ski Hut or at Ostrander Lake Ski Hut.

For information on all ski facilities, contact Badger Pass, Yosemite National Park, CA 95389, ph (209) 372 1330. For an update on all conditions, ph (209) 372 1338.

Skating
There is an outdoor ice rink at Curry Village, and rental skates are available.

Fishing
Licences are required for everyone over the age of 16, and can be obtained without any fuss from the Mountaineering School at Curry Village, or the Sports Shop in Yosemite Village. Trout is the main catch.

LIST OF MAPS

California	8-9
Missions of California	14
Downtown Los Angeles	44
Hollywood	66
Orange County	120
San Diego Area	147
Carmel	200
17-Mile Drive	203
Monterey	207
San Francisco (East)	222-223
San Francisco (West)	250-251
San Francisco Regional Guide	262
California's Wine Country (North)	272
California's Wine Country (South)	273
Napa Valley	280
Sonoma Valley	286

INDEX

General

Accommodation 36-37
Business hours 29
Car hire 38-40
Climate 22-23
Communications 27-28
Credit cards 28
Crime 29-30
Drink 42
Earthquakes 31
Embassies 26-27
Emergency telephones 32
Entry Regulations 25-26
Food 41
Health 29
History 10-13
Holidays 25

How to get to California 33-36
Insurance 29
Language 24-25
Liquor laws 31
Local transport 37-41
Missions 15-22
Money 27
Population 24
Religion 25
Shopping 42-43
Sport 43
Tipping 30-31
Travellers cheques 28-29
Trivia 32

Cities, Towns & Attractions

Alcatraz Island 241-243
Anaheim 121-127
- Accommodation 122-123
- Eating out 124
- How to get there 121-122
- Local transport 124
- Shopping 125-126
- Sightseeing 126-127

Balboa Park 149-151
Berkeley 265-266
Beverly Hills Golden Triangle 90
Big Sur 196-197
Buena Park 127-131

Cable cars 226-228
Calico Ghost Town 170
Cannery Row 213-214
Carmel 199-204
- Accommodation 201

- Eating out 201
- Shopping 201-202
- Sightseeing 202-204
- Tourist information 199
Catalina Island 104-105
Central Coast 171-198
Channel Islands 174
Chinatown (LA) 78
City Hall (LA) 76

Desert Museum 165
Disneyland 109-119
Dodger Stadium 78-79
Downtown Los Angeles 74-79

El Pueblo de Los Angeles
Historic Park 74-76
Exposition Park 78

Fisherman's Wharf
(Monterey) 215-217

Fisherman's Wharf (SF) 239-241
Forest Lawn 85-86

Gene Autry Western
Heritage Museum 86-87
George C. Page Museum 89
Getty, J. Paul Museum 98-99
Golden Gate Bridge 255-256
Golden Gate Park 249-254
Greek Theatre 88
Griffith Park 86-88
Griffith Observatory 87

Hearst Castle 193-196
Heavenly Valley 300-301
Hollywood 79-90
Hollywood Bowl 68-70
Hollywood sign 81
Hollywood Studio Museum 88

Joshua Tree National
Monument 167

Irvine 133

Knott's Berry Farm 127-129

La Jolla 154
Lake Tahoe 294-301
- Accommodation 296-297
- Beaches 301
- Eating out 297-298
- How to get there 295
- Sightseeing 298-300
- Ski fields 300301
- Tourist information 296
Little Tokyo 77
Long Beach 103-104
Los Angeles 45-96
- Accommodation 46
- Downtown 74-79
- Eating out 58-63
- Entertainment 64-70
- How to get there 45
- Local transport 54-58
- Shopping 71-74
- Sightseeing 74-90
- Spectator sports 9394
- Sport & recreation 91
- Tourist information 46
- Tours 94-96
Los Angeles Coast 97-108
Los Angeles County Museum
of Art 89

Los Angeles Zoo 86

Malibu 97-99
Mann's Chinese Theatre 81
Marina Del Rey 101
Marine World Africa USA 266
Max Factor Museum 88
Melrose Avenue 88
Mission Bay 152-154
Mojave Desert 169-170
Monterey 206-217
- Accommodation 208
- Eating out 208-209
- Entertainment 209
- How to get there 206
- Shopping 210
- Sightseeing 210-217
- Sport & recreation 217-219
- Tourist information 208
Monterey Bay Aquarium 214-215
Monterey Peninsula 199-219
Movie & TV studios 82-85
Movieland Was Museum 129-130
Muir Woods 268-269

Napa Valley 271-285
- Accommodation 275-276
- Eating out 276-277
- How to get there 274
- Sightseeing 277-281
- Tourist information 275
- Tours 284-285
- Wineries 281-284
Newport Beach 133-136
- Accommodation 133-134
- Cruises 135-136
- Eating out 134
- Sightseeing 134-135
- Sport & recreation 136
Nob Hill 246

Oakland 263-265
Ojai 175
Orange County 121-136
Oxnard 171-176
- Accommodation 173
- Eating out 173
- How to get there 172
- Sightseeing 174-175
- Sport & recreation 175-176
- Tourist information 172

Pacific Grove 205
Palm Springs 160-169

INDEX

- Accommodation 161
- Eating out 162-163
- Entertainment 163-164
- How to get there 160
- Local transport 162
- Shopping 164
- Sightseeing 164-167
- Spectator sports 169
- Sport 168-169
- Tourist information 160-161
- Tours 167-168

Paso Robles 191-192
Point Lobos 197-198

Queen Mary 103-104

Rancho La Brea Tar Pits 89

San Diego 137-158
- Accommodation 139-143
- Eating out 145
- Entertainment 145-146
- How to get there 137-138
- Local transport 143-145
- Shopping 146-148
- Sightseeing 148-155
- Spectator sports 157
- Sport & recreation 155-157
- Tourist information 138-139
- Tours 157-158

San Diego Wild Animal Park 154
San Fernando Valley 106-107
San Francisco 220-261
- Accommodation 220-225
- Eating out 232-234
- Entertainment 234-237
- How to get there 220
- Local transport 225-232
- Shopping 237-239
- Sightseeing 239-261
- Sport & recreation 258-259
- Tourist information 220
- Tours 259-261

San Francisco Bay area 263-270
San Gabriel Valley 107-108
San Luis Obispo 187-191
- Accommodation 187-188
- Beaches 190
- Eating out 188
- Entertainment 188
- How to get there 187
- Sightseeing 189-191
- Tourist information 187

San Pedro 101-103
San Simeon 193-196
Santa Barbara 176-185
- Accommodation 177-178
- Eating out 178-179
- Entertainment 178-179
- How to get there 176-177
- Shopping 179
- Sightseeing 180-183
- Sport & recreation 183-185
- Tourist information 177

Santa Monica 100
Santa Ynez Valley 185-187
Sausalito 243-244
Sea World 152-154
17-Mile Drive 202-204
Sierra Nevada 294-307
Solvang 186
Sonoma Valley 287-293
- Accommodation 288-289
- Eating out 289
- How to get there 288
- Sightseeing 290-292
- Tourist information 288
- Tours 293
- Wineries 292-293

Squaw Valley 300
Stearns Wharf 182

Tiburon 269-270

Union Station 76
Universal Studios 82-84

Venice 100-101
Ventura 175

Walk of Fame 79
Westside 90-96
Westwood Village 90
Wilshire Boulevard 88
Wine Country 271-293

Yosemite National Park 302-307
- Accommodation 304
- How to get there 302
- Sightseeing 304-306
- Sport & recreation 306-307
- Tourist information 303-304

Monday – ~~3rd~~ 4th Sept. Labour Day.
Leave SF head to Lake Tahoe.
Stayed. South Lake Tahoe. 200mi

Tuesday ~~4th~~ 5th Sept.
Leave S. Lake Tahoe. Goedeard L Tahoe
head towards. Carson City. + Yosemite Pk.
250 miles. to Mariposa.

Wed 6th Sept.
Spent day going around Yosemite
went up to Glacier Point. Saw
deer + squirrels. Stayed Mariposa
146 miles

Thurs. 7th Sept.
Left Mariposa – Merced – Monterey
went via. Chowchilla + Dos Pablos.
226 miles. Arrived Monterey lunchtime
parked at the Marina + went to see
Fisherman's Wharf. Booked into the
Driftwood Motel. Then went to Cannery
Row + The Aquarium. Called to see
Betty + Bruce.

Friday 8th Sept.   50 miles
Drove to Carmel + along 17 mile Dr.